PIERRE BOURDIEU AND CULTURAL THEORY

Theory, Culture & Society

Theory, Culture & Society caters for the resurgence of interest in culture within contemporary social science and the humanities. Building on the heritage of classical social theory, the book series examines ways in which this tradition has been reshaped by a new generation of theorists. It will also publish theoretically informed analyses of everyday life, popular culture, and new intellectual movements.

THE TCS CENTRE
The Theory, Culture & Society book series, the journals *Theory, Culture & Society* and *Body & Society*, and related conference, seminar and post-graduate programmes operate from the TCS Centre at Nottingham Trent University. For further details of the TCS Centre's activities please contact:

Centre Administrator
The TCS Centre, Room 175
Faculty of Humanities
Nottingham Trent University
Clifton Lane, Nottingham, NG11 8NS, UK
e-mail: tcs@ntu.ac.uk

Recent volumes in the Theory, Culture & Society book series include:

Cyberspace/Cyberbodies/Cyberpunk
Cultures of Technological Embodiment
edited by Mike Featherstone and Roger Burrows

Spatial Formations
Nigel Thrift

The Body and Society
Explorations in Social Theory
Second edition
Bryan S. Turner

The Social Construction of Nature
Klaus Eder

Deleuze and Guattari
An Introduction to the Politics of Desire
Philip Goodchild

PIERRE BOURDIEU AND CULTURAL THEORY

Critical Investigations

Bridget Fowler

SAGE Publications
London • Thousand Oaks • New Delhi

First published 1997

Published in association with *Theory, Culture & Society*, Nottingham Trent University

SAGE Publications Ltd
6 Bonhill Street
London EC2A 4PU

SAGE Publications Inc
2455 Teller Road
Thousand Oaks, California 91320

SAGE Publications India Pvt Ltd
32, M-Block Market
Greater Kailash – I
New Delhi 110 048

British Library Cataloguing in Publication data

A catalogue record for this book is
available from the British Library.

ISBN 0 8039 7625 9
ISBN 0 8039 7626 7 (pbk)

Library of Congress catalog record available

Typeset by Photoprint, Torquay
Printed in Great Britain at the University Press, Cambridge

Contents

Acknowledgements

I should like to acknowledge the encouragement of Pierre Bourdieu and to express the hope that I have not distorted his views. A huge debt is owed to David Frisby, whose learning and patience have been greatly appreciated. Richard Jenkins and Mike Featherstone also read the entire manuscript and made wise suggestions for improvement, while Terry Lovell's support convinced me once more that the project was worthwhile. I have been sustained by conversations with Lindy Barbour, Esperança Bielsa, Harvie Ferguson, Barbara Littlewood, Paddy Lyons, Kirsten and Scott Meikle, Mick Scott, Paul Stirton, Stephen Thomson and Hillel Ticktin. Robert Rojek has been a most tolerant and approachable editor and Carol Woodward generously helped with French translation problems. Lastly, I have been both heartened and stimulated intellectually by my family. To all of these, my thanks.

INTRODUCTION

Situating Pierre Bourdieu

In the Anglo-American world, there have been two moments of Pierre Bourdieu, the first in response to the English translation of *Reproduction* in 1977 and the second at the time of *Distinction*, also in translation, in 1984.[1] Thus although there has been recent acceptance of his importance in the fields of education, consumption and leisure, there has been no sustained analysis of his cultural theory nor any attempt to analyse works such as *Les Règles de l'art* (1992) in the light of all his other works. This book will therefore examine his sociology of culture, with especial reference to his analysis of literature and painting. My contention is that Bourdieu's approach is the most comprehensive and sophisticated available at present and that it is more profoundly antagonistic to idealist thought than is the work of poststructuralists such as Derrida and Foucault. Bourdieu has developed an impressive new synthesis of classical social theory in the light of late capitalism. He offers a welcome relief to anyone suffering from post-Lacanian excess on the issue of the subject.

Bourdieu's personal trajectory is well known from the small number of other critical works on him that have appeared (Harker et al., 1990; Jenkins, 1992; Robbins, 1991). I will summarise briefly. The son of a postman in a village in the South-West Pyrenees area of Béarn, in France, Bourdieu is very like his late contemporary, Raymond Williams, in being from the marchlands of a metropolitan country, that is to say, in a peasant area within a late capitalist society. In these juxtaposed worlds, he has himself experienced some of the contrasts between pre-capitalist and capitalist life that he writes about in his works. This class and spatial marginality was enhanced by experience of the bitter confontation between coloniser and colonised in his period in the French Army. Here he managed to secure the time and, more bizarrely, the *entrée* to start the conversion from philosophy student to ethnographer: one mark of his radicalism in the war being the inclusion of revolutionary songs at the end of *The Algerians*. After field-work in Algeria, he returned to France, undertaking work for his doctorate (*agrégation*) at the University of Lille. He refused to take this partly because of the pedestrian type of knowledge on offer and partly due to the hegemony of Stalinism. However, he became a university teacher at Lille, where a number of his first studies of local cultural life were undertaken, along with his early studies of school and university students. From there he progressed to the

École des Hautes Études in Paris, where he has had a major effect on the nature of research in sociology, not least by the breadth and imagination of his own work. Since 1981 he has been Professor at the Collège de France, perhaps the most consecrated position within French sociology (Jenkins, 1992: chap. 1; Robbins, 1991: Intro.). *Distinction* has become a popular work in France, with over 100,000 copies sold, while Bourdieu has increased his accessibility with lengthy television interviews.

Bourdieu's sociology has been labelled, with only a little exaggeration, 'not only the best, but . . . the only game in town' (Lash, 1993: 193). In my view, this is because he has combined elements of structuralism with approaches less hostile to the transformative potential of human beings. By these means, he attempts to gather in again the lost harvest of structuralist promise. What he has repudiated is 'the prison-house of thought' (Hall, 1986: 532) in which recent forms of social theorising have been artificially polarised into extremes. Bourdieu has often recited a litany of positions to be transcended – subjectivism versus objectivism; quixoticism versus 'fixism'; idealism versus determinism; existentialism versus structuralism – all dichotomies which resemble that between structuralism and culturalism in British cultural studies. Going beyond structuralism he has proposed the notion of men and women as agents, not merely because they are determined in their relations to production, but because they are elements of a structure which exists in and through signifying practices (see, for example, *Language and Symbolic Power* (1991), where it is proposed that such practices are the stakes in struggles over meaning, and *The Logic of Practice* (1990a: 15)).These are the classifications or representations of the world through which meanings are possible and which are embedded in each individual through the doxic or taken-for-granted ways of living which socialisation confers. Bourdieu does not use the Althusserian term 'imaginary' conditions of existence, but he does write of the principle of vision and division which organises the world for each agent and, as in Durkheim and Mauss's *Primitive Classification* (1963), these are enfolded in the habitus as a form of 'doxic knowledge'. The reproduction of the dominant class, as well as extended forms of social structure, occurs through these principles, located within a historical framework (see especially the chapter entitled 'The Historical Genesis of the Pure Aesthetic' (Bourdieu, 1993a: 254–66)).

But the active side of sensuous human practice, which culturalism draws on, is also renewed in Bourdieu. Hence his important conception of improvisation and strategy, explained by recourse to jazz playing or to the quarter-back's feel for when he should take the ball and scramble. Such divisions of labour, which signifying practices instil through the rules of combination and opposition, are never smooth and unproblematic. The mistake of structuralism was to see events through observers' rather than the natives' eyes. This enhanced the expectations of rule-following and under-estimated the degree of creative disorder from which advantages might be derived (as in the process of stretching conceptions of genealogical units, so that parallel cousin rules of marriage might be said to govern them). This was the reason for Bourdieu's original break with structuralism – he refers to it as 'French flu' – and the source of his appeal to subjective understanding: that is, to the Goffmanesque world of games, strategy and the disjunctures of back- and front-stage. Hence his demand for an end to the 'repression' of Durkheim through the 'softened, sweetened, euphemised' forms of the Durkheimian heritage (Bourdieu et al., 1985: 89). Retaining a concept of rupture and transformation, he has progressively returned in recent years to a radicalised idea of anomie, that is, to a discrepancy between expectations and experience with its potentially politicising effects. Thus while he hangs on to the structuralist notion of the political unconscious, which is acquired with the habitus, he also possesses an understanding of practice in the sense of 'experience', which is by no means merely a passive effect of taken-for-granted ('doxic') knowledge (see, for example, the recent work on the Front National militant or the scientist (1993b)).[2]

I shall argue that this concept of practice is immensely fertile. It avoids the dilemmas of necessity and choice that have bedevilled sociology and Marxism. It allows us to understand how social imperatives prompt individual position-taking in a manner which, avoiding a mechanistic model of determined action, appeals to an order based on 'feeling'. Principles of classification are described as being laid down within us, rather as an old house exerts its pleasurable order from an accumulation of things, and in distinction to the pristine purity of the interior designer.[3] Bourdieu's practice thus operates on the same principle as works of art themselves, that is to say, that they unify a multiplicity of discrete objects (Loesberg, 1993: 1037–8),[4] harmonising imperatives based on biological needs with social imperatives. Further, although practice is actually experienced as 'unwilled necessity', it is neither the consequence of mere mechanical reproduction nor the working out of the seed of inspiration. In an unrecognised act of understated subversion, Bourdieu has made artists' action the model for all normal skilled practices accomplished in everyday life:

> The coherence without apparent intention and the unity without an immediate, visible, unifying principle of all the cultural realities that are informed by a quasi-natural logic (is this not what makes the 'eternal charm of Greek art' that Marx refers to?) are the product of the age-old application of the same schemes of action and perception, which, never having been constituted as explicit principles, can only produce an unwilled necessity which is therefore necessarily imperfect but also a little miraculous and very close in this respect to a work of art. (1990a: 13)

But what marks out Bourdieu's work most clearly is his very full conception of class and of culture as a response to class experience. He must think both how the dominant linguistic classifications create a common world for all classes and how these are distinctively inflected for the subordinate class with its closer experience of material urgencies. It is this which he discusses vividly with Darnton in relation to a violent demonstration of apprentices' disaffection in 1762:

Darnton: [T]he workers who manipulated the common code were able to mock their bourgeois superiors without the latter grasping this.
Bourdieu: It seems that this differential use of common codes, along with all sorts of strategic and complex games made possible by the juxtaposition of understood and misunderstood parts, is a product itself of differentiated worlds. (Bourdieu et al., 1985: 92)

This is an extraordinarily difficult project. Bourdieu has been criticised for portraying an oversimplified working-class culture, so constrained by the 'taste for necessity' that other principles of choice have been neglected (Frow, 1987: 71; Shiach, 1993: 214). Grignon and Passeron, in particular, have developed his problematic by undertaking a 'double reading in which culture can be seen as at once ideological and autonomous', using the example of consuming food (1989: 73).

Bourdieu has himself begun to undertake such a project in regard to gender. It is clear that an elaborate set of gender meanings has actively sustained working-class lack of choice. Because 'the idea of masculinity has one of its last refuges in the identity of the dominated classes' (1993c: 4), male *bourgeois* consumption can be repudiated as effeminate. In other words, there must be an immensely subtle negotiation of the sign so that its inflection fits with the experience of life (as in the conception of Voloshinov's multi-accentuated linguistic sign or Bakhtin's popular culture as 'gay laughter'[5]). But it is extraordinarily difficult to combine smoothly both the Durkheimian tradition of representations and the Marxist tradition of class ethos, especially with Bourdieu's insistence that popular language only acquires a counter-hegemonic freedom in the highly limited areas of pub and prisons.[6] Bourdieu has consistently underemphasised working-class freedom (versus constraint) and the culturally creative energies that can come from underneath, as opposed to the many permutations of psychological domination. In this respect, Bourdieu might be contrasted with Walt Whitman in nineteenth-century America, who saw popular slang as the active yeast fermenting in the dough of language and insisted that linguistic development had its bases from both broad and low (1969: 103–4). Similarly Medvedev and Bakhtin were keen to stress the *centrifugal* nature of the novel ('the novel is uncanonical by nature'), which was, they said, generated from beneath and renewed by popular energies (1978: xxi), an insight quite foreign to Bourdieu's conception of the best-selling novel. In contrast to both these, Bourdieu's concept of habitus attributes much more causal force to the action of the dominant class. His is a self-conscious anti-populism which stresses the power of great families, great schools and even great buildings in an endless form of symbolic violence. But it possesses a fatalistic consequence, particularly acute in depicting the subordinate class, whose habitus is simultaneously defensive and the product of a colonised sense of inferiority. Although Bourdieu's theory *is* preferable to individualistic versions of rational action theory, and although it is too harsh to say of Bourdieu (Jenkins, 1992: 97) that there is *no* strategising in his conception of strategy, these difficulties weaken his sociology of culture.[7]

Bourdieu's emphasis on symbolic domination confers on him a tragic wisdom. But apart from his studies in decolonisation, he has never undertaken the sort of protracted discussion of *transformation* – in the form of long revolutions or slave rebellions – that distinguishes the work of, say, Barrington Moore. Bourdieu is at his best exposing the pretensions to change by unveiling a whole 'highbrow' culture which is dedicated to a purely rhetorical militancy or revealing the hijacking of revolutionary terms for the purposes of distinction (1980a). But the absence of any analysis of structural transformation is a gap in his work.

There are other difficulties with Bourdieu's project (although some alleged problems reveal more about the deficiencies of the critics than of Bourdieu). It could be said that all these issues stem from the *relative devaluation of the subjective moment* in Bourdieu's theory, in order to reveal the tragedy of institutions which is played out behind characters' backs. There is a Sophoclean arbitrariness producing the fate of reproduction that we are condemned to bear in this conception of class and gender. It has been attenuated in very recent years by allusions to the rejection of 'destiny', but in terms that draw upon the register of radical theories of anomie rather than classical Marxist images of the ranked masses of the Left. Thus I wish to raise a range of issues dealing with the alleged over-determinism of Bourdieu, which cluster around the problematic diagnosis of contradiction and conflict in his work.

Calhoun has raised the difficulty of characterising Bourdieu's work as an inheritance from Marx, in that although it clearly lays bare inequality, it fails to characterise adequately the difference between capitalist and pre-capitalist societies (1993: 68–9). In fact Bourdieu does go some way toward this by identifying the difference between the market and a good-faith economy, or, again, between *impersonal* power based on exams and education as against *personal* power acquired by family networks, rifles and honour. However, Calhoun is on firmer ground in arguing that there is an inadequate theory of contradiction in Bourdieu. Now, his critics have failed to understand that contradictions are often masked by being presented as natural differences, so that, for Bourdieu, paternalism is the paradigmatic magical form of enchantment of inequalities (1990b: 10). Furthermore, Bourdieu has presented contradictions as perceived social antagonisms *in his recent work* (for example, 1989), but, save for Wacquant, this has gone unnoticed (Wacquant, 1993a: 240). In particular, he has developed a theory of anomic experience which has many of the qualities of 'class conflict' elsewhere, as in his account of the resentment of unpromoted staff faced with the rapidly increased student body in Parisian universities (1988a); his comments on 'school sickness'; and his exploration of violent, frequently racialised confrontations (1993b). Despite this, he has been taken to task for failing to compare economic capital and its accounting practices with other types of impersonal power (Calhoun, 1993: 68; Garnham, 1993: 185–7).

This point is well made. I believe that Bourdieu's work does, however, derive from what might be called the 'peculiarities of the French' –

especially the relative strength in French history of a 'state nobility'. This meritocratically selected group of higher civil servants and professionals was the target of Bourdieu's critical intervention in the public sector strikes of 1995-6, when he claimed that it was their interests that the Juppé government voiced. Consequently, an immense gulf separated them from the people, despite their professing to know 'where lay the happiness of the people, against their will' (*Le Monde*, 14.12.95).

Bourdieu's recent work has identified the contradiction between the state nobility and the industrial or finance capitalist fraction, especially in terms of the fate of their different styles of education, the hierarchical position of different educational institutions according to the relative power of each fraction within it and the antagonisms between them expressed as absolute oppositions of taste (1989, 1994b).[8] Moreover, nobody who has read his books since 1988 can miss the struggle for survival and open conflict that he depicts both at an individual, departmental and faculty level, within the academic world and within the cultural field more broadly (1988a, 1992). But part of his pathos undoubtedly lies in the truth to which he bears witness, that conflicts of social interests are frequently detectable only through the costs of individuals' adaptations, as in the case of the large number of peasant inheritors. Their economic plight he shows as simultaneously expressed and masked through a clumsy 'unattractiveness' and a consequent vulnerability to celibacy (1990a).

There is, further, confusion about the philosophical status of Bourdieu's *reflexive* sociology or 'constructivist structuralism' (1994a: 122). Bourdieu has argued for three stages of analysis: first, the objective exposure of invisible (objective) determining relations, of which the agent is often unaware; secondly, the retrieval of subjective perceptions or experience, including a focus on the active making of collective groups such as classes; and, thirdly, a second-order historical construction of the spaces from which perceptions and perspectives derive (1994a: 130). This is only possible if the sociologist breaks with naivety by monitoring his/her social understanding, not just in relation to the interests known to be linked to class, gender and ethnicity, but in relation to relative deprivation within a field (political, sporting, artistic, etc.).

Some sociologists have argued that Bourdieu's ultimate position is that of perspectivism (Lash, 1993), others, that it is realism (Wacquant, 1993b). The second is, in my view, more persuasive. But it should be said from the outset that, in explaining these sources of confusion, Bourdieu's heuristic principle of 'bending the stick the other way' should never be underestimated. It is this which requires grasping his work as a whole rather than any small part of it.

This applies particularly to reflexivity itself. As Bourdieu's sociological focus has extended to the heart of the academic institution, it has been progressively concerned to provide a reflexive discipline.[9] In his study of the division between types of capital and types of intellectual, Bourdieu has provided us with new insights into the Nietzschean world of *ressentiment* or compensatory rationalisations of bad fortune, as well as the Mannheimian contrast between ideology and utopia. He has refused, however, the easy opt-out which led Mannheim to exonerate intellectuals from being themselves distorted in the positions they adopt over academic and social struggles. Yet ultimately, he believes that there are some saving graces which can rescue us from the irrationalism to which such relativism appears to lead. These do not permit sociologists to go back to their 'regal positions', but they do permit the knowledge of *ressentiment* to become a discipline of self-investigation that allows the sociologist – and indeed any social agent – to interrogate him- or herself as to his or her own envious distortions and rationalisations of interest. In this way the knowledge of the social world might be put to new uses, not excluding a rational utopianism (Bourdieu and Wacquant, 1992: 212, 254).

Other objections have been made to Bourdieu. He has been held to exhibit an 'individualism of . . . world-view', possessing no conceptualisation of a social group and dissolving mind into a mere function of the body (Jenkins, 1992: 93). In the light of his emphasis on the (political) 'unconscious' and its historically changing collective outcomes, this is an odd claim, which has been too seduced by one dimension of Bourdieu's idea of strategic agency. He has been criticised for producing in *Distinction* a work of 'cultural voyeurism' (Robbins, 1991: 129). He has been condemned for his 'labyrinthine theory of practice' which is 'a machine for the suppression of history' (Jenkins, 1992: 97). These are strange views that I don't think can be sustained by an exhaustive assessment, especially of both early and very recent work. They gain their impact in part from the genuine difficulty of synthesising all Bourdieu's different projects.[10]

There are certain key areas of Bourdieu's cultural theory which have provoked problems that should be taken more seriously. Although there have been two single-authored books on Bourdieu so far, and important essays, especially by Lash, Garnham, Lipuma and Calhoun (see Calhoun et al., 1993; Crowther, 1994; Moi, 1991; Wilson, 1988), Bourdieu has not yet had the depth of attention he deserves in the field of sociology of culture. Admittedly, there has been a critical reception of Bourdieu's work in the narrower compass of studies of the school, which it is outside the scope of this volume to consider (Bernstein, 1975: 161, 176–7; Bredo and Fineberg, 1979; Halsey et al., 1980: 141–6; MacDonald, 1979/80). But within the broader sphere of cultural theory, his subversive approach to legitimate aesthetics has not been properly understood. In particular, Bourdieu's attempt to retrieve classical Marxism from routinised banalisation has involved an attack on literature and art as ideologies and it is the logic of this attack which his critics have often failed to grasp.

Indeed, recent commentators on Bourdieu, in my view, have entirely misunderstood his meaning. Thus, despite my great admiration for Jameson, I cannot follow him when he sees *Distinction* merely as a study in conspicuous consumption (1991: 131). This dismissive judgement is unexpected since Jameson, like Bourdieu, also uses the combined approaches of Marx and Durkheim and has a comparable interest in the changing place of modernism in relation to power. I should mention also Roger Huss, whose *Times Literary Supplement* review of Bourdieu's cultural theory succeeds only in caricaturing Bourdieu when it describes him as a 'modest aristocrat' engaging in a '*kulturkampf*' against the cultural resentment of the masses (1993: 11). Lastly, Garnham and Williams have made some illuminating comments on Bourdieu's implicit valorisation of a popular aesthetic in *Distinction*. Yet they have misunderstood his view that the techniques for the decipherment of canonised works might be broadly diffused, rather than class possessions (1986).

In the chapters that follow I aim to remedy these deficiencies. I intend to do so by two routes. First, I shall provide a hermeneutic interpretation of Bourdieu's writing insofar as it is relevant to theories of culture. Here I shall argue that Bourdieu has indeed rescued cultural production from simplistic social theory which viewed the artist in reductive and passive terms:

> I had to take back from idealism the active side which the materialist tradition, notably with the theory of reception, had abandoned to it. (1987a: 14)

This statement will be explored in terms of Bourdieu's unmasking of various ideologies of cultural creativity and reception, which together constitute areas of magical 'belief' in contemporary societies. Secondly, I shall address through a number of substantive issues the lacunae in his thought or the areas that suffer at present from an over-schematic presentation. By these means I hope to stimulate further research following in the wake of Bourdieu, whose project is conceived as an important renewal of a rich tradition.

Bourdieu's more recent work (1993b) differs from practices he has developed in the past to restore to the subordinate class or subaltern group the same importance and complexity of motivation that is attributed to canonised authors or the political élite. There are therefore unexplained methodological shifts over precisely how to 'democratise the hermeneutic' (1993b: 923). In part, Bourdieu's cultural theory has used methods that depend on interpretative analyses of texts, biographical materials, etc., as well as innovative content analyses of essay comments or *agrégation* reports to shed light on the binary classifications deployed by academic or critic. But the questionnaire which he once used has now been excluded – even demonised – as the crass instrument of the domination of the masses. In the absence of any auto-criticism of his earlier work, this is confusing, especially since an early work like *The Love of Art* cloaked its thin and patchy data on the subjective experience of art with an imposing array of mathematicised analyses of people's behaviour in galleries (Bourdieu and Darbel, with Schnapper (1991 (1968)). However, from the point of view of the sociology of culture, three main problems exist: descriptive status in relation to relevant comparisons, conception of the canon and the controversy over popular art.

(1) Comparative studies

While *Distinction* in particular has been praised as a rich ethnogaphy of contemporary France (Brubaker, 1985), the scope and meaning of its assessment of the role of cultural capital in late capitalism have been questioned (Giddens, 1986). In fact, even the textual meaning of *Distinction* itself is fundamentally contested. Thus Robbins, who emphasises that Bourdieu's sociology 'is a concerted attempt to rescue and to celebrate the authenticity of the behaviour of ordinary people' (1991: 4), has argued that *Distinction* is a 'politically dysfunctional work' (1991: 129) that can only accentuate the divergence of tastes it describes. Garnham, on the other hand, has read *Distinction* as 'the revenge of the French rural working class' (1993: 181), deciphering its main thrust as a defence of popular culture (see Fowler, 1991: 215–16). The national limitations in Bourdieu's findings have been emphasised recently in a fascinating comparison of the contrasting class ethos of the French and North American upper middle class by Lamont (1992). She has stressed the divergence of views about the salience of the aesthetic (or high culture) relative to either moral values or economic success, by contrasting both a Parisian sample with a provincial Clermont-Ferrand bourgeois group, and two groups from New York and Indianapolis. She identifies certain key differences between France and America, especially the smaller class fraction dependent on economic profits in France, the greater French central government expenditure as a proportion of gross domestic product (45 per cent versus 26 per cent), the more significant proportion employed by the State in France (31 per cent versus 16 per cent) and the more centralised French educational system, with its smaller educated élite (1992: 144). Such differences, she argues, have resulted in greater inequality of wealth in France, fewer chances of social mobility, less ethnic diversity – and also in less stress on money as a form of social closure than on differences based on cultural distinction. In her view, inequalities of knowledge have been overemphasised by Bourdieu:

> Indeed in France, cultural barriers are only slightly more important than other types of boundaries and they predominate only in Paris and not in Clermont; even if Bourdieu is not concerned with the American case, it is useful to stress again that many [upper-middle-class] Americans do not show signs of cultural goodwill, do not acknowledge the legitimacy of high culture and the importance [of] knowledge about it. (1992: 186)

She concludes that Bourdieu's sociology has not been *sufficiently* reflexive in examining the distinctiveness of its own perspective, that of Parisian intellectuals or cultural and social specialists.

But is this so? An alternative explanation of Bourdieu's rationale is that he wants to emphasise precisely the differences between the metropolis and even large towns in the periphery and that Paris has a typical significance for him as the location of the most extreme examples of the ideology of 'natural' intellectual gifts and the legitimate mode of consumption (1993a: 37). Thus a comparative study might not refute Bourdieu but would confirm the very trajectories and strategies that are at stake when he writes of the control over space and time that the Parisian haute bourgeoisie possesses. Be that as it may, it is clearly important to explain these divergencies (of gender as well as national and regional origin) and to unravel their meaning. The reception research used in my earlier study (1991) of women readers in the peripheral location of Scotland confirms the extent of cultural stratification. But, like the work of Lamont (1992), it questions the degree to which aesthetic formalism, or the absolute primacy of style, is apparent, even for those fractions, such as the higher professions, that are rich in cultural capital. These issues are taken up in chapter 7.

(2) The canon

Bourdieu has criticised the essentialist view of art by showing that its proponents stress the universality and timeless qualities of works of art while simultaneously excluding as valid sources of aesthetic pleasure both the charm offered by the objects of popular pleasures and the purely cerebral playfulness of the court. Hence what Bourdieu himself christens his ' vulgar' critique (1984: 485) shows how the economy of symbolic goods offers scarce resources (the taste for consecrated art) to serve as the basis for a strategy of distinction. Such a strategy must favour the dominant class because of the built-in class specificity of Kant's speciously universal judgements. Bourdieu has been taken to task for this, both on the (Kantian) ground that *analytical* arguments about the judgement of art are not affected by *empirically existing* differences in taste (Giddens, 1986) and on the ground that art, on this view, cannot be distinguished by its intrinsic value but only by its magical aura or 'fetish' character in social action. Such a view would detract from artists' historical importance in resisting the demands of the culture industries (Bürger, 1984: 24). Both these arguments have *some* force. Bürger is certainly right that the canon has been at least in part constituted by the work of dissident artists. Yet he has failed to understand Bourdieu's assessment of fetishism, which is founded on a similar critique to his own of art's status as a 'sacred island' in a bourgeois society. Nevertheless, I think there is a tension between Bourdieu's views of artistic goods as *fetishes* and his view that artists are *prophets* (1992). I shall argue that there are grounds for applying the concept of prophet with more substantive social referents than Bourdieu does and that consequently the approach to artists adopted in his writings has paid too little attention to their motives and subjective meanings. I shall suggest that the process he describes as the artistic internalisation of the high/low divide by artists fails to assess adequately the historical differences in the groups of avant-garde artists. My approach in chapter 5 specifically takes up his case-study of Manet and Impressionism as an avant-garde movement, which, I shall argue, Bourdieu misleadingly associates solely with a turn to formalism.

(3) The problem of popular art

Finally, it has not escaped critical attention that Bourdieu has excluded any popular art from his category of canon or consecrated culture (Shusterman, 1992: 172; 1993: 155), even though it is not clear why this should be. Bourdieu regards the emergence of modernism as a period when the possession of culture was axiomatically equated with the monopoly of an élite minority. Except for a few folk fossils, the masses have been literally culturally dispossessed, a process which ranks at the very least for him with the stripping of peasants of their land and which we can now perhaps hardly recall with its full terror. The attempt to produce a few claims to the title of 'working-class art' is to make the mistake of falling into pastoral mode, that is, of confusing intellectuals' accounts of the people with the people's own view of themselves.

This book will explore the limitations of such a position. It will question whether the ironic interpretation of early capitalist aesthetic discourses has not caused Bourdieu to erect a historical construction of canonical closure which is too complete and too impermeable. It will suggest further that the restricted spatial arena of Bourdieu's studies has blinded him to the existence of authorship within the popular art-forms that a concept of rediscovery can bring back to our gaze. The analysis of middlebrow and popular writers contained in chapter 6 suggests new perspectives on this problem.

I shall suggest that these are areas where a reassessment of cultures of resistance would be appropriate, and that this cannot be done without an examination of the gendering of genres. I shall look especially at the obstacles for women in acquiring recognition within avant-garde movements, and the emergence of women writers with considerable cultural capital in the middlebrow sphere, especially in the inter-war period. It is proposed that their works continued to make an impact on what has been called – following Felski (1989) – the feminist counter-public sphere. Arguing that some of the insights of Bourdieu's *Photography* could provide the basis for a fertile approach to working-class and peasant art, I take up some of the best-selling genres he has neglected. I shall also question Bourdieu's view that in capitalist modernity there is no popular art, a position which has been ably criticised by Shusterman (1992: 192). I shall assess this in the light of British Chartist novels, working-class industrial writing and other more recent popular literature. This will suggest that literature has a variety of roles for popular readers which Bourdieu's contrast between the formalism of the aesthetic attitude and the glitz of the naive gaze has neglected. Bourdieu's reception theory denies neither that writers and artists are autonomous nor that they are capable of 'singular achievements', but it does deny that culture is now an instrument of social change. It will be contended that he has underemphasised the potential for art and literature both to be critical and to imagine new alternatives.

Notes

1. *Reproduction* (written with Passeron) appeared in French in 1970; the edition used is the second English one (1990). Similarly *Distinction* was first published in 1979.

2. For this reason I cannot agree with Jenkins when he claims that 'his theory becomes a machine for suppressing history, banishing it with an eternal ethnographic present' (1992: 97).

3. This seems to me rather similar to Gramsci's notion of action in accordance with common sense, in which he defines the latter as deploying fragments of old philosophy and popular maxims.

4. Loesberg (1993) has emphasised the degree to which the habitus itself has been delineated in terms which have drawn on Kant's theory of art as purposiveness without purpose. However, he has omitted the fact that such aesthetic elements are translated by Bourdieu into a theory of social regulation which owes its origin to Durkheim.

5. Bakhtin is, of course, invoked by Bourdieu himself in relation to popular culture (1984: 491).

6. This point has been made by Codd (1990: 135); it is also raised in Garnham and Williams' critique of the quietist aspect of his thought (1986).

7. I should clarify that I do not regard Giddens' structuration theory as any more successful in this respect, despite its similar moves to Bourdieu. It should be noted that although all the assumptions of mechanical Marxism have been eliminated, Bourdieu still regards a constructive and reflexive social science as a renewed source of rational transformation, and believes that its conclusions should be disseminated through the media.

8. Frow makes several important points about Bourdieu's earlier weaknesses in addressing the over-determined character of intellectuals' views, but he is surely wrong to believe that there is a difficulty in converting economic capital into cultural capital, as Bourdieu claims takes place (Frow, 1987: 59).

9. In this respect, he shares a general conception of the sociological craft with C. Wright Mills and Alvin Gouldner, while also stressing, like Habermas, that the process of participant observation serves to enhance sociologists' own reflective self-consciousness (Habermas, 1988: 92–3).

10. It is only necessary to note Bourdieu's essay 'The Historical Genesis of the Pure Aesthetic' in *The Field of Cultural Production* (1993a: 254–66) and all his early work on Algeria to realise the oddity of this claim.

PART I
INTERPRETATIVE STUDIES

1
SITUATING BOURDIEU: CULTURAL THEORY AND SOCIOLOGICAL PERSPECTIVE

It is only possible to grasp Bourdieu's work on art and cultural reception if we understand the comparative analysis on which his whole work pivots. His childhood in the peasant area of Béarn and his time as an anthropologist in Kabylia (Algeria) shaped his analysis of the transition from pre-capitalist to capitalist forms and of the distinctive patterns of domination associated with modernity. My aim here is to start with Bourdieu's early studies in Algeria to show what historical preconditions are necessary for specialised and autonomous cultural fields to emerge. I shall then introduce, via his major works, the theoretical areas in which he has made decisive interventions. My main claim is that he has superseded various problems that have perennially plagued sociology as a critical social theory and that, at the present moment, this is the most original and cogent modelling of the social world that we have.

The Kabylian World

Bourdieu's early work on ethnography already shows unusual scope and an innovative departure from the authorised and mechanistic materialism of 'Histmat' or Stalinist historical materialism (1961, 1963, 1964 (Bourdieu and Sayad), 1966a). These books explore the breakdown of the equilibrium between artisan towns and the peasant countryside, following on the emergence of both the class society and the ideology of race instituted by colonialism. Although Bourdieu is not listed as one of the intellectuals who signed the Manifesto of the 121, he wrote in the midst of the Algerian War and may well have contributed to the events which led to resistance to service in the French Army (Alverman, 1960: 46; Anon., 1960: 196–7). In drawing on traditions normally insulated from each other, Bourdieu's approach bears the traces of the profound influence not just of Durkheim but also of Weber. Even more decisive are the marks of the famous Vol. I, Part 8 of *Capital*, especially where Marx deals with the importance of colonialism for increasing proletarianisation.

Bourdieu points out that traditional tribal Algerian societies such as the peasant Kabylia compensated for their weak mastery of nature by elaborate and detailed social organisation:

> By a sort of phenomenon of compensation, to the imperfection of techniques there is a corresponding exaggerated perfection of the social order – as if the precariousness of its adjustment to the natural environment was counterbalanced by the excellence of the social organisation. (1961: 6)

This is also evident in the artisan and merchant towns, where a leisurely daily period within the public sphere developed – at least for men – ' the art and culture of social relations' (1961: 62). By such statements, Bourdieu reveals that the colonialist or Orientalist discourse is subverted within his writing. Thus he stresses the democracy of Kabylian tribal organisation and the logic of social honour or symbolic capital which takes the place of the accumulation of economic capital in the Kabylian life-cycle. In general, his ethnographic analysis effectively undercuts any facile belief in the 'barbarism' of the Islamicised Algerians.

However, Bourdieu sometimes verges on the undiscriminating nostalgia that is implicit in some representatives of *négritude*. I refer in this context to his discussion of gender divisions, where he seems to me to 'bend the stick too far in the other direction' by stressing the multiple forms of *de facto* power available traditionally to women, despite their condition of male tutelage (1964: 187). He claims, for example, that although the position of the women of the Shawia tribe was one of extreme subordination, they possessed countervailing influence deriving from their extraordinary gender solidarity. Those who had been widowed or repudiated by their husbands could resist extreme patriarchal controls by judicious resort to the magical rhetoric of the evil eye. Less contentiously, he states that it is not traditional custom but recent urbanisation and rural displacement that has led to the imposition of the veil and the segregation of women within the house (1964: 131–2). Yet he also acknowledges the ceaseless labour of the Kabylian women he lived amongst and their disappearance from all public life as soon as they marry. Even if the effects of uprooting have massively constrained such women's everyday lives, Bourdieu's conclusions suggest a fraught and uneasy stance towards the traditional division of labour at this point. His perspective is better grounded in the evidence of a marked level of legally monopolised male power rather than of the existence of extensive freedoms for women.

Algerian traditional society did not lack endogenous change.The Mozabite tribe in the desert cities, whose predestination beliefs and ascetic rigour Bourdieu compares to Weber's Puritan dissenters, are the main protagonists of this drama of capitalist entrepreneurial activity and industry. However, Mozabite modernity did not serve – like the icy waters of egoism in the West – to drown the heavenly chorus. Rather, the profane centre of the market is viewed by Bourdieu as having *supported* the sacred centre of the mosque, while the success of the entrepreneurial action of male migrants to the cities fostered the family and communal life of the countryside.[1] Bourdieu's writing thus stands in the anti-Orientalist tradition of Maxime Rodinson (1974) in explaining the lack of internal development of capitalism through the strength of a dominant military stratum which has been committed to the resilience of non-capitalist forms, rather than the influence of Islam itself.

However, the main emphasis of the ethnographic studies is on the end of the old paternalist order of the great families and of its stable balance between city and country. Instead, the dialectic of colonialism leads remorselessly from the appropriation of the most fertile soil by the French to the subsequent dispersal of the Algerians on to marginal land, followed by rapid urban proletarianisation, the re-groupments of the War and the explosive growth of the unemployed (1964). The city is now stripped of its public sphere, with its daily routine of rational communication. Only its worst conditions are shown to its new inhabitants, whose lives (outside the new bourgeoisie) become ones of utter privation: 'the art and culture of social relations' cannot survive the epidemics, absolute want and overcrowding of the distended urban centres (1961: 62).

In the country the concentration of property and consequent sharecropping had preceded colonialism, but was greatly strengthened by it, particularly since European law legitimated individual ownership of land. This not only facilitated European takeover, it also led to an accelerated decline in tribal-owned land (one-fifth in 1961). '[T]his means the death sentence of the tribe', Bourdieu comments, noting the atomisation or 'social vivisection' it produced. More profoundly, it provoked a shift from the 'gift and counter-gift economy' to the money economy (1961: 84). It is necessary to understand this clearly for Bourdieu views the gift economy as sustaining solidarity. Its abandonment was partly due to a forced modernisation, partly a response to the hegemony of French culture. Rural Algerians (fellahs) had a long time-perspective in which the future was perceived as close to the present. Thus the fellah has almost a 'mystical' attachment to the soil:

> [L]and is an end in itself not a mere means of existence and work is not a way of living but a way of life. (1961: 103)

Money was a unit of value before colonisation, but it was not used as an abstract value. Specifically, it did not serve as speculative credit for the purpose of capital accumulation, because the future was not conceived as new or different. Only with the impoverishment of the fellah was there the rise of the 'new men' of the cities, stripped of their families and dispossessed of that temporal sense and 'art of life' founded in the land. From now on, even the peasants will express the contradiction between the old and the new. Agriculture has lost its dignity – its capacity to inspire a 'sacred terror' (1964: 95). Even on the land, a crisis has affected the 'peasant spirit':

> What separates the 'unemployed' from the 'peasant' [is not the actual time spent working, it] is the refusal to consider as work what is not paid for by a wage . . . . (1964: 68)

Thus the French had precipitated 'a transmutation of values' (1961: 118).

It is crucial to understand Bourdieu's view of this representative non-Western pre-capitalist culture in order to grasp his view of the place of the aesthetic in modern Western life. Self-expression in the West has spawned constant vigilance to a 'dialectic of distinction'. Such individualism is absent in Kabylia, as is evident in the demarcation of tents by red and black colour within a social classification. Moreover in Kabylia, the cliché is desirable as part of a culture of politeness (set against the normal logic of practice) in which the cultural apprenticeship is 'to guard against . . . any improvisation . . . in behaviour' (1961: 96). Typical in this respect is oral poetry which annuls the passage of time so as to make the young aware of the noble actions of their ancestors. It thus allows the perpetual re-experience of the past within a present only weakly opposed to it. Yet more striking, in Kabylia, craft has not become degraded by contrast with high art.

The Algerians ends with a recent collective development of poetry: the songs of resistance composed anonymously during the war against the French. From this society 'sliding into the dizzy abyss', then, there was also salvaged a small compensation, a new culture. Within this, there was not only a popular culture of poems registering the common experience of loss but a new French-language novel, expressing the 'sense of anguish' of the educated Algerian class 'between two worlds'. Bourdieu frequently returns to these linked themes, the erosion of all the old communal forms through both capitalism and colonialism and the compensatory dream of setting apart a sacred aesthetic sphere.

In his subsequent studies of Kabylia (1977, 1990a), Bourdieu first introduces the ideas that have had an extraordinary impact on later sociology. I shall discuss first the concept of practice, which for him means an agent makes decisions and moves his or her body in a 'regularised improvisation' like jazz (1977: 11).

The idea of practice has been developed extensively in Bourdieu's later work. To what extent does this concept, associated as it is with his conversion to structuralism, successfully withstand the criticisms levelled against this approach? Remarkably well. Bourdieu manages to abandon the unacceptable Enlightenment conception of native thought as irrational (like that of the mad and children) (Ferguson, 1990: 16–21). But he saves the equally important notion of the submission of ideas to a rational procedure of truth-claims as the distinguishing feature of scentific rationality, or 'theoretical practice'. It has certainly been argued that Bourdieu's conception of scientific habitus embeds scientific thought in the same concern for the 'game' and in the same aesthetic sense of adequacy which governs practice in everyday life more broadly (Brubaker, 1993: 230–1). But this is hardly faithful to the complexity of Bourdieu's *Logic of Practice*. For while in this work he compares practice with the aesthetic and especially with taste, he locates practice as a feature of the *everyday* life of modernity. When he comes to use the term in relation to specialised fields, for example law or science (1987c; 1994b: 91–7), he assumes that the 'intuitive' 'feel for the game' takes place within the procedural principles that constitute the field itself, as part of its professional modes of operation.[2]

Despite his acknowledgement of conflict and its socio-genesis, Bourdieu has repudiated the irrationalist position that lurks in Brubaker's argument. Indeed, for him, sociology is in itself a prophylactic against irrationalism. His most recent study of sociological method explicitly uses the term 'realism' (1993b: 903), thus associating himself with a tradition of thought about social science which rejects the relativist perspectivism of Kuhnian or Lyotardian paradigm theory (Bourdieu and Wacquant, 1992: 155).[3]

It is one of the most attractive features of Bourdieu's sociology that he has transcended the sterility of the objectivist versus subjectivist debate within social theory, along with the one-sided alternatives of both structuralism and existentialism, of mechanical materialism and rational action theory. Bourdieu roots his theory of 'structural constructivism' in the materialism of Marx's *Theses on Feuerbach* (see Colletti, 1977: 23; Bourdieu and Wacquant, 1992: 11). He locates the role of objective structures in setting limits to agents' choice of goals as well as blinkering their perceptions of reality. A theme constantly reiterated in relation to Sartre's existentialism and to Schutz's and Garfinkel's phenomenological 'accounts of accounts' is that these lack a sufficient grasp of historically developing objective conditions within which humans' social constructions can occur. Sartre, for example, neglects any analysis of revolution in terms of a response to objective conditions and constraints, making it instead a feature of a willed act of the imagination alone. But most strikingly, Bourdieu has understood social structures as operating not just via internalisation but through incorporation. Thus the submissiveness of Kabylian women is embodied in the curvature of their spines towards the ground. It is not just that social learning is ingrained on the body, like the scars sometimes signifying transition to adulthood, rather it is imitated *unconsciously* through specific bodily actions. This stress on the unconscious and bodily expressions of the social ('hexis') (1990a: 74) does not deny the emergence of complex forms of resistance but it does stress the durability of the earliest actions learnt through example or apprenticeship, that is, through the mastery of practice. In this respect it parallels the beautifully demonstrated idea of Elias (1978) that the repressive controls over the body must be understood not just psychogenetically, but historically, that is, as internalised forms of compliance to the influential classes or nations which are the bearers of social rules. Thus Bourdieu proposes a similar socio-genesis of bodily hexis in the context of a *pre-capitalist* society, while Elias had merely argued that there is a 'civilisation curve' in Europe, in which bodily controls become more intense from the period of *the courtly aristocracy* onwards. But to grasp his thinking on this point properly, it is necessary to understand the concept now virtually synonymous with Bourdieu for some: that of the habitus.

Habitus has been variously defined in Bourdieu's theory but it is put most simply in *Reproduction* as '[the] system of schemes of . . . perception, thought, appreciation and action which are durable and transposable' (Bourdieu and Passeron 1990: 35). Given that this implies that the subjective world is constituted in a stable pattern, Bourdieu then goes on to link habitus to a material or structural position, not unlike the Lukácsian notion of world-view. Yet whereas the Western Marxist position has identified existence within the dominated class with a utopian or revolutionary world-vision, Bourdieu has stressed also the modes of *ressentiment* and especially resignation associated with deprivation. The habitus of the dominated frequently leads them to choose actively what they are objectively constrained to do. Thus they 'make a virtue out of necessity', as in the case of women who adopt high standards for the housework that they are constrained to undergo alone. Aspirations are therefore limited, as revealed in the phrase 'That's not for the likes of us'.[4]

What are the schemes of perception that order the Kabylian habitus? Bourdieu has portrayed some of the crucial principles in the diagrammatic descriptions of the Kabylian house and agricultural calendar. These guide how things should be done. In terms of strict logic, they are based on principles that flout the rules of contradiction. However, in a key passage, Bourdieu stresses that the 'polythetic' rationality of the Kabylians inheres in their conception of a logic of practice regulated by a longer and more episodic conception of time (1990a: 12–13, 261). Polythetic logic is based on strategic consideration of interests in the broadest sense and exists in all societies. In contrast, the more 'monothetic' rationality, characteristic of a tiny minority, particularly of scientists and philosophers in late capitalism, derives from the typical capacity to view things abstractly, stripped of all temporal embeddedness in events and presented in the written form which makes for theoretical understanding.

Successful practice requires the actor both to operate within a specific habitus and to act creatively beyond the specific injunctions of its rules. Put another way, the habitus supplies a regulated set of perceptions and actions, within which improvisation typically occurs. Bourdieu himself likes to use the examples of football or tennis to explain this: the player has literally a 'feel for the game' such that 'in the heat of the moment' he or she will make the right moves or calculations. This loose linkage with the rules and what has been done before is also pointed to in the field of painting: thus the painter not only acquires a sense of how other artists fit together in the chain of producers, but also masters the medium practically by solving the problematic issues present at any given moment (1990a: 55). This often distinguishes him from the art critic, who frequently lacks awareness of such difficult practical skills.

It seems to me that – like Giddens – Bourdieu has been struck by the sheer level of expertise involved in run-of-the-mill human accomplishments. Despite the existence of doxic or taken-for-granted knowledge (that which cannot be spoken), this complexity of calculation is what he sees as an endemic feature of action. It is this rejection of the mechanistic model of humans as mere bearers of structures that led Bourdieu to break with the 'happy structuralism' of the period up to 1963, and to re-interpret the oppositions which he had earlier deployed to characterise the rituals and symbolism of the Kabylian world (1968). Crucial in this respect are two criticisms he makes of Lévi-Strauss. First, the latter assumes that ritual and myths are 'eternal answers to eternal questions' rather than the solution to practical problems:

> Beneath its air of radical materialism it is a form of idealism affirming the universality and eternity of the logical categories, while ignoring the dialectic of social structures and structured, structuring dispositions. . . . (1977: 203)

Thus Lévi-Strauss reifies into separate aesthetic or spiritual episodes actions which have both wider significance and a precise material function. Linked to this, Lévi-Strauss fails to connect ritual meanings both to material experiences and to the subjective principles of vision and division to which these gave rise:

> The Kabylian peasant does not react to 'objective conditions' but to these conditions as apprehended through the socially constituted schemes that organise his perception. To understand ritual practice, to give it back both its reason and raison d'être without converting it to a logical construct or a spiritual exercise means more than simply reconstituting its internal logic. It also means restoring its practical necessity by relating it to the real conditions of its genesis. . . . It means describing the most brutally material bases of the investment in magic, such as the weakness of the productive and reproductive forces, which causes a life dominated by anxiety about matters of life and death to be lived as an uncertain struggle against uncertainty. (1990a: 97)

It is also abundantly clear that Bourdieu has rejected the alternatives to this position, by which I mean the 'rational choice' theory of Elster, or, earlier, the Sartrian ideas of 'authentic action' or good and bad faith.

In each case the reasoning is the same. Both these approaches lack a proper sense of a *social institution*. Thus, on Sartre he laments that

> from the reified state of the alienated group, to the authentic existence of the historical agent, consciousness and thing are as irremediably separate as they were at the outset, without anything resembling an institution or a socially-constituted agent having been observed. . . . (1977: 76)

From Elster he has taken the 'sour grapes' syndrome, but he sternly rejects the pretensions of this type of re-reading of Marxism, with its over-calculative, rationalist conception of human action. For Bourdieu, practice is

> informed by a kind of objective finality without being consciously organised in relation to an explicitly constituted end; intelligible and coherent without springing from an intention of coherence and a deliberate decision; adjusted to the future without being a product of a project or a plan (1990a: 50–1)

It will perhaps now be clear that Bourdieu's characteristic way of resolving the stalemates in academic social theory is by refusing both rival positions that compete for intellectual authority, whether in terms of problematics raised outside Marxism or in terms of issues that produce the same dilemmas within it. He transcends the existing antinomies by pioneering a third alternative position or method in a manner that often seems extraordinarily fertile. I shall briefly map out how he has done this.

Symbolic capital

Both pre-capitalist and capitalist societies are organised around symbolic capital – to achieve recognition as one of the great is its ultimate mark. Algerians have a vigorous sense of honour, reputation or dignity, which is in part regulated by the sexual division of labour. It is honour, rather than the accumulation of money or capital, which principally motivates them. Although Bourdieu uses the term 'symbolic capital' as an analogy to economic capital, he has sometimes provoked misinterpretation on this score. Symbolic capital is not necessarily the outcome of a 'market'-based, or a calculative competitive, struggle, as he himself acknowledges (1994b: 161–4). However, although sociology may unveil interests in disinterestedness, it is my view that an important category of the possession of symbolic capital may simply mean the achievement of a *human* existence – as in Kabylian sexual honour – which is differentiated from animal action and which is potentially open to all humans. Thus its absence is best seen in certain types of deviance, possibly only the subject of myth, and not the zero-sum competition inherent in the modern Western conception of 'status'.

It is true, as Bourdieu points out, that in class societies every type of symbolic capital is filtered through the prisms of class domination. Action is based on collective strategies to ensure the interests of the great families, in France as much as Kabylia and through marriage as well as production. But in Kabylia symbolic profits demand the repayment of favours to retainers and are destructive of capital accumulation as an end in itself. In France, however, symbolic capital is *typically* converted through a circuit rather like the conversion of money into value or capital and back into money again; there is, however, no necessity to this circular transformation and acquisition of symbolic and economic capital can in principle be separated.

Bourdieu's theory of symbolic capital is often arrestingly phrased and owes much to the need to move beyond a crude economic reductionism in Marxist thought. It is not always transparent in its clarity, however, and one area I wish to introduce here will prove difficult when discussing the field of culture. I refer to the notion of 'symbolic profits'. Are these perceived and shared by the agent and does he/she gauge his/her action to achieve them? Or are 'symbolic profits' the product of an objective analysis of a whole social process? If so, who is the observer and how has he/she managed to attain such a uniquely privileged, totalising perspective? Despite Bourdieu's awareness of this problem in general in his criticism of Lévi-Strauss cited above, it is still a source of difficulty in relation to his attribution of interests in symbolic capital to modernist artists.

Time and practice

Bourdieu's recent work has expanded his notion of the sense of practice. It characterises not just those activities especially near to material necessity, but every action in which time is important so that it is undertaken with a sense of urgency. Even science has been interpreted as a set of activities involving mastery of specific rules (which also master the scientist). The theoretical mode in which contradictions are isolated and rejected is now seen as only one aspect of science. In this way activities, such as sociology, can be viewed *also* as a craft.

As we have seen, Bourdieu emphasises that the fuzziness of polythetic thought, with its elaborate cosmological meanings for social differences, is rational in a context where activities are separated by the passage of time. He goes on to argue that such systems of differences survive in advanced capitalism in the shape of ultimate values (1990a: 1). These inform also a set of meanings – 'taste' – which allows very diverse areas to be described with the same contrasting terms: cooking, personal appearance and philosophical essays can all be differentiated by certain major oppositions, such as brilliant/dull, bland/scintillating or noble/common. These are retained with the greatest complexity in the sphere of art, for art operates by means of images drawn from popular analogies or textual references and it is these images which trigger mythological evaluations:

> As a belated small-scale producer of private mythologies, it is easier for him [the poet] to cut through dead metaphors and go straight to the heart of mythopoeic practice. ... (1990a: 94)

Time, capital accumulation and art

In order to understand political economy as ideology, Marx had to deconstruct it and show how the mutually dependent social relations of the agents of capital and the agents of labour had come into being. An interest in capital accumulation for its own sake has to have other objective conditions: Bourdieu's work has reminded us that these are absent in Kabylia, as they are everywhere where there is no unadulterated pressure for profit as an end, and consequently no perception of labour as an abstract and depersonalised unit of time. Bourdieu insists that in Kabylia the man who tries to get through his agricultural work very fast and without regard for the calendrical regulation of different jobs is thought to be crazy. Moreover, since everyone 'takes pains with nature' in his/her labour, there is no conception of a timed interval of labour for a particular given task. Finally, even after the emergence of capital accumulation, it is a 'fairy story' to assume that the same objective conditions exist to make *everyone* concerned with it. There is an unequal distribution of the 'right to pre-empt the future'. In this context, the peasants of Kabylia offer

> the art of living raised to an art for art's sake, founded on a refusal to acknowledge the 'business is business' or 'time is money' on which the

unaesthetic lifestyle of the harried leisure classes in so-called advanced societies is based. (1977: 195)

By contrast, in advanced capitalism, the concern for money so dominates the whole of life that art stands out as one of the few areas where things operate differently:

> The denial of economic interest . . . finds its favourite refuge in the domain of art and culture, the site of pure consumption – of money, of course, but also of time convertible into money. The world of art, a sacred island systematically and ostentatiously opposed to the profane world of production, a sanctuary for gratuitous, disinterested activity in a universe given over to money and self-interest offers, like theology in a past epoch, an imaginary anthropology brought about by the denial of all the negations really brought about by the economy. (1977: 197)

Cultural capital: the inheritance of consecrated culture

In this section I want to explore these issues more deeply, before going on to look specifically at Bourdieu's theory of the perception of art. Bourdieu introduces in his earliest works a theory of symbolic violence and misrecognition, which he returns to as late as *Language and Symbolic Power* in 1991 (French editions, 1982–3). In effect, this *is* his theory of ideology and there are indeed some quite striking parallels between Bourdieu's conception of ideology as both theory and 'material practice' and that of his teacher, Althusser. For both thinkers the school is the major modern ideological base, not least through the ritual of examinations. However, I want to show that Bourdieu has virtues that Althusser lacked. Although Bourdieu went through a structuralist stage in which his thought was also weakened by positivism, he nevertheless developed and revised his theory as Althusser was unable to. Thus where Althusser was vulnerable to a powerful critique of his essentially functionalist and idealist conception of ideological domination, as in E.P. Thompson's *The Poverty of Theory* (1979: 272–3), Bourdieu cannot be criticised in the same way.

Bourdieu's sociology is a pincer-like attack on both objectivism and subjectivism. Breaking with subjectivism, he accepts that there can be causes of social action of which the individual subject is not fully aware. But challenging also the objectivist structuralism of his own earlier work, he proposes a theory of practice which, as we have seen, is based on both collective and individual strategic activity. This is inevitably an uneasy combination, but it does get beyond the sterility of conceiving ideology as a whole ensemble of social relations. While this takes the rational kernel of Althusser's emphasis on collective representations and their coercive character in daily social relations, it repudiates Althusser's neglect of the whole vocabulary of interest. The virtue of Bourdieu is that he combines a theory of class interest[5] and misrecognition of such interest with a theory of stable structures and social relations which comes from his Durkheimian inheritance. This in turn strengthens his conception of contradiction, which, along with symbolic violence, has remained a pivotal category in his work. Although he has always stressed that commodity fetishism – with its associated pursuit of maximum profitability or exchange-value – does not magically create social antagonisms or even fragmentation, his sociology has always unmasked contradictory *interests* and exposed conflict, especially in the arena of the school and the university. In this respect he has moved far beyond Althusser's over-socialised conception of humanity.

To summarise, then, Bourdieu, from *Les Héritiers* (The Inheritors) (1964)[6] onwards, has insisted, like Giddens, on a *duality* of structure. Thus people (agents), collectively or individually, transform or reproduce their social structures, but they do so within specific social conditions, including those that are internalised as part of their habitus even at the very moment of revolution. Domination, therefore, occurs through a variety of means, from the economic operations of the market, to symbolic intimidation (in this context Bourdieu is surely right in seeing success in exams as a modern equivalent to the sign of grace). Even the gentle violence exerted by dominant families in their marriage arrangements ensures the satisfaction of diffuse interests.

Les Héritiers has an Orwellian tone to it. Things are not really what they are said to be. This is signalled dramatically right from the start, where the prologue introduces us to the Omaha Indian method for the discovery and recruitment of new sorcerers. Everyone must compete to be a sorcerer and for this reason they must spend a period away in the wilderness awaiting a vision. But although everyone has visions, some have more authentic visions than others and, curiously, these are the members of the sorcerers' own kin! Bourdieu reveals the similar importance of social origins in academic attainment within so-called advanced societies. It is through the family home that the cultural capital of the school is accumulated and the absence of such cultural capital for working-class youth is a much more immoveable barrier to social mobility than material poverty. Consequently, only 6 per cent of French university students were recruited from the children of farm labourers, peasants or industrial manual workers (Bourdieu and Passeron, 1964: 18).

Paradoxically, free culture is accumulated when the reality principle has surrendered to the principle of pure pleasure. Moreover, behind the apparently random leisure choices of the students of the dominant class lie all their early family training, a training which disciplines their interest in artistic form even in the most popular genres like cinema and jazz. From these experiences and modes of thought emerges an ethos of preciousness and irony, a fascination with the exotic and a desire for distinction. Even within the choice of art which 'liquidates the bourgeois experience' (Bourdieu and Passeron, 1964: 29) there is concealed a cultural good-will, a 'conformist anti-conformism' (1964: 69). For the children of the dominated class, on the other hand, free culture has a quite different impact. Lacking the close familial contact with consecrated culture, their experience of mass culture is informed by a popular aesthetic which serves to divert them further from academic success. Consequently:

> The school is the royal way to the democratisation of culture if it does not consecrate these same inequalities through reproaching students for being too scholarly . . . this has the effect of devaluing the culture of the educational curriculum . . . by replacing it with the inherited culture. (1964: 35)

This is the first formulation of the theory that those who most criticise the culture are also those most likely to benefit from it. Criticism presupposes cultural mastery. What is more, the most materially secure children of the haute bourgeoisie display their 'spiritual grace' in our period not by thrift or frugality but rather by their casual ease and heretical tastes. In other words, by showing the signs of unworldly disinterestedness, they appear distant from the 'common' display of effort of the less privileged students. There has been a transmutation of the Protestant Ethic's basic values.

Clearly, this is the origin of Bourdieu's later theory of the dominated fraction of the dominant class: a conception which has undoubtedly illuminated his subsequent approach to artistic groups such as the late nineteenth-century aestheticists. Already, in *Les Héritiers*, we note the 'conformist anti-conformism' which leads the children of the haute bourgeoisie to their adherence to the modernist canon (Valéry, Proust, Sartre). But in more anthropological manner, Bourdieu and Passeron stress that the root of their approach to the educational curriculum lies in their distinctive place in space and time. Despite the material privileges these students possess, there is also a much greater individualism among them and, compared to working-class students, a lack of secondary associations or wider communal ties. Yet if in this respect they are typical of the 'cool' deracinated bohemian of the metropolis they also have a nostalgia for integration and a cult of the utopian community. The students of the dominated class, on the other hand, are closer to material urgencies and also more traditional in their conception of space and time. They have both more experience of the serious nature of social reality and less commitment to the '*game* of seriousness'. Bourdieu thus initially sketches out a number of the antinomies found subsequently in his work on cultural reception.

This is a fascinating theory and it seems perverse to criticise it when it emphasises the significance of the private sphere. It stresses the powerful emotional transmission of cultural sensitivity, as with the child who learns Beethoven from the mother's playing. Moreover, Bourdieu and Passeron are clearly attuned to gender difference. They refer to women being more susceptible to the authority of university professors, such that their greater attentiveness and docility facilitates them more easily than men for upwards social mobility. For all this, there are still signs that Bourdieu was himself under the impact of '*la domination masculine*', which he only unravelled much later (1990b). He blunts his notion of socialisation when, despite emphasising that home is the main site for the growth of the classificatory mesh through which all subsequent educational ideas must be passed, he neglects the skilled labour (especially of women) which goes into this educational matrix.

The division between work and leisure is identified here with the Freudian dualism between the reality principle (or necessity) and the pleasure principle (sexuality, gratification). For Bourdieu and Passeron, the sphere of leisure and the pleasure principle is the terrain for the acquisition of the heretical culture that later turns magically into an investment in consecrated knowledge. But, taking apart the pleasure principle, it becomes apparent that it involves also that all too familiar but still significant area, invisible domestic work. Are we to assume that all the pains taken with the bringing-up of children can be discussed under the heading 'pleasure' ? Are not these sacrifices in the form of time and care for children also a kind of 'labour of love', which has as its issue the cultural capital from which the child benefits? Bourdieu and Passeron pass over these questions, discussing only their public effects in terms of scholastic accomplishments when it is a matter rather of the survival of the pre-capitalist 'good faith' economy within the home. And yet, when we pull back the veil on these mundane matters, what an extraordinary profusion of methods and modes is found. It takes work like Davidoff and Hall's *Family Fortunes* (1987) to reveal what the middle-class rationalisation of domestic labour really meant, as in the systematic inculcation of the work ethic with the use of the abacus for infants or the minute classification of the kitchen and garden like that of natural science.

Reproduction belongs to a happily brief ultra-positivist formulation of problems, which Bourdieu came later to pose in a more satisfactory way. This book is particularly important for showing how a cultural arbitrary is imposed in education, which, because of its remoteness from the culture of the dominated class, tends to reproduce the existing class order. In it, Marx is bounced off Weber (and sometimes Durkheim too) in a very creative manner. In particular, the Weberian notion of legitimation is used to stress, in Marxist fashion, that the act of legitimating a ruling class does not just convert power to authority but increases that power, while Weber is upbraided for ignoring the fact that the misrecognition of the culture of the dominators tends to have independent social consequences. More problematically, in my view, Bourdieu argues against a 'utopian' rationalism: symbolic violence is necessary, he contends, since all teaching depends on an *arbitrary* cultural choice in which only one perspective from the permanently clashing interests in advanced societies is elaborated. I would want to contest the inevitability of cultural domination along Habermasian lines, holding that arbitrariness could be replaced or reduced by undistorted communicative competence.[7]

The teachers themselves have two possible relations to this culture. They can either rest on the charisma of office, or they can see themselves rather as prophets, with their authority coming from within themselves. This is the first delineation of the notion of *heterodox* leaders, so important in Bourdieu's broader theory of culture. Yet the conception of the teacher as prophet, who may articulate a message critical of the social practices of those with economic and social capital, is unelaborated. For although the model adopted to illuminate the nature of the legitimate culture is that of the alien rule of colonialists over natives, and although some of the rhetorical force derives from this vision of the sharply conflicting interests into which the school is inserted, nevertheless there is a massive over-simplification at the level of meaning, especially of teachers' motivations. In particular, while the 'cultural arbitrary' begins to explain the powerlessness of the dominated to determine their own children's education, the problem with the book is its silence precisely about why the 'natives' don't become 'restless'. Moreover, the prophetic type of teacher potentially implies the existence of educational pleasures attached to schooling for the working class, which then act as inducements. In my view, the school is not *just* the site of authoritarian rituals with educational canons, as the authors imply by quoting Marx on exams:

> The examination is nothing but the bureaucratic baptism of knowledge, the official recognition of the transubstantiation of profane knowledge into sacred knowledge. (quoted in Bourdieu and Passeron, 1990: 141)

Rather the school culture works because it can connect precisely to aspirations within the working class. Teachers see themselves as rescuing 'bright' children from the harsh deformities of poverty even while simultaneously employing categories of educability that favour the dominant class. It is this cultural pleasure or hope which explains the collusion of the dominated with the school. It only continues to work its legitimating magic to the degree that some of the dominated do indeed appropriate the educational culture and that this conferral of a changed mode of existence is viewed by the dominated as a sacrifice of their children for the sake of their material future. *Reproduction* also neglects a key dimension which reduces the gap between the culture of the school and that of the dominated. This is the mediation of the national culture, with its anti-aristocratic baggage (discussed subsequently in 1991: 46–8) As Renée Balibar has shown, the revolutionary formation of a French national identity was crucial in spreading a whole culture of popular manuals and popular fiction in which Parisian French was used against regional dialects to spread useful knowledge (Balibar, 1986; see also Anderson,1983). It is teachers' invocations of such 'imaginary communities' which the stiff anti-functionalist positivism of Bourdieu fails to grasp yet this philosophy exists as a crucial part of the motor fuelling French schooling, despite its undeniably reproductive mechanisms. In brief, while the notion of 'prophetic' educators could have been used to point to the complex nature of the subjective realities at stake, it was never exploited. In an understandable eagerness to reveal the objectively more favourable position of the children of the dominant class, Bourdieu fails to explain precisely how concealment of this fact is made possible by the (real) chance that marginal benefits may even be won by the children of the working class, especially for those who comply with the rules of the game.

Yet we can already see that the concept of habitus has begun to acquire the flexibility and richness that has made it one of Bourdieu's trademarks. For whereas early on he welds together a concept of class world-view or consciousness as a set of regulatory dispositions, which are the basis for the individual's improvised and skilled accomplishments, here he begins to apply his theory of rationalisation or cultural autonomy to habitus. In other words, in Western societies the school is the bearer of a distinctive culture into which even the children of the dominated class can be trained if they are given a sufficiently early, Latin-based *lycée* schooling. Two or three cryptic remarks indicate that in France specific conditions enhanced the syncretic aspects of the educational habitus, particularly the powerful impact of the Jesuits in providing the transmission belt for a worldly *secular* culture and that of the Jacobins in underwriting a Latin-based schooling as a revolutionary organic ideology. In other words, the Revolution of 1789 enhanced the power of the intelligentsia by making a classical education part of a cultural mission to the people. This notion of an elaborated educational habitus is fundamental, not least because it is the seed for Bourdieu's later idea of an artistic habitus, with its distinctive set of professional competencies.

Secondly, the belief in meritocracy is immensely powerful, as Bourdieu indicates. It leads to the self-exclusion of the excluded. Even dissenting teachers are affected by it, in that any break with canonical knowledge can lead to the accusation of providing a devalued education. However, even in this early work, we notice a tendency for Bourdieu and Passeron to attribute a greater influence to the rules of consecrated culture than actually exists. While it is quite true that consecrated culture has undermined much folk art, it is misleading to suggest, as they do, that the culture industry is staffed solely by those with legitimate culture. In fact, the excluded popular culture is hardly analysed in this text. Later events suggest that the media and culture industries need more analysis: indeed, the subsequent conflicts within television suggest a very *insecure* hegemony for consecrated culture (Garnham, 1993: 189–92).

Language and Symbolic Power (1991)

The essays collected under this title represent not only a contribution to the philosophy of language, but also a rich series of interpretative concepts for the generation of middle-level theory. Both these initiatives allow Bourdieu to make a significant intervention in a sector which has been dominated by the subjectivism of ethnomethodology to such an extent that it has produced only a sterile vacuousness equivalent to much linguistic philosophy. Instead Bourdieu's thinking brings together objective forces, such as the possession of scarce linguistic resources, and reveals what consequences emerge from these at the level of linguistic style and meaning and to what extent a linguistic dimension exists within some partially unconscious struggles.[8]

First, he introduces an extension to the idea of economic markets, that is, linguistic markets. Such linguistic markets occur wherever language operates as an independent aspect of social interchange. Bourdieu is concerned here not with the politics of colonial linguistic domination, but rather with the hegemony of certain linguistic codes, which, when viewed as cultural capital, are linked to the dominant class.[9] Thus in the advanced societies, where there are constrained linguistic markets, high linguistic capital brings high symbolic profits ('the profits of distinction') (1991: 55). The social reality of the existence of linguistic capital is that some feel authorised to speak, that is, they have the social assurance of possessing a mastery of language and, unlike the hypercorrectness of the insecure petty bourgeoisie, have the temerity to flout selected rules (1991: 62–3).

Secondly, a few 'free linguistic markets' persist where the dominant code does not produce symbolic profits. Of these, the most unconstrained occur in the contexts of closed institutions like the prison, where developed subversive codes exist, as indicated through the use of nicknames, blasphemy and slang. Other institutions like pubs, clubs and adolescent peer-groups also permit a subversive code (1991: 98-9). Thus the manner of the publican (or the DJ) is to facilitate the sense of well-being gained from self-expression by stimulating it through the use of common language, colloquialisms, etc. The subversive code operates by neutralising the effects of the euphemisms so characteristic of the dominant code, especially by unmasking their inappropriate, arbitrary or even counter-factual status.

Bourdieu advances a further variant of the thesis that high linguistic capital brings high profits of distinction. This is his argument, elaborated subsequently as 'the Heidegger effect', that specific profits derive from mixing the imposition of form with the use of popular speech. Symbolic profit in this case springs from the combination of the rarity of the mastery of form together with the signs of a disinterested good-will towards the popular (1991: 148). However:

> [S]tyle, whether it be a matter of poetry as compared with prose or of the diction of a particular (social, sexual or generational) class compared with that of another class, exists only in relation to agents endowed with schemes of perception and appreciation that enable them to constitute it as a set of systematic differences . . . . (1991: 38–9)

As this suggests, dominant class membership is thus joined by other social bases for the acquisition of linguistic capital. Since empirical research shows that French working-class women swear less than their men (1991: 265), Bourdieu suggests that this more 'tight-lipped' use of language from the feminine '*bouche*' places them in a stronger position for chances of upward mobility than the rough language from the '*gueule*' of the working-class male (1991: 86–8). But if women's bodily constraints paradoxically place them in stronger position vis-à-vis the dominant linguistic code, we should also recall the silence of women. This is not a literal silence, but rather relates to the consequences of women's exclusion from the public sphere. It is surprising that Bourdieu fails to link his valuable category of 'authorised language' to women's speech, which, in lacking those markers of educated or democratic debate (points of order etc.), has been disqualified from seriousness for this reason.

Thirdly, Bourdieu notes the social consequences of the 'nationalisation' of language, that is, in France, the emergence of the Île de France dialect in the seventeenth century as the official language and the consequent degradation of regional speech. The phenomenon of the Revolution, he remarks, was to carry much further this initial work of the Jesuits, that is, the unification and purification of the official language (1991: 48). The devaluation of the superseded *patois* was intensified from that time through the mastery of both Parisian and regional codes by the aristocracy and professionals. The national language thus sets up another arena for struggles for distinction, not least in the accompanying usage of 'strategies of condescension'; that is, the acquisition of populist credentials by the conspicuous use of the vernacular (1991: 68).

In brief, where sociologists see *either* the truth of consensus *or* the truth of coercion, Bourdieu's 'constructivist' sociology sees both. Where Chomsky agrees with Saussure in seeing language as a universal treasure, perhaps the most graphic expression of the collective consciousness, Bourdieu emphasises language use as a sign of salvation by a secular elect (parallel to the linguistic prerogatives of males at bar mitzvahs). Such a theory of linguistic representation can be extended to (vulgar) Marxists, whose rhetoric also serves to obscure the degree to which social divisions, as in the case of classes founded on production, must counter pre-existing solidarities and may exist cohesively only on paper. Hence Bourdieu's frequent theme: 'We must classify the classifiers!' (1984: 467; 1991: 242), that is, a reflexive sociology must examine the interests – political as well as economic – in constructing groups in certain ways. Just as Marx questioned who might educate the educators, Bourdieu is here concerned with the structural location of those who provide a facile romantic account of social revolution.

I have argued at various points in this chapter that Bourdieu's sociology is directed towards the work of critique by *extending* the labour of materialism associated with Marx. One area in which this is shown most innovatively is in his analysis of politics. Thus *Language* complements Marx's commodity fetishism with a concept of political fetishism, analogous to the former in that politicians' discourses also conceal the social relations and interests in which they are embedded (1991: 27). One crucial factor in this process is that of mandated authority (1991: 203). Bourdieu asks who is mandated to speak for a group and how they legitimate their authority. Perhaps we can apply this more widely to the theory of culture. Following on Bourdieu's comments about the linguistic legitimacy of being in touch with the popular mind, much more discussion is needed of how the linguistic forms aspiring to be popular are embedded within various genres. Stuart Hall, for example, has discussed the journalism of the tabloids as a 'ventriloquism' of the popular voice (1981). Such a concept could be elaborated in other forms of culture, especially where a novelist assumes a popular style for commercial effect, as in Bourdieu's category of types of literary production for the large-scale market.

Heretical discourses are also politically mandated. Bourdieu breaks with a residual individualism in Weber by arguing that even the charismatic prophet must attract a following (1991: 249–50), since this is the pre-requisite for the 'prophecy of bad fortune'. The 'labour of denunciation' or dramatised deprivation then enhances a crisis which produces the potential for a major change of social identity. Here Bourdieu uses Voloshinov's conception of the clashing class or ideological accents as an inherent element of linguistic discourse, stressing that words can never be neutral. But when is the labour of denunciation using the vernacular also a strategic form of 'condescension' with its own symbolic rewards? What are the marks of such strategies and how might we distinguish the false prophecies motivated by distinction from true ones? On these crucial issues Bourdieu is quiet.

In the labour of denunciation, the forms of discourse seeking to rescue the subordinate can themselves be transitional. Again, this is a context in which studies of popular culture are illuminating. Denning has shown how the American dime novels of the 1870s to 1890s appropriated feudal titles, but with a new content, as in the phrase 'Knights of Labour' (1987: chap. 9). At stake, then, is the emergence of linguistic responses to stigmatisation and literary cultures of resistance taking popular forms.

The sociology of the academic profession

While the campus novel is an established genre, there has been little sociological analysis of the makers of consecrated culture and their social origins. Nor has there been any extended study of *the conflict of the faculties* based on the discordant fragmentation of different disciplines. I shall show how in this arena there appear many of the same structural conflicts and fractures that occur in Bourdieu's analysis of the art-world, not least between different fractions of the bourgeoisie. Finally, the analysis of the crisis of 1968, which acquired its distinctive aspect as a crisis of late capitalism, can be shown as being triggered by conflicts over cultural consumption. The May Events of 1968 are important in Bourdieu's sociology in part as an unsuccessful revolution, the relative frequency of which in modern French history perhaps gives his sociology its characteristic pessimism.

Bourdieu has undertaken a number of studies of cultural production. While my main interest is in his pioneering position within the field of sociology of literature and art, I want first to situate this within the broader context of his studies of intellectuals responsible for innovation and diffusion. It is necessary to state these first in relation to power and action. In the simplest form of pre-capitalist social order such as the Kabylia of the 1960s, thinkers such as poets were not segregated, but were venerated by the whole society for their influence as repositories of knowledge (Bourdieu and Mammeri, 1978: 53). Even within traditional societies these powerful figures began to be differentiated, as in the Weberian opposition between priests and prophets, and it is from this classification that Bourdieu has highlighted the underlying structural forces shaping modern intellectuals and artists. A key division, as we have seen, is between those who are 'doxosophes' (expounders of legitimate knowledge – lawyers, doctors, etc.) and those who are 'prophets' – dissenting scientists or artists.

In his studies of universities, Bourdieu deploys the concepts of the four types of capital which are by now almost synonymous with his approach, that is, social capital (power gained by the sheer number of family members, retainers or network of supporters), symbolic capital (reputation or honour – including intellectual honesty), cultural capital (distinction within the autonomous fields of art and science; intellectual or educational qualifications) and economic capital (ownership of stocks and shares, or, more generally, of monetary rewards). These clearly echo Weber's categories of party, status and class, although, unlike Weber, Bourdieu argues that in modernity these are not accidentally connected but – over time – necessarily linked. Thus, as we have seen, symbolic capital is, in modern societies, typically reconverted into economic profits.

Homo Academicus (1988a) is organised around three intersecting oppositions within French universities, which elaborate on the earlier Kantian idea of a conflict of faculties. These can be stated succinctly as, first, between the 'social' pole and the subordinate pole; secondly, between those in control of social reproduction chances and those with scientific authority; and, thirdly, between established and obscure intellectuals.

The first pole concerns the 'taste for order' (1988a: 51) of those directly concerned with temporal power, as in the modern faculties of medicine and law. Because of their significance in the smooth running of the dominant order, these academics are much more likely to be given State honours, such as the Légion d'Honneur. Typically from the haute bourgeoisie, they are married to women with high social honour, have large families, don't divorce and are usually Catholics. They are thus part of a wider social élite that has, simultaneously, a commitment to the spirit or ideal of the traditional university élite, a visceral sense of its own importance, and even a typical posture (the 'indefinable somethings' by which others recognise them: 1988a: 56). Against them, the subordinate pole lacks temporal power, is linked to the Faculties of Science, Social Science and the Arts, and is constituted by members who have low social origins or belong to ethnic minorities, such as Jews (1988a: 49). They are associated with dissent. Perhaps curiously, they have smaller families and more divorces, as well as being less often religious. As members of the Left, their politics have been shaped by their lower social origins and by their experience of stigmatisation, the passage through state rather than private schools, etc. The social pole is active in the ceremonies of the wider society; the subordinate pole is autonomous from these (1988a: 49–51).

The second key division is between the leading players in universities' internal regulation ('reproduction') and those devoid of institutional status but possessing scientific authority (especially from high citation rates) (1988a: 75). Even a title such as professor can be distinguished in these terms as well as according to the age, seniority and institutional or scientific status of the title-holder. Finally, Bourdieu distinguishes between those whose rise has established them as Establishment *consecrated intellectuals* and those who are *obscure* and are unconcerned with winning traditional honours. The Establishment figures are

> crowned with scholastic glory . . . the ultimate product of the dialectic of acclaim and recognition which draws into the heart of the system those most inclined and able to reproduce it without distortion. (1988a: 83)

Against them are the figures who deny the orthodoxy of their day: detached, wayward, stubborn scholars. Here again,we note the great trajectory from obscure freethinkers or 'heretics' to consecrated figures most likely to create an impact on future curricula. But paradoxically, those who have the most independent social power are those who tend to become heretics – and, later, consecrated heretics. Material ease gives them the social assurance that permits innovation, often through the transgression of disciplinary boundaries. Here again is introduced the theme of the dominated fraction of the dominant class, so indispensable in understanding the class background of artists. Further, in this context, a distinction is made between 'true' and 'facile' radicalism, that is, between figures such as Hyppolite and 'bogus' iconoclasts such as Barthes (one might mention Derrida). For such academics gain their following not by substantive innovations but only by playing off one game against another, that is, by deploying the originality and imaginative flair attractive in the Arts Faculty in an ostensibly scientific set of concerns (1988a: 111–12). Genuinely path-breaking intellectuals may not acquire the number of postgraduates of other more central academics, but reveal their distinction in attracting adherents from a series of wide-ranging fields, thus permitting an indisputable impact on posterity. Yet even lacking this, all such senior staff possess spectacular control over the time of their subordinates, for it is their business to dictate the schedule through which the lengthy thesis will be submitted and examined, as well as their manipulation which matches students with completed theses to new job-openings.

The timing and explosiveness of the crisis of 1968 was thus, for Bourdieu, provoked in part by institutional meltdown – concentrated outside the well-endowed faculties of law and medicine. Precipitated by converging flash-points of structural conflict, this was initially an educational collapse that spilled over into a wider conflict within certain homologous sections (1988a: 175). Most poignant, here, particularly on the part of those with temporal power in the Arts Faculties, was the attempt to retain the traditional élite origins of new recruits, at the price of extending membership to women academics and older *agrégés* from the dominant class. This objectively confined a large number of young lecturers to permanent non-promotion and caused in turn the breakdown of the protracted French thesis system of 10 to 15 years' preparation. The crisis was amplified through other linked groups, most conspicuously, by degree-holders with manual jobs, by media professionals or cultural producers whose occupational roles made them sympathetic to academic staff, and by the more educated sections of the working class, whose expectations had also been disappointed (1988a: 165).

If *Homo Academicus* deals with crisis, resistance and (successful) preemptive reform, Bourdieu's case-study of a prophetic figure, Heidegger, takes as its theme unemployed and proletarianised scholars, intellectual formalism and the dislocations of established fields by means of successful conservative revolution. *Homo* shows patrician academics undermining dissidents' claims through awarding them glittering prizes: in brief, by consecrating and incorporating them. His other work published in that same year, but on inter-war Germany, shows, in contrast, how such patrician intellectuals had themselves been undermined by a different order of heretic, but with even more fateful consequences. A figure such as Heidegger possessed a capacity for powerful manipulation of scholarly forms. This guaranteed an academic respectability denied to the plebeian thinkers who formed the populist base of a conservative revolution.

'The illusion of autonomy' and academic euphemism: the case of Martin Heidegger

Most studies of artists are of figures who lack temporal power. Bourdieu's case-study, Martin Heidegger, is, however, an important departure from this pattern, for the subject of this monograph is a figure who, as a successful philosopher and Rector of Freiburg University, had reached the commanding heights of academic policy-making. It is therefore of vital importance to establish how such a position within the autonomous university field was used to develop a regressive political critique, not least because of the rise of certain parallels today to the popular politics of the 1930s. What was at stake in Heidegger's Rectorship as an active member of the Nazis was their strategic gain in acquiring a backer who would lend them legitimacy. Heidegger's case is also important because both the ambiguity of his disavowal of Nazi support, and the recurrent appeal of his radical existentialist ideas, makes it essential to study under what conditions an illiberal, antisocialist ontology can nevertheless have an allure for a very diverse set of social theorists. Even the early Bourdieu himself was not unaffected by it, although his later combination of elements of Heidegger with Marx certainly strips off its messianic cult of a future leader.

For Bourdieu, the real clue to Heidegger's academic success lay in his 'imposition of form' (1988b: 3). It is the importance of form, or the elevated style, which consistently masks a discourse which is otherwise identical to that of his conservative plebeian contemporaries. It is form that also makes for a notable kinship between Heidegger, with his irrationalist antimodernism, and certain poststructuralists, such as de Man.

The urgency of Bourdieu's own recent studies of the links between the language of euphemism and the practice of social domination now appears more sharply. His interest is in criticising not just the logic of Heidegger's own thought but also the logic of the university field. For in this, Heidegger achieved both the following of a cult-leader and also the respectability of academic power. Indeed, parallels are made between the position of Heidegger and that of some consecrated heretics among modern artists. Bourdieu points out that Heidegger *knew what he was doing*: in terms of another key opposition of the cultural field, Heidegger was like the professional painter, as opposed to the 'primitive' discovered by a more sophisticated avant-garde. Indeed, the true parallel in terms of form between Heidegger and others is with Marcel Duchamp, who also derived symbolic profit from introducing the popular objects of everyday life into the formal language of serious art. Bourdieu suggests Heidegger should be read as constructing similar 'retranslations' (1988b: 34) or 'philosophical ready-mades'.

The other good reason for discussing this case-study is that it is one of the first examples of the development of Bourdieu's mature cultural method. Any adequate interpretation of Heidegger must be linked to a genetic analysis of his texts, in other words, to a focus on the class position of the thinker and on the objective changes in the university field. Chief among these was the growth of a 'proletarianised intelligentsia'. But Bourdieu's vital insistence is that it is necessary to look at Heidegger's capacity to achieve social power by means of an 'alchemic transformation' of the contemporary field of university philosophy. Let me explain what this entails.

First it is necessary to identify Heidegger in terms of structural forces. As the son of Black Forest small rural craftspeople, Heidegger was drawn to portrayals of the *Volk* and was deeply critical of urban egalitarianism. But a structural analysis also reveals the emergence – for the first time in modern years – of trained intellectuals without university jobs, that is, a proletarianised or sub-proletarian intelligentsia. Such plebeian writers, influenced by figures such as Jünger, Niekisch and Spengler, possessed a conservative vision, with a Romantic quest for values that would compensate for the emptiness detected in Enlightenment conceptions of the individual ego. Their thought subverted the major oppositions of the period:

> [B]etween culture and civilisation, between Germany and France . . . as a paradigm of cosmopolitanism; between the 'community' (Tönnies' '*Gemeinschaft*') and the 'people' ('*Volk*') or the incoherent masses; between the *Führer* . . . and liberalism, parliamentarism . . . ; between the country or the forest and the town or the factory . . . between life or the organism ('*Organismus*') and technology or the dehumanising machine . . . between ontology and science or godless rationalism. (1988b: 21–2)

Heidegger's role was not to be the direct mouthpiece of these objective social forces, even if his artisan origins linked him structurally with them. Bourdieu insists that, on the contrary, Heidegger's identity was stamped decisively by the field of professional philosophy. What is at stake is a double refusal. On the one hand Heidegger rejected the naivety of the revolutionary conservative plebeians and produced an esoteric discourse with a distinctive ontology. On the other hand, Heidegger was a 'vertical invader' within philosophical circles, who profoundly disturbed the patrician milieu of the dominant neo-Kantianism (Cassirer and other liberal philosophers). Even his appearance, with his penetrating eyes and his 'existential suit', marked him off as a heretic, a prophetic figure who disturbed the everyday consensus over routine forms.

Thus Heidegger's philosophical discourse and its imposition of form produces a 'ritual distance' (1988b: 127) from the crude populism of anti-modernist thought. It rather 'euphemises' the latter, by its dense metaphorical language and its invocations of 'Man' without ethnographic substance.

More significantly, in inserting himself within the philosophical oppositions of the period, Heidegger alternated between an erudite, abstract ontological rhetoric and sudden reversions to popular language, so as to depict the loss of craft tools, the aimless chatter of modernity or the visionary eyes of the leader. This is what Bourdieu means by the use of 'readymades', which feature as a return of the repressed and command extraordinary emotional force:

> Heidegger reintroduces into the domain of academically-acceptable philosophical thought . . . topics and modes of expression – and in particular an incantatory and prophetic style – which were previously confined to those sects encamped on the margins of the field of academic philosophy, where Nietzsche and Kierkegaard, George and Dostoevsky, political mysticism and religious fervour, met and mingled. (1988b: 69)

Thus the double significance of Bourdieu's analysis is that it mobilises a *genetic structuralism* which, first, stresses the class habitus of the thinker, secondly, shows the distinctive university mode of production in relation to the formal nature of the text – including its lack of intersubjective falsifiability – and, thirdly, isolates its structure as a revolutionary combination of high and low culture, which can be read as a response to the premium on form in the university.

In these ways, Bourdieu allows us to unmask the illusion of autonomy of the philosophical field. He offers implicit analogies with contemporary prophetic discourse concerning the transcendence of high and low in the postmodernist thought of Baudrillard and Lyotard.[10] But, throughout his writing, he has also 'saved' one element of Heidegger. Paring off his theological and metaphysical trappings, especially his neo-conservative critique of modernity, he has smuggled from his works a useful contraband: the phenomenological perspective on (subjective) time-consciousness or modes of temporality of Being. Thus he amalgamated Heidegger's project of understanding the nature of everyday experience with his own realist framework on social relations. For when Bourdieu explores social agents in the subjective life-world he will never fail to remember Heidegger's precepts that spatiality is a specific way of Being and, more crucially, that the past and the idea of the future constantly affect the experience of the present of individuals, whole generations and – Bourdieu will add – classes (see especially his 'Avenir de classe et causalité du probable' 1974; Heidegger, 1962: 41). Through all his thinking, Bourdieu uses control over time as a vital social power and considers its absence indicative of social dispossession. He thus enhances Marx's critique of abstract social labour (see 1974).

La Noblesse d'état (The State Nobility) (1989)

This work contains Bourdieu's anatomy of the ruling class and the reproductive strategies it has employed. Like most of his studies it is empirical, being based on samples of prizewinning students in the *grandes écoles* in the 1960s and 1980s and a content analysis of examiners' reports on doctoral theses.

In brief, Bourdieu explores the ways in which the modern division of labour parallels that of the medieval world (1989: 211). The medieval strata – those who pray, those who wage war and those who labour – can be linked loosely to the modern division between mental and manual labour, while the mental labour performed by the bourgeoisie is itself fragmented into an entrepreneurial fraction, an autonomous intellectual fraction and a State technocracy. Parodying the division of the nobility into the *noblesse de robe*, *de cour* and *d'épée* in the period of French absolutism, Bourdieu introduces the category of '*noblesse d'état*' or 'cultural nobility' (a kind of nomenklatura (1989: 210)). Through this, he registers the great expansion of the bourgeois political and bureaucratic élite in the post-war period, as a necessary overhead permitting a more stable bourgeois rule (1989: 409). The segmentation itself is associated with the reproductive strategies of the French haute bourgeoisie and the dominance of certain higher educational institutions. Thus the story of the struggle for power from the late 1970s in France is told obliquely by Bourdieu through its impact on the 84 *grandes écoles*. The dominance of the Sorbonne and the École des Hautes Études (and even the École Nationale d'Administration) has been undermined by the rise of the more applied, vocational centres such as the Institut d'Études Politiques, the Paris École des Mines and business schools. The correlative of this has been the decline of both the autonomous intellectual and the State nobility (although not of economists, as Bourdieu has recently made clear (*Le Monde*, 14.12.95)). Linked to it is the rise of the power and economic capital of the entrepreneurial and top managerial strata of the bourgeois class (1989: 304).

In addition, at the 'little gate' schools of St Cloud and Fontenay (as opposed to the more illustrious 'great gate' schools such as L'École Normale Supérieure and L'École Nationale d'Administration), the numbers of students from the popular and middle classes decreased from the Third to the Fifth Republic (1989: 296). Thus it is possible to isolate a change of educational strategy which has its major impact on the weight of the different class fractions, and their relationships of cultural to economic capital (1989: 314–17).

The most fateful manoeuvre in this respect is the accumulation of material resources through the use of cultural capital, coupled with the end of the formal exclusion of women from the professions and top business. This means substituting a reproductive strategy *based partly on highly educated women* for one based on good marriage. By employing women in these well-paid jobs, members of the dominant class have been able to offset a decline in their relative material position vis-à-vis other classes (Bourdieu and Saint Martin, 1978; 1989: 271–5). Thus this new spread of a rhetoric of individualism to women has actually been accompanied by a new mode of reproduction of class privileges, although sociological theory has been distracted from perceiving these consequences by its focus on relics of sexual inequality.

In brief, for Bourdieu, the cleavage between class fractions has profound consequences, since the intellectual fractions high in cultural capital value disinterested knowledge, while the fraction high in economic capital values vocationally relevant education. Such an approach also illuminates antinomies over universities and cultural policy in Britain in the last 20 years:

> If the conflicts over education take the form of antinomies unresolved by resort to ultimate values, it is because what is at stake is the means of mastery of the instruments of cultural and social reproduction, the reproduction of the very foundations of domination, of existence and the values of the dominant groups . . . . (1989: 235)

Students' choices, then, reflect the constitution of the family's capital. Occasionally 'cross-trajectories' occur, as in the case of professors' sons in commercial schools. Where this happens the children tend to drop out (that is, a rectification over time occurs). But here Bourdieu fails to take an opportunity to theorise transformation or change, for if social determinism reasserts itself eventually, in the short run it still creates minorities that can have a disproportionate impact on events. Such a tragic vision has its own blind spots. In particular, it does not theorise the ways in which those demanding social change have drawn historically on cultural sources to express their economic disappointments. Might not the cross-trajectories mentioned above be viewed as creating marginality which, under certain circumstances, can foster a different kind of transformative vision: a dissidence shorn of the facile radicalism of the fashionable dilettante?

La Misère du monde (*This World of Suffering*) (1993b): proletarian emiseration revisited

In his studies of the university and of the *grandes écoles* (1989), Bourdieu has dissected the body of the French ruling class. In 1993, however, he published an extraordinary collective work which turns back to the dominated class and especially takes up from *Language* the plea that those who invoke 'the people' need to turn to the Algerians, Portuguese and Moroccans, who experience most sharply the deprivations of the advanced societies (1991: 91).

What is important in this book is that while Bourdieu has been conducting his recent attacks on vulgar Marxism, he has also continued to develop a critical sociology, which revolves around the social relations of production, around capital (both economic and symbolic) and its effects. Hence while he undertook the neglected analysis of the ruling class in the work of the 1970s and 1980s, we see here, in his return to the analysis of the subordinate class and 'race', the subtlety and power of a sociological approach which combines both the analysis of production relations in the broadest sense, and the sophisticated exploration of reification, incorporation and systems of classification, with their Durkheimian and Lukácsian provenance.

La Misère du monde is made up principally of interviews undertaken in the North of France, an area of de-industrialisation and of conflicts between the migrant population and the native working class. The sharp fall in factory employment has provoked simultaneously an intensified struggle for educational qualifications and a perception of the failure of the school in meeting the needs of most working-class children, bringing about a 'crisis of reproduction'. Emblematic of these disasters is the Rue des Jonquilles, introduced by Bourdieu, with its low-paid and unprotected employment for some native French, its sub-proletariat of debt-burdened families from the Maghreb, its closed factories and steelyard.

The transcribed interviews convey graphically the nature of social reality experienced at the level of many neighbourhoods but through the successive filters of a theoretical and empirical understanding. Intermingled here are both 'great' and 'little' miseries: for Bourdieu's view is that if advanced societies have rolled back absolute poverty (although less than is commonly supposed), the social order of contemporary France has 'multiplied through social differentiation the forms of little misery ' (1993b: 11). Thus this book is Bourdieu's exposition of the major types of deprivation – both dissatisfaction relative to reference groups and more stark forms of social distress, together with his mature analysis of the social contradictions within which a neo-liberal state and economy take shape.

Considerable sections of this book assess the breakdown of relationships between migrant families and native French, despite the emergence, too, of friendships across ethnic groupings. Conversations with both parties of warring neighbours of the tower blocks reveal a deterioration provoked not just by unemployment, but also by economic and domestic anomie. ('We're like pieds-noirs now', said one migrant woman. 'We go back there, and we're not Algerians, we stay on here, we're not French either . . . ' (1993b: 20)). Bourdieu, in a series of perceptive socio-analyses, reveals the *ressentiment* experienced by respondents from the native French residents, such as the old woman who objects to the smells of her neighbours' cooking, which he reads as the displaced anger of the socially isolated member of the native working class concerning the rich family ties and friendships of the Maghreb incomers. The illuminating interview with the Front National militant succeeds in revealing with great poignancy the fantasies of the anti-migrant in the face of a common fate of unemployment: 'The poor bloke from Ghana, he can always come here, but the poor Frenchman, what's he going to do?' (1993b: 577).

A characteristic mark of Bourdieu's sociological vision is his capacity to observe with the subtlety of a Simmel the detailed forms or interstices of life coupled with the penetrating gaze of economic and other objectivist approaches. He investigates the structures of space, as he has elsewhere, but notes here how the structures of the new urban social space intermingle with physical space.Thus, in assessing the public housing schemes in the areas of urban aid, he reveals how the 'dignified' parts of the society have been dramatically reduced and relocated (1993b: 159). There is a reconstitution of the city through the emergence of an intensified class segregation, broadly based on the geographical division between East and West. Class divisions are thus mapped onto the city as if in two homogeneous structures, the elegant munificence of the haute bourgeois areas being thrown into relief by the deprivation of the working-class corrals. The delineation in *La Misère du monde* of the world of goods is simultaneously of cities fractured by a dualism resembling that of the colonial cities of the nineteenth century, such as Cairo (see Said, 1993: 154–5).

These different experiences of time and place are also matched by the 'end of a world': the decline of the 'red neighbourhood' (1993b: 407). Bourdieu here suggests that while much channelling and controlling of the working-class areas went along with the hegemony of socialists within them, this counter-socialisation has been virtually destroyed by the flight of employment. Again this is of key significance for popular culture. Thus within the housing schemes a 'crisis of reproduction' (1993b: 16) has occurred, marking the young inhabitants with 'the effect of destiny' (1993b: 86). At its most accentuated, the devastation of the urban areas and the disappearance of jobs for skilled males has created a vicious circle where the two meanings of 'reproduction' are in fact superimposed. In Bourdieu's view, these young migrants and native French youths cannot attract women and marry because of their stigmatised existence. It is especially in the 'malaise lycéen' that there are encapsulated many symptoms of the wider distress. For here is exposed the 'aggrandisement of the school', that is, the penetration of the *school* standards and the school *consecrated culture* into the culture of those strata who previously had only to achieve a minimal educational level in order to get an apprenticeship. In the absence of the factory, these now have to stay on and pursue ever-increasing academic qualifications for the sake of further accreditation. As Bourdieu defines it, the school offers 'salvation chances' to the dutiful members of the working class: 'the school excludes . . . but she keeps in her bosom those she excludes' (1993b: 602). The school gains the power to undermine the cultural dignity of manual labour. Within the heightened aspirations, disappointments in the school abound:

> This school sickness is linked to the problems of the housing schemes and to fantasies about immigrants. Those who dramatise the school sickness and link it to the sickness of the city schemes touch unknowingly on one of the fundamental contradictions of the social world, especially in relation to the consumption of material, symbolic or even political goods. (1993b: 603)

Bourdieu once insisted that *Distinction* should only be read alongside *The Logic of Practice*. I suggest also that *La Misère du monde* should be read as a critique or expansion of *Distinction*. The dominant class, in *Distinction*, acquires its legitimacy, but at the psychic and economic cost of more and more children being exposed to the pursuit of educational capital, which only a few can win (Model A). *La Misère du monde* shows the long-term tendency of the reappearance of the law of value, or of market competition (de-industrialisation, pruning of the State, etc.), the rise of a new mandarin fraction and the decline of the old (Model B). But Model B is also increasingly unstable, leading to dependence on the seductions of market consumption for an ever-decreasing number and the violence of State coercion for embittered minorities. In other words the 'overheads' of the non-market services are increasingly stripped down, but at the cost of increasing problems of legitimacy. Reliance on the dull economic compulsion of compliance is not – for Bourdieu's team – the long-term solution to these problems of social fragmentation (*pace* Abercrombie et al. (1980) and other 'classical materialists'). Rather, the evidence from this study implies that the resort to pure economic logic is increasingly being supplemented by Model C – the reappearance of a proletarianised intelligentsia who focus on nations as 'imaginary communities', with all the inevitable consequences for ethnic conflict (see 1988b).

I do not want to point here to some of the omissions of this masterly work, although inevitably some exist, particularly in its silence about the way the increasing economic independence of women has affected at its roots the old basis for masculine domination and has instituted instead fragile and unstable forms of new household structure. However, the prophetic dissidence of this extraordinary collective intervention marks practically every page such that it would be churlish to dwell on its negative elements. Perhaps what is most remarkable in this work is that as a prophecy of bad fortune it is still nevertheless rooted in a scientific methodology. Bourdieu here has literally rethought positivism after the critique of ethnomethodology, within the heart of the ethnographic enterprise itself. He has pioneered a new form of 'paradoxal' thought, neither complicit with the dominant class, nor comfortably denunciatory of the miseries of the impoverished (1993b: 159).

In its model of 'participant objectivation' (1988c: 784; 1993b: 8), *La Misère du monde* describes how a constructivist sociology ('une construction réaliste' (1993b: 915)) is forged out of quite revolutionary methods of working. Bourdieu uses all his accumulated knowledge about symbolic violence in order to suggest a method in which it can most nearly be eradicated (1993b: 903–25). This bears little resemblance to the shoddy goods passing for scientific or market research techniques, which often reveal more about the questioner than about the respondent; on the contrary, this technique requires a 'spiritual exercise' in which the questioner must lose himself so as to make the other's perspective shine through (1993b: 909, 914). It liberates the need for self-expression on the part of respondents: in fact, the test of the method is its capacity to identify with the interests and needs of the dominated class. It is by this criterion that he aims to avoid the 'imposition effect' in which the questions asked are so distant from the concerns of the subjects that their answers are arbitrary and ill considered. By recovering the speech of small shopkeepers, workers, etc., he claims to offer a richer cultural document than the novels and songs held up as popular culture:

> By virtue of the exemplification, concretisation and symbolisation that they operate with, and which confer on them sometimes a dramatic intensity and emotional force close to a literary text, these interviews have something of the effect of a revelation. . . . In the fashion of parables in prophetic discourse, they . . . make more perceptible the objective structures which the scientific work strives to expose . . . . (1993b: 922)

I have completed the initial project of presenting a general survey of Bourdieu's themes in order to situate his science of culture without one-sided abstraction. It is to consider this cultural theory in more detail that I now turn.

Notes

1. The comparison is with the Protestant Ethic but the more apt analogy would have perhaps been with traditional Judaism, in which business rationality was developed within a context of integrated family and community life (Weber, 1952: 344–5, 382, 424).

2. Bourdieu sought to provide a genetic (historical) development beyond structuralism. The model he may have drawn on, via Piaget, was Lewin's field theory of the 1930s, which aimed to incorporate within it the study of essential relations or deep structures. These were conceived as forces operating within a field over time and exerting either positive or negative effects upon the trajectories of the groups within it (Piaget, 1971: 99–101). Borrowing models from Einstein, Lewin had insisted on the importance of mathematicised diagrammatic modelling or mapping of fields (Schellenberg, 1978: 69). It is this, I suggest, which is the source of the visual representations of fields as in 1984 or, again, in 1993a, in which Bourdieu plots the relationships between genres or tastes and social determinants. The causally effective forces appear in these diagrams as the amount of cultural or economic capital (inversely related), with political alignment as a mediating factor.

3. It is not without interest that the late Ernest Gellner also proposed before his death a theory of native traditional thought which relies on substantially the same distinction as Bourdieu's classification of monothetic and polythetic logics (see 1990a: 83–4). Like Bourdieu, Gellner argues that the fuzziness of this mode of thought fails to be a problem when the defined objects are separated in time or place (1988: 44–5).

4. Bourdieu does not pose the question that is raised systematically in a work such as Barrington Moore's *Injustice* (1978), that is, given the experience of (material) injustice, when is a revolutionary response rather than one of *ressentiment* more likely? While Bourdieu states that crises that produce a revolutionary response emerge from the disparity of subjective expectations and objective conditions, he rarely specifies what provokes such crises. Nor does he consider the role of the imagination or desire in heightening crises, especially in contrast

with Ricoeur's or Habermas's philosophical analysis of the role of art. I return to this point in chapter 7 and the Conclusion.

5. In recent work, he has added a theory of bureaucratic interests in power, see *Raisons pratiques* (Practical Reason) (1994b).

6. *Les Héritiers* is co-authored by J.-C. Passeron.

7. Bourdieu hints that cultures institutionalised by dominant classes are arbitrary in the sense that they operate chiefly as rhetoric (as in the case of the institutional Catholic Church in medieval Europe). But orthodox or institutionalised culture is not always arbitrary in this sense, or, rather, there are limits to its arbitrariness. For example, it was no accident that during the whole period of Nationalist-imposed apartheid, only in one instance did a black South African make a critical film (Tomaselli, 1989: 23).

8. There is a clear fit between this area of Bourdieu's enterprise and that of Raymond Williams: see, especially, *The Long Revolution* (1965).

9. Although Elias is not cited in these essays, there is an obvious link between his analysis of linguistic codes of '*civilité*' and Bourdieu's linguistic markets.

10. For an unambiguously critical analysis of the exaltation of Heidegger and Nietzsche, and the emergence in philosophy of an 'aestheticism of transgression', see Bourdieu and Wacquant (1992: 154).

2

BOURDIEU'S CULTURAL THEORY

In this chapter I shall be primarily concerned with the effects of literary and artistic canonisation and with the ways in which this has cemented the claims to power of the dominant class through its superior grasp of certificated knowledge. In particular, it will be shown through *Distinction* that appreciation of modernist works is restricted to other artists and to those with high educational capital. I shall try to show, through highlighting Bourdieu's transgressive method, that knowledge of modernism requires a grasp of iconography that can only come from understanding the old. Moreover, it will be shown that the same taste (avoidance of the facile, refinement, originality, etc.) permeates wider decision-making in the sphere of consumption and leisure and that it requires specific social and material conditions. I shall then show that if modernism has now become hijacked to add to the dignity of the dominant class, Bourdieu's understanding of its rise accounts for it differently, that is, in terms of modernist artists as a heroic group who preserved the autonomy of the artistic field from the laws of the market. The laws of this autonomous artistic field will then be explained, along with Bourdieu's claims to have a method for the science of literature and art which is more effective than that of his rivals. A brief assessment of its hidden debts and its weaknesses concludes this chapter.

Art and the ideologies of natural gifts

Throughout all his cultural works Bourdieu aims to unveil the mystification caused by ideological distortion. Three linked ideologies have been the object of his recurrent dissection: the ideology of the fresh eye, the ideology of the charismatic artist and the ideology of natural taste. In terms of classic *Ideologiekritik*, he shows that these three attitudes systematically favour the dominant class. Thus there is an equivalence between Bourdieu's approach and Marx's method in *Capital*, which also aims to show that economic ideology contains religious or magical vestiges. Bourdieu's method is to use Marx's critique in another sphere of production in the bourgeois period, that of cultural goods. The prevalent approach to cultural production is represented by an essentially religious attitude to the operation of a mystery. Cultural production is therefore defined as the expression of transcendental genius, and is elevated both beyond the human and beyond analysis. Yet cultural reception is also *naturalised*, so that it appears the consequence of innate distinction. It follows especially from the first that Bourdieu's demand for a return to the social relations underlying culture means that there is no 'essence' of a text, that is, no single set of interpretative rules which dictate the terms under which a text unambiguously yields up its treasures. Perhaps it is not surprising that it was also Marx who said – à propos censorship – 'Who are to be the authorised producers? And who are to be the authorised readers?' (cited in Prawer, 1976: 47). The punishment of death is no longer used to induce compliance to the range of canonical books protected by papal imprimatur, but it is Bourdieu's view that secular canons of consecrated culture still serve authority, even at the cost of symbolic violence.[1]

Bourdieu draws on descriptions of novels or poems as abstracted or fetishised commodities, in other words, as products that are sold on the market and viewed as things, independent of the specific social relations of production underpinning them. Just as Marx showed how the ideology of classical economics, with its Holy Family of land, labour and capital, depended on a magical manipulation of categories, so Bourdieu shows that a similar magic is at work in doxic discussions of the objects of cultural consecration:

> Consequently . . . a rigorous science of art must, *pace* both unbelievers and iconoclasts and also the believers, assert the possibility and necessity of understanding the work in its reality as a fetish; it has to take into account everything which helps to constitute the work as such, not least the discourses of direct or disguised consecration which are among the social conditions of the work of art *qua* object of belief. (1993a: 35)

Bourdieu presents the aristocrats of culture as 'justified' men, who are, in this respect, the heirs to the arrogant self-made men of the early industrial bourgeoisie. Indeed, even by characterising culture in terms of consumption, he desacralises objects which have become the focus of veneration. This is particularly marked in the case of the 'high priests', those professors of English who recoil from the crude language of 'production and consumption' for the hallowed objects of their studies. However, unlike the Nietzschean refutation of Christianity as a whole secret machinery of salvation erected on suffering (Nietzsche, 1961: 200), Bourdieu does *not* conclude that the objects of artistic awe are merely the product of mystification. Rather, the title of his work *Les Règles de l'art* (1992) (The Rules of Art (1996)), suggests that it is possible to redescribe art so as to valorise it without the distortions of individualism, perhaps rather as Durkheim (1995) thought religion might be revalued as an expression of the transcendence of the social over the individual. For the use-value of some works may be retained after their fetishistic aspect of literary creation has been stripped from them:

> [O]ne might, by . . . [a] willing suspension of disbelief, choose to 'venerate' the authorless trickery which places the fragile fetish beyond the reach of critical lucidity. (1993a: 73)

Thus his approach to literary analysis also provides the prerequisites for an adequate understanding of the 'singular vision' of Flaubert or the profundity of the symbolic revolution initiated by Manet.

But first, we need to understand the approach of *Distinction*. The method deployed most conspicuously in this work entails the scandalous transgression of critically esteemed categories, particularly the subversion of the boundary between sacred and profane. Where Kantian conceptions of high culture are premised on an undisputable boundary-line between the works of artistic genius and everyday products – signalled by the difference between the difficult and the facile – Bourdieu insists on the prevalence of such oppositions within modes of perception and appreciation in a wide variety of areas of living. For example, he links artistic consumption and production to that of food and insists on mapping tastes across these rigidly patrolled frontiers (1984: 13, 100). This irreverent viewpoint reveals that the adoption of a preference in each of the various parameters of cooking – sweet/sour, pungent/bland, crude/delicate, etc. – is also the template of choice in the area of mainstream aesthetics. Tastes might be systematically elaborated in the areas considered 'high' because they are more abstract or pure, such as for some types of music, but they are still subject to the same oppositions that prevail in the arena of more *sensuous* pleasure. The main source of these tastes or needs is the habitus, a set of attitudes engrained in agents so early that they acquire an unconscious compulsive force. As one such instance, Bourdieu reports that working-class men dislike fish because it conflicts with the rules of vigorous masculinity, the bones necessitating a more delicate operation than the hearty mouthfuls felt to be proper for a manly man (1984: 190). In this case, bourgeois men occupy the opposite 'feminine' pole, opting for delicate cultivation rather than earthy directness. In other areas, such differentiations revolve less around taste for an object or indifference to it, than around how it is used. The enjoyment of inventive form rather than the celebration of the family in photographs;[2] the preference for a Romantic landscape combining the wild with the cultivated rather than the more formal aesthetic with its rigid segregation; visits to galleries to see artists other than those celebrated in contemporary trends: all these are interconnected choices springing from the initial acquisition of a cultural ethos (1991: 57). In this context, the preference for imaginative disorder rather than repressive order marks an aesthetic opposition which Bourdieu notes as rooted in the unconscious. It indicates a fundamental division between the secure and relaxed stance of the 'old rich' and the rigid self-discipline of the petty bourgeoisie (1974: 20–1).

The same principles of perception, cognition and appreciation inform all areas of cultural choice, both in the scholastic culture of duty and obligation and in the 'free' culture of leisure. Moreover, in opposition to Kant, Bourdieu claims that such choices are not merely cerebral but are, literally, embodied. Even music – Kant's highest and most intellectual art – moves us, seizes us in the stomach ('ravishes' us), while we may also be 'nauseated' by a wallpaper or interior colour scheme.

The habitus, from which such conscious and unconscious ordering devices derive, can be summarised in the dichotomy between the 'aesthetic gaze' and the 'naive gaze'. This distinction takes various guises, not just in relation to general differentiations of consumption according to class and in the opposition between professional painter and untaught painter in the field of art (1992: 349). The aesthetic gaze prioritises style or the mode of representation. It is concerned not with registering or morally evaluating the nature of the empirical world but with a self-sufficient form of play, concerned therefore with the way images are deployed or narratives are constructed. Linked analytically to Kant's 'judgement of beauty', the aesthetic gaze is part of a *game of form* from which certain people are excluded:

> It is barbarism to ask what culture is for; to allow the hypothesis that culture might be devoid of intrinsic interest, and that interest in culture is not a natural property – unequally distributed, as if to separate the barbarians from the elect – but a simple social artifact, a particular form of fetishism; to raise the question of the interest of activities which are called disinterested because they offer no intrinsic interest (no palpable pleasure, for example), and so to introduce the question of the interest of disinterestedness. . . . [T]here is practically no question of art and culture which leads to the genuine objectification of the cultural game, so strongly are the dominated classes and their spokesmen imbued with a sense of their cultural unworthiness. (1984: 250–1)

Those possessing a naive gaze – like Rousseau in Kant's account – refuse to evaluate the beauty of a great house independently of their moral disapproval of it as a site of exploitation. They enjoy the artistic celebration of commonplace enjoyments, such as sunsets or a mother and her child. The status groups that can manipulate a rare as opposed to a common or shared cultural heritage derive symbolic profits from this. For Bourdieu the same overarching polarisation is at stake, for in the formalism of the aesthetic gaze is demonstrated also a concern for individuation or differentiation, whereas in the naive regard there is an expression of what the group shares in common. 'Barbarism' therefore embodies the collective consciousness of the social group, or rather of those classes in which the collective consciousness is most unadulterated by the social forces for distinction.

The habitus of the aesthetic gaze is engendered by the distance from material necessity. Like all pure gazes, it is observation which has acquired dignity from being detached from participation and action. It is the object, moreover, of time and rigour (1984: 183). Here again we see Bourdieu developing a perspective which owes much to Marx. If Marx had a labour theory of value, in which the value of a commodity was based on the amount of labour-time used in its production, the consumption of symbolic goods can also be measured by the time and rigour necessary to master them (1984: 350). The heart of the aesthetic is the long mastery of old texts. For it is only through this lengthy education that there can be an appreciative awareness of the power to startle which is possessed by the really new. Thus the aesthetic gaze which is fascinated with the signifier, as in the Surrealist and Dadaist avant-gardes, has as its prerequisite the saturation in earlier forms of art. It follows that the twentieth-century avant-garde concern for intertextuality, with its nostalgia, pastiche and melancholy, is merely the *ideal type* of the aesthetic gaze. Since the aesthetic gaze is the product of the closeness to old things, such as inherited paintings and furniture, it is the attribute of the haute bourgeoisie and aristocracy. Paradoxically, despite the iron cage of instrumental rationality constructed by a bourgeois world, a *gentrified* status ethic reigns in the arena of taste.

A further principle is counterposed to the time perspective fundamental to the aesthetic attitude (and epitomised in the Proustian 'waste of time'). This is the perspective of space. A spatial axis that differentiates the culture of distinction from the more traditional solidaristic cultures is demarcated by the separation of the industrial from the peripheral arenas of the world-market, favouring particularly the metropolis (1984: 250). The Parisian haute bourgeoisie is also contrasted with its class equivalents in regions such as Lille, who possess predilections closer to the pole of 'bourgeois art' (timeless, therefore *déclassé* works celebrating social harmony) or middle-brow, petty-bourgeois taste (a pleasure in the older classics and in 'pre-digested' forms of culture).

One further point here. To the mental classifications such as sweet–sour, coarse–fine, banal–refined, there is a a linked group of categories setting the dominant class apart from the dominated (high–low, noble–common, etc.). It is these distinguished expressions of noble feeling which are associated with the serious pleasure offered to the aesthetic gaze, while the simple sensuous charms of popular entertainment are linked to the naive gaze. Popular culture, in contrast, derives its force partially from the transgressive laughter of the carnival, (especially from the iconoclasm of the grotesque body (Bakhtin, 1968)), and partially from an anti-aesthetic aesthetics, based on the absolute supremacy of the moral and political in plebeian criticism (Proudhon) (1984: 491). What is it that engenders with such stability both the historical ethos expressed in the aesthetic attitude and the popular culture of the naive gaze? Only a specific time–space axis which is rooted in material existence or lived experiences could acquire such power. Its origin is to be discovered in the possession or absence of a future which is conferred in turn by wealth (more precisely, access to surplus-value) and especially by the sense of possessing rare skills:

> This is the difference between the legitimate culture of class societies, a product of domination predisposed to express or legitimate domination, and the culture of little-differentiated or undifferentiated societies in which access to the means of appropriation of the cultural heritage is fairly equally distributed, so that the culture is fairly equally mastered by all members of the group and cannot function as cultural capital. . . . (1984: 228)

Among sociologists profoundly influenced by Marx, Bourdieu is unusual in his anthropological inheritance, which leads him to emphasise the importance of socialisation into cultures from a very early age. There are two sites of the aesthetic habitus: domestic transmission and scholarly culture. The earliest tastes are formed through the family and take on an emotional bodily resonance which is ineradicable: works like Bach's *The Well-Tempered Clavier* are indissolubly linked with emotions of secure happiness when introduced to the child from early infancy through the 'musical mother' of bourgeois autobiography (1984: 75). Thus the route-map through which to decipher the confusing landscape of inherited music and art is early and effortlessly imparted to the bourgeois child. The school, in transmitting this canonised culture, organises it within a specific pedagogy. Where this curriculum is rational, it democratises the inherited culture; where a rational pedagogy is absent, it diffuses the culture to a select few, thus reproducing the social structure. Bourdieu's point about contemporary France is that there is an invisible curriculum, underlying the scholarly curriculum, which 'fills in' the school-imparted knowledge and which is generally available only to the offspring of the dominant class. The children from the subordinate classes who surmount the obstacles of the *lycée* selection and subsequent examinations become, in Bourdieu's words, 'miraculous survivors'.

I have discussed so far the major division within consumption: between the sacred of the pure aesthetic gaze and the profane of the popular gaze. There are also subordinate disputes at stake in cultural struggles. Within the aesthetic attitude, there is the division between the gentlemanly or aristocratic ethos, originating at the court, and the more scholarly culture of the liberal professions. This is an antagonism of seminal significance in Bourdieu's cultural theory. In a move he himself labels 'vulgar', he notes the homology between the structure of Kantian aesthetics (which valorises the complex analytical play of the mind as against the appeal of the senses) and the world-view of the dominated fraction of the dominant class, to which, as a professor, Kant belonged, and which preserved its distinctive virtue from its rigorous opposition to the worldly ease of the aristocracy. This becomes pivotal in Bourdieu's later work, for artistic production itself is linked to the subaltern fraction of the dominant class, deracinated by primogeniture from the possession of temporal power. The dissident culture of the youthful haute bourgeoisie, rich in cultural capital, but lacking economic capital, is a recurrent subject. At the heart of his view of modern France, therefore, there is a series of potent contradictions or conflicts. Of these, the division between the *noblesse d'état* – drawn most often from the aristocracy of culture – and the entrepreneurial fractions of the dominant class is especially fateful. For the cultural critique of capitalism often gains its force from those who articulate an organicist and hierarchical alternative or who express an élite's pessimistic disenchantment. It is these antagonisms which are played out in the struggles between the consecrated and the new avant-garde, as well as between the Left and the Right, which are represented in the mild parodies or drawing-room comedies of the Right Bank as against the social criticism of Left Bank intellectuals:

> Whereas the dominant fractions of the dominant class (the 'bourgeoisie') demand of art a high degree of denial of the social world and incline towards a hedonistic aesthetic of ease and facility, the dominated fractions (the 'intellectuals' and

'artists') have affinities with the ascetic aspects of aesthetics and are inclined to support all artistic revolutions conducted in the name of purity and purification . . . . (1984: 176)

The transgressive modern intellectual is to be described later as the equivalent of the Renaissance fool. The *licensed inversion* of the authoritative claims of the dominant class is at once the source and limitation of such intellectuals' radicalism.

Bourdieu's notion of cultural goodwill, or the affirmative attitude towards legitimate culture, also plays a major part in his analysis, especially in relation to the middlebrow consumption of the old petty bourgeoisie. It is conditioned by his conception of time, for it is especially time that controls the upward trajectory of the socially mobile office-worker in the form of a 'lost present':

In the end these altruistic misers who had squandered everything on the alter ego they had hoped to be . . . are left with nothing but resentment – the resentment that always haunts them in terms of being taken for a ride by the social world which asks so much of them. (1984: 353)

Perhaps the most well known is Bourdieu's work on the *new* petty bourgeoisie: educational failures from the dominant class who use their dominant taste to become the 'need merchants' of the new market for cultural and symbolic goods. This group – psychiatric professionals, aromatherapists, social workers, etc. – possess a 'fun ethic' and a taste distinguished by its catholic expansiveness. Bourdieu is especially perceptive in noting the iconoclastic aspects of this world-view, which permits an eclectic alternation between the more creative and modernist elements of popular culture and the more accessible legitimate culture. In this mix, the body also becomes the site of a worldly discipline, depicted in language reminiscent of the Nietzschean critique of the sick moralism of earlier bourgeois culture.

Despite the many misplaced attempts to classify Bourdieu as an advocate of postmodernism, it is odd that nobody has yet pointed out how he has creatively reworked Durkheim, especially in his studies of the ideology of the culture of capitalist modernity.[3] Durkheim's *The Division of Labour* is in part concerned with the decline of sumptuary laws, that is, the regulation of dress, food and other codes for specific occasions and social estates (consequently, the nobility alone might wear ermine or gold; items for feasts and fasts may not be eaten everyday, etc.). Bourdieu emphasises that the 'statutory signs of distinction' in matters of cultural goods were abolished in the nineteenth century with the increased writing for the market done by the de Kocks, Feuillets and others (1971: 1359). However, he stresses that consumption today is *still informally structured* despite the removal of all fetters or 'Chinese walls' against the free movement of commodities (Marx, n.d.: 53). For consumption is controlled by the habitus. Within such dispositions, differentiated by gender and class, are laid down the pleasures which later lead the actor to occupy a specific position. As Bourdieu explains, this is largely an unconscious process. The typical child from the dominated class experiences through the habitus both the exclusion from the dominant class and, more surprisingly, the willed acceptance of his/her subordinate position through visceral repulsion from the style of life of the bourgeoisie (1984: 169–75). *Taste* is the principle through which individuals occupy a certain social space:

> It continuously transforms necessities into strategies, constraints into preferences, and without any mechanical determination, it generates the set of 'choices' constituting life-styles. . . . (1984: 175)

In other words, when supernatural and moral sanctions lose their power, it is through taste, style and even pleasure that we come to accept certain occupations and kin positions. The habitus creates an active willed choice to occupy certain spaces, even if behind this choice there is also necessity.[4] My argument, then, is that Bourdieu has taken Durkheim's 'sumptuary freedom' and replaced it with his notion of 'free culture' or 'domestic culture'. In an enterprise of demystification not unlike that provoking the *fin-de-siècle* angst of Durkheim, Bourdieu emphasises the bizarre conjuncture of social forces such that academic work based on the pleasures of luxury is converted into the educational laurels implicit in categorisation of 'brilliance', 'refinement' and 'originality'. Such educational classifications euphemise and disguise the underlying social classification (1988a: 218). But the more menacing dimensions of these individuated social processes are never very remote. *Distinction* might emphasise the 'Discreet Charm of the Bourgeoisie', like Buñuel, but symbolic violence and the reproduction of inequality are never far beneath the surface. They are thrown into relief by the ceaseless struggle of self-exploitation and self-limitation on the part of the petty bourgeoisie. And even many children of the haute bourgeoisie in the university, who possess all the signs of grace, are nevertheless plagued with doubts comparable to those of Calvinists in their counting-houses as to whether they have acquired salvation (see also Bourdieu and Passeron, 1964: 74).

As the synthesis of all Bourdieu's earlier writing, *Distinction* provides the most sustained analysis of artistic and non-artistic culture. It offers an extraordinary depiction of the ethos of cultural consumption of groups differentiated in space and time, and, beyond these, in their relation to the material urgencies of life. The book cuts between a Proustian perspective on the part of the aristocrats of culture and a Proudhonian aesthetic on the part of the skilled working class, in a dizzying exercise of perspectival thought that has the scope of a modernist novelist like Musil.

The liberation of art

Parallel to the analysis of authorship by Barthes and Foucault, Bourdieu proposes a sociological account of artistic genius. The artist represents, for him, the prophet in a theodicy of bad fortune. He/she is thus the descendant of the Old Testament prophets who upbraided the Ancient Jewish tribes for neglecting the moral law. Prophets, such as Isaiah and Amos, spoke of the social group as a totality, through their concern with its inner life. Transformed in modernity by the break with tradition, artists have become similar austere voices of doom and visionaries of the social order,

The Jews possessed a 'special contract' as a chosen people, with a God who is nevertheless a universal God. As Max Weber pointed out, what came to distinguish the Jewish pastoral people was their highly unusual interpretation of their history.[5] He categorised this as a theodicy of bad fortune. For the more the Jewish people seemed neglected by their God and subjected to a whole array of catastrophic miseries, the more they believed that they alone were saved. It is this conception of the value of suffering for salvation that Bourdieu calls on in his conception of the bohemian artist. The real writer establishes his reputation only through risking rejection and experiencing suffering. Thus the invention of the bohemian artist derives from their need to project onto the beyond of posterity a solution to the present time-lag between artists' 'supply' and the consumers' 'demand' (1971: 1359).

From salon to bohemia (France, 1850s)

In the aftermath of Louis Napoleon's seizure of power, an autonomous art-world emerged. More precisely, the art-world splits: on the one hand into the market for restricted production and on the other into the market for large-scale production, the commercial organisation of the 'culture industry'. Within the restricted field there is in turn an opposition between the bourgeois art of the official artists in the salons and the avant-garde art of 'bohemia'. For bohemia can be considered a 'reversed world' or a 'society within a society' (1992: 86), founded on a fundamental rupture with the ethos of the market and the dominant class. The bohemian principles of erotic and alcoholic excess, love and opium create a culture of transgression, further sustained by songs, linguistic puns and jokes (1992: 88). The artistic habitus most characteristic of modernity is shaped by knowledge of this oppositional history and the lived experience of heterodoxy. Balzac had divided the world into three orders: he who works, he who does nothing and he who contemplates a masterpiece. The bohemian does nothing (1992: 87).

What then determined this 'empire within an empire' (1992: 90)? Briefly, profits and persecution. Bohemia emerges within an economic boom of 'profits without precedent', with the rise of the Talabots, Wengels and Schneiders and the accelerated entry of domestic workers into factories (1992: 77). While Bourdieu retains the notion of fetishism to describe this aggressively capitalist turn, he also sees proletarianisation and bohemianisation as twin processes, organically tied to increased market freedom, with bohemia as a protective sanctuary *against the fate of free labour*. Its occupants inherited their insouciance from the remaining artisan cultures of wandering 'masterless men': magicians, clowns, jugglers, singers. But the Bonapartist regime after 1850, as a dictatorial state, was itself founded on the suspension of parliament and union activity: it exerted a rigid censorship with the imprisonment of political dissidents, amongst whom artists were included. Both Flaubert's and Baudelaire's works were the subject of trials. From such repression was born the 'heroic period' of bohemia (1992: 76)

Bohemia was 'the world turned upside down' of the haute bourgeosie in particular, for it was opposed both to the salon and to the Academy. It thus has some parallels with the subversive rituals of carnival, although carnival was a popular holiday from the noble principles of vision (and division), whilst bohemia was a movement of internal exiles, initially from both dominant and dominated classes. Unlike the best-selling artists of contemporary novel factories, bohemian artists despised economic rewards.[6]

Bourdieu insists that bohemian artists and writers have to be understood also against the backcloth of the changes in the artistic field itself, not least the increase in the number of artists and their concentration within Paris. This itself was a response to the new compulsory education, producing new mass publics. Such a heterogeneous development in the number of producers with interests in the field created internal structural reasons for the new division of the artistic world. This recapitulated in many ways the earlier sectarian critique of social forces hospitable to dominant material interests. Nor was the analogy with the sect lost on contemporaries. Stendhal was to comment: 'I am a sectarian' (1993a: 122). Bourdieu borrows here from the views of Weber, stressing the utility of his theories of charismatic leaders and prophets for approaches to the cultural field, but it is noteworthy that he does so in different terms to Weber. Despite Weber's stress on the continuities between art and religion, his *theory of religious interests* treats the emergence of charismatic prophets as though they are entirely independent individuals. For Bourdieu, more convincingly, if the Weberian trinity of priests, prophets and lay professionals is to be deployed in the cultural field, it must be without the assumption that these figures are structurally undetermined and therefore explicable only in terms of personality, leadership qualities, etc. (1987b). *Specific social preconditions* are necessary for the emergence of secular artists as bohemian figures, while the charismatic bohemians in turn legitimate their arts with the knowledge that it is the needs of the masses of which they alone speak.

The changes cited above in the wider power relations and their impact on cultural production explain the genesis of a formally autonomous field. Its subsequent development is by means of disruptions in the field, which can be viewed as symbolic revolutions or transformations which have the long-term effect of the 'purification' or aestheticisation of literature and art. This can be characterised as a movement from the initial Romantic bohemia of the 1830s, to the second 'Realist' bohemia, constituted largely by plebeian intellectuals (1840s onwards). This is then followed by the bohemia of the 1850s and 1860s, drawn from the dominated fraction of the dominant class, which was to reject 'realism' and to turn instead towards style (1992: 110–11, 118). It is this moment of the conquest of artistic 'autonomy' which particularly interests Bourdieu, characterised as it is by a dual change, the initial appearance of a set of relations which change the artistic habitus, pushing the writer towards a more allusive text, for example, and also the shadowed ideological expression of this in the charismatic view of the poet or painter (1992: 92).

The trajectory of each individual artist – Gautier, Baudelaire or Flaubert – he links not merely to their class origins, or, as Sartre does, to their position in the family and in the family romance. In order to make the trajectory of each artist totally explicable it is also necessary to depict the artist's action within the autonomous art-world. Such strategies take as their backdrop the 1850s 'invention of the life of the artist', that is, the artist's disinterestedness, the Christ-like suffering that is the proof of extraordinary vision and the dialectic of distinction (or the logic of perpetual surpassment). Thus the unmasking of artistic ideologies means that the highly spiritual self-presentation of the artist must be coolly scrutinised in the light of his/her artistic interests, as well as the characteristics of the field of power. Within the new artistic field, the artist with cultural capital, and especially with knowledge of the collective inheritance of art, is alone capable of becoming a powerful player. Unresourced by rent and undercapitalised with education, rural plebeian intellectuals are only eclipsed by the brilliant circuits of their more favourably placed rivals. The fate of the plebeians was typically to retreat from the metropolis and to seek refuge outside it, as the writers of regional novels etc. It is for these reasons that the bohemia of autonomous art is based on a 'double rupture' (1992: 115), a simultaneous recoil both from bourgeois culture and from popular culture. Bourdieu thus clarifies with this second bohemia the exact dimensions of the trend towards artistic formalism.

The Realist bohemia then represents a parallel to the 1848 political movements within the artistic field. The social art of Champfleury, Bonvin, Courbet, Duranty, Castagniari and Desnoyers is captured in the '*bohème dorée*,' so christened by Henri Murger, which was the home both of deracinated bourgeois groups and of stigmatised minorities. Baudelaire is an active figure of revolution within this circle; Flaubert a more peripheral presence. This was a circle dominated by artists of artisan or poor petty-bourgeois orgins (1992: 134). Being thus absolutely constrained by time and money, they had no opportunity to accumulate in leisurely manner the capital in terms of a knowledge of art history which is one mark of the artistic habitus.

This moment of creative realism, which leaves its great remains in Courbet's reworkings of popular woodcuts and in Baudelaire's visions of metropolitan fragmentation and abandonment, is a transitional phase only. To it is owed Baudelaire's negative image of the future as the 'puerile utopia of art for art's sake' (1992: 89). The pure art which superseded it has to be understood as both rejecting the alliance with the people of the 'Realist' bohemia but at the same time as rejecting extreme formalism, in which the exposing ethical gaze of the artist is silenced by means of an exclusive focus on the means of representation alone.

There is a tension between the two presentations of the proletarianised intelligentsia in this account of bohemia. On the one hand there is a continuing structural conflict between the recruits from the dominant class and those from the subaltern classes within the bohemian space. On the other hand these antagonisms can be periodised. Thus the 1848 February Revolution represented a temporary recapitulation of the 1830 Revolution, with the bourgeoisie ranged against the finance aristocracy in an alliance with the people. It was the moment also for the proletarianised intellectuals and realism (1992: 40).

The 'double rupture' – with both the dominant class and the people – is the generating principle of Flaubert and Baudelaire's art after 1850. It ushers in the aesthetic of modernity, a pure art which repudiates both engagement and false idealism. In my view, the originality of Bourdieu lies in his description of this pure art and its recuperated fate in a way which seeks to transcend the false dichotomy within Marxist aesthetics between the epistemological naivety of Lukácsian realism and the modernism of Adorno. Bourdieu's theory of artistic capital, productive freedom and the long timespan for disinterested success claims that in the restricted field the artists who have acquired reputations have been those who derive from the dominated fraction of the dominant class, and not from the subordinate class. Consequently, this has entailed the perpetually 'fragile alliance of artists and people' (1994a: 146). In this alliance, success in terms of the 'dialectic of distinction' constantly removes the painter or writer from the mass base he or she aims at. The typical fate of artists is that they progressively reinterpret their concerns in terms of 'how it is said' rather than 'what is said', that is, they are increasingly concerned with the distinctiveness of their means of representation (1992: 197).

Bourdieu's major emphasis is thus on the 'contradictory class location' of the artist, a space which is simultaneously dominated and dominant. This site engenders a sense of marginality which leads artists to develop their analytical potential in an artistic way of seeing and to perfect new techniques as artistic means of production. At the same time their location threatens constantly to reduce their accountability to the widest public and to narrow their world-vision to that of the cultivated members of the ruling class, due to the structural limitation imposed by the field of restricted production. This tragic vision of art is sufficiently flexible to permit not only the celebration of an individual modernist like Flaubert, but also an unambiguous description of the perspective to which the viewpoint of pure art corresponds.

The bohemia of pure art has not discarded what has gone before:

> But [Baudelaire] never renounces what he has acquired by his passage through the most disinherited regions of the literary world, which are thus the regions most favourable to a critical and global perception – disenchanted and complex, criss-crossed by contradictions and paradoxes – of this world itself and the whole social order. Moral deprivation and misery, even while they constantly threaten his mental integrity, appear to him as the only possible site for freedom and the only legitimate principle of an inspiration inseparable from an insurrection. (1996: 60)

Hence Baudelaire's integrity was sustained through this opposition to the world of power despite the dandyism and blasphemies which separated him from the respectable working class. His suspicion of the people is an endemic feature of the 'elect élitism' of the second bohemia.

Flaubert's goal of extending the scope of the novel led him to distance himself simultaneously from best-selling fiction, which won its acclaim by flattering the public, and also from the classical gaze which insists on noble forms and noble subjects. Instead he wants 'to write well about the mediocre' (1992: 140) and to work on the level of form to make the real apparent (1992: 142). This 'realist formalism' requires a new intertextuality of the novel – a revalorisation of the great writers of the past whilst challenging the conventions of the former Academic monopoly.

This required the 'institutionalisation of anomie' or the de-regulated championing of the new in art: '[E]ach creator is authorised to introduce his own nomos, with works bearing – without antecedents – their own norms of perception' (1992: 103; 1993a: 333). In reintroducing the term 'anomie' (the absence of rules) in connection with the second bohemia, Bourdieu again explicitly connects the artistic formations of modernity with Durkheim's pioneering explorations. Further, his discussion of the division of the artistic field between restricted and large-scale production, which is the result of the increase in the numbers of cultural producers, also resembles Durkheim's description of the increased density (of population) which brings about the organic division of labour. Durkheim is the brooding theoretical presence behind much of *Les Règles de l'art* from its title onwards, but Bourdieu draws on the 'radical Durkheim', who stresses the connection between social structures and mental classifications, not the structural functionalist Durkheim. Durkheim was himself aware of the exposed structural location of artists and writers, since it is these groups he explicitly links to suicidogenic currents.

More important, for Bourdieu, is Durkheim's image of anomic modernity which takes – and inverts – contemporaries' fears of the mob or crowd. For Durkheim, social development is inextricably tied to the twin phenomena of the lonely figure who rejects tradition and demands the pursuit of new paths, and the supportive crowd, whose collective effervescence suspends normal categories and legitimates the new (1995).

Bourdieu extends the idea of an artistic new nomos through his studies of Flaubert and Baudelaire, the Symbolists, Marcel Duchamp, etc. The bohemians have a collective identification with a 'niche of madness', in which there is a reversal of the economic world (1992: 141). Their works have a transgressive force. They obtain the pure pleasure of breaking the rules, but also – like the fool – they lay bare illusions, and in this lies their value.

Thus, taking *L'Éducation sentimentale*, Bourdieu moves from an orthodox reading which stresses the author's position as a novelist of disillusionment to a reading of the text as a more serious 'model of social aging' (1992: 61). On this account, Frederick, in his pilgrimage through Paris and Le Nogent seeking to find love, creativity, friendship and material sufficiency, is doomed to discover only their monstrous incompatibility. *L'Éducation sentimentale* is, for Bourdieu, the presentation within a literary text of a sociologically realist model of social life.

Frederick himself expresses the social divisions of modernity. For Mme Arnoux he feels an uplifting love which can never become sensual. For Mme Dambreuse, the wife of a powerful banker, he feels a mesmeric attraction which can never be resurrected once she becomes a destitute widow. For Rosanette – the courtesan and his social and educational opposite – he experiences a sexual passion which can never be resolved other than through madness. Politically, his actions are equivalently self-cancelling. Like many bourgeois, he turns to the Revolution at the outset of 1848, but his role is one of passive support, not active engagement on the barricades. He distances himself from the stupidity of procedings in the radical political clubs and casts his die with the Dambreuse banking circle, only to become disgusted by their imprisonment of their enemies and their use of money to buy political advantage. *L'Éducation sentimentale* is therefore the literary unmasking of the real nature of Louis Napoleon's farce and Frederick is, for Bourdieu, emblematic of the unheroic nature of the political opposition to the Emperor's Eighteenth Brumaire.

For Bourdieu, then, *L'Éducation sentimentale* cannot be read, as Lukács suggests, as a novel, which, by interiorising events rather than by expressing them through objective action, fails to reach the triumphs of the earlier critical realism of Stendhal or Balzac. It is not simply that the artist has now become a passive observer rather than an active force in history, as Lukács suggests in *Studies in European Realism* (1978). Rather, for Bourdieu, the bohemian novelist is a realist, although the term itself has become a stake in the struggles over the aesthetic arena. What Flaubert reveals through the image of Frederick's hesitations and his clashing avowals to different social worlds is not so much the weakness of this personality but rather the fragmentation of the social order. Within the highly structured fields of power of modernity, Flaubert depicts a world in which only tragic individual distortion or exploitation is possible. In an allusion to Weber, Bourdieu suggests that Flaubert also lays bare the mutual incompatibility of salvation through erotic sensitivity, artistic creativity or business success. Within these social worlds – polarised in terms of their possession of temporal or spiritual power – Frederick is the image of a homeless wanderer who cannot choose between such values. Even the artist himself becomes a monstrosity 'above all of humanity' (1992: 151). Pure art is like pure love: both are disembodied and hence opposed to life and to practical necessities; both are sterile perversions (1993a: 157).

In representing Frederick as a type like himself, Flaubert neither simply reflects his social world nor merely depicts his own hesitations. Going beyond these unhappy alternatives, he offers a sociological view of things, though one concealed by literary form. Sociology lays bare what fiction creates in veiled form. In this respect, *fiction subdues the terror of the present*. Flaubert said, 'I will have done true writing, which is rare' (1992:

140). Like the adolescent, the writer denies reality by constructing an imaginary world. But through this fiction two purposes are served at a stroke. First the writer reveals the complex structures of the field of power. Secondly – and here Bourdieu recalls Adorno – artistic practice opens up the possibility of anticipating alternatives, precisely because literary form depends on the imaginary universe of illusion.

This literature is 'the reconciliation of the irreconcilable' in the dominant representation of art (1992: 115) in the sense that it possesses not only an affinity with art for art's sake but also a deeper social or ethical commitment, going beyond the conventional expressions of the ethical in 'social art'. In his disenchantment, Frederick's aphorisms such as ' fraternity is the great invention of social hypocrisy' actually operate as an ethical penetration of the stale rhetorics through which Left careerism is concealed. Bourdieu sees in Flaubert an 'art for art's sake of transgression and revolt'. To this end, Flaubert destroys the pyramidal construction of the earlier novel form and disrupts the simplicity of perspective (1992: 164). For him and for subsequent modernists, a condition of penetrating to the essential relations, which exert the strongest causal force, is the abandonment of the simplicity of a single viewpoint. The consequent multiplicity of perspectives, the fragmentation of the personality and the notion of space as aggregated rather than unified, represent the decline of Enlightenment conceptions based on the Cartesian rational subject (1992: 163):[7]

> That text which in refusing to 'make a pyramid' and to 'open up perspectives' declares itself as a discourse of the here and now, and from which the author is effeaced (though like Spinoza's God he remains immanent and coextensive with his creation), there, then, is Flaubert's point of view. (1996: 112)

I quote this passage because nothing clarifies more the degree of finality of the break with Lukács at this point. Bourdieu is not arguing that Flaubert's art is a lesser form, as Lukács believed, psychologically enriched but, in relation to the critical realists, socially reduced. He certainly accepts Lukács' view that Flaubert's novels represent the product of contemplation rather than an active sense of being in the world, while he shares his conclusions about the artist's loss of popular appeal, but this does not represent for him a loss of artistic scope. Thus Bourdieu uses Lukács' own criterion for literature – that it should *understand the essential relational connections of modern society* – as a critique of the narrowness of Lukács' own literary canon, just as in the 1930s Brecht had turned Lukács' critique of modernist formalism into a critique of Lukácsian formalism.

Bohemia and social origins

Flaubert is typical of bohemians of the modernist second period in being the son of a member of the liberal professions. His father, a surgeon, encouraged his son's protracted education, supporting his travels in Egypt and the Middle East. In hinting at an anti-bourgeois family world-view, Bourdieu suggests that Flaubert's own antipathy to this politically dominant class had deeper roots than the writer's structural opposition to market and utilitarianism. He is a member of the dominated fraction of the dominant class, because he was temporarily impoverished in the 1848 period, an heir who had not yet inherited and who thus depended ignominiously on allowances from home. Yet, as Bourdieu quotes Zola, this merely meant that 'rent took the place of sales' (1992: 124). Distance from commercial writers and from the need to get a living by discovering the taste of the wider public was thus granted by the inner assurance of economic independence. Such freedoms could permit more artistic experiments and the accumulation of other elements of cultural capital. This point is crucial for Bourdieu's structural depiction of the bohemian artist, the equivalent in the cultural field of the politician who lives 'for' politics rather than the politician who lives 'off' politics (Gerth and Mills, 1947: 85–6). The bohemian affiliation permits the fullest development of the artistic habitus, or the particular pattern of cognition and appreciation prevalent at the time. A precondition for this is mastery of the collective labour of the field, that is, the literary inheritance. It is only as a consequence of socialisation into the 'cultural mode of production', with its norms imposed constantly on each productive member, that significant productive advances are possible, in Bourdieu's account, and a new nomos can be created. This requires social *time* due to the slow process of acquisition of this collective labour and is only available to the children of the dominant class. Additionally, it requires a certain social place. Bourdieu insists that it is only on condition of deserting their country existence and coming to the city that the possibility for a creative contribution to modern art can occur.

Courbet and Champfleury are emblematic of the alternative possibilities, divergent from Flaubert or Baudelaire. Both became members of the first bohemia but their resulting social trajectories are profoundly different. Courbet represents the last great successful Realist painter, in Bourdieu's view. His reputation is made before Louis Napoleon's seizure of power and is thus connected to the progressive bourgeoisie's engagement with the 'social question'. Further, Courbet was able to be a larger-than-life rustic in Paris, a figure whose conviviality and common speech heightened the identification of the painter with the peasantry (1992: 366–7). However, his choice of Realism is explained not by his peasant origins, but by the opposition within the restricted field to the spiritual character of bourgeois art.[8]

In the case of Champfleury, on the other hand, although writing at a time when literature was still comprehensible to all those who were literate, it was impossible to compensate for distance from the metropolis. He attempted to develop the Realist novel as Courbet had Realist painting, but his lack of new writing led him only to take up with ponderous slowness positions which had been adopted quicker by others. Champfleury's failure to acquire recognition led him to accept, out of necessity, another strategy: that of becoming a regional or 'peasant' novelist. By becoming successful in this, he became cut off from literature in the restricted field. Champfleury is the model for all lower-class writers who abandon their rural roots in the modernist period without being able to compete successfully in the city. It is also in this light that Bourdieu emphasises the passage of time which leads some members of the Parnassian Symbolist group to participate by turning to the production of psychological novels (1992: 176).

Given the prevailing field of power and their position within the time–space axis, it is the sons of the dominant class who are poised to take possession of the aesthetic field. It is these social origins which alone confer on the writer or artist the necessary resilience to become the 'accursed' figures of the poet or modern painter. If bohemia is, then, the enclosure of madness, there still persist within it inequalities in the chance of receiving recognition as charismatic. Only those who are buttressed by material supports can endure the perils of initiating a style which has not yet been 'banalised'. It is only through the process of routinisation of the avant-garde, when the works literally become readable, that such artists acquire the fruits – or symbolic profits – of their iconoclastic action. So Bourdieu argues, using Duchamp's image, that each avant-garde movement is like a double-barrelled shotgun: it is fired once at its start but then goes off again after a long period of social ageing (1992: 227). This dual reception depends on the social formation of an art-loving public, for they are the instrument through which the movement can be consecrated. It also depends on the fusion or interlocking of the art-world with the world of power, a process which in itself is the signal for a new avant-garde to surpass the old. Bourdieu's distinctive use of the term 'banalisation' thus refers to the gathering 'refamiliarisation' of a 'defamiliarising' art-work (1992: 198–9).

Consecration, then, is not merely a process of the routinisation of a defamiliarising vision, it it the subjection of meaning to the authoritative interpretation of those with linguistic capital and other forms of temporal power. The analogy of avant-garde prophets depends partly on the dialectical movement of prophetic sects into churches, accommodated to the world. But there are also overtones in Bourdieu's banalisation of 'symbolic revolution', of Weber's poignantly dystopian reading of the necessary dilution of socialist practices after revolutions. The mass of hangers-on drawn into a movement once it looks like being on the winning side not only have material interests in the movement, they also possess a rhetoric that itself 'banalises' the genuinely defamiliarising content of the renovating original message. I shall draw attention to this issue later.

'*Permanent revolution*', or symbolic revolutions as a structural feature inherent in art itself, develops only after 1850 with the 'institutionalisation of anomie' (1993a: 52–3). Art now proceeds through a process of 'purification' which inevitably separates ' pure art' or 'literature' from those who possess only primary school education. Such revolutions in 'ways of seeing' require the same kind of dedicated labour as that of the professional scientist. Bourdieu insists that what is at stake in such a revolution is never negligible, for it affects the mode of perception of every actor, the liberty to use the name 'artist', to police boundaries to exclude pretenders but also to impose their world-vision on everyone:

> To define boundaries, defend them and control entries is to defend the established order in the field . . . the great upheavals arise from the eruption of newcomers, who, by the sole effect of their number and their social quality, import innovation. (1996: 225)

The logic of the artist's position is structured by the delicate balance between originality and disinterestedness. For the artist complies with the social needs expressed in the terms 'spiritual' or 'altruistic', which have been displaced from everyday social production by the rationalisation of the capitalist economy. This draws artists towards 'an alliance with the people'. Hence one of the glittering prizes in terms of reputation is an association of the author or the movement with popular art. For Bourdieu, such strategies obscure the question of who the real bearers of the movement are. Taking such claims at their face value risks identifying such art with popular culture, which is itself restricted to a naive gaze. For the possession of the artistic capital necessary to make a successful career in art also cuts off artists from the workers and political revolutionaries whom they had once championed. The real dilemma is whether to remain popular (that is, comprehensible) or whether to appear to abandon the initial public by going for a more difficult form. It is the nature of the cultural field itself – and also the relatively privileged social origins of bohemian artists – that leads them to associate true disinterestedness with rarity. They seek distinction, not solidarity. The quest for distinction is in part unconscious, for those artists coming from the old haute bourgeoisie already possess a 'natural' distinction. The art dictated by such concerns is incompatible with production for the masses. So consecration and banalisation of a movement generate a new wave.[9]

The pursuit of distinction is therefore created by a multiplicity of social mechanisms, being the consequence of occupying both the field of power and the social field of art. The act of taking a position in the restricted field of literary or artistic production exposes the writer to the logic of that game or *illusio*. Only the extraordinarily resilient individual can resist throughout a whole working life the judgement of the institution 'art' which bestows recognition of his/her works. In this sense, Bourdieu's exploration of the art-world emphasises the penetration of the social into even the most apparently private and isolated of acts and reminds the reader of Durkheim on suicide or of Goffman on madness.

Deviant cases: Zola and Rousseau

If Bourdieu's theory of modernism is to be plausible, it must account for cases of writers who were exceptional in gaining critical acclaim *and* a popular following. The only candidates for this are those who have emerged to prominence after the expansion of the reading public: Dickens and Balzac are thus inadmissible.

Zola's reputation seems genuinely anomalous. How could he have acquired simultaneously enormous sales for his books, prominence in defining the life of the intellectual, and eventual literary recognition? The answer, in Bourdieu's view, lies in the historical contradictions exposed in the Dreyfus Affair. For in the defence of the Jewish military officer condemned to death, it was Zola who redirected the attention of the authorities, with his celebrated manifesto *J'Accuse*. By such a courageous *political* intervention, Zola thus became transformed into a *literary* figure (1992: 185-9). His novels, which had attracted notoriety for their application of a scientific investigatory method to subjects that had been thought to be lacking in dignity, became suddenly recuperated for Literature. Moreover Bourdieu shows Zola's initial adoption of the field of large-scale production as the chosen terrain for his activities to have been itself exceptional. It was because of the early death of his father and his consequent lack of an inheritance that Zola was forced to move into the more commercial popular genre of the novel in the first place. His marginality in this sector ultimately permitted his recuperation.

The consecration of the naive painter, such as Henri (Le Douanier) Rousseau, is also a special case. If there is a refusal of bourgeois and working-class taste and standards of excellence in modernism, how is the emergence of the naive painter to be understood, for there seems to have been a series of such painters (Alfred Wallis could be mentioned in the case of Britain, Grandma Moses for America, etc.)? The answer suggested by Bourdieu is that the naive became a part of a couplet in modernism. He/she was the *plaything* of a field dominated by the professional modernist artist (1992: 339). We can only really understand Rousseau if we grasp that the essential relations in which he was placed within the cultural field led him to become the counterpart of Marcel Duchamp, a figure in whom is crystallised the most pure form of the subversive strategies of the new oppositional avant-garde. Hence the *playful* 'destruction' of the *Mona Lisa* and other venerated cultural icons and the insistence on the role of *chance* in the adoption of the signature 'Mutt', rather than the over-serious suggestion that this might be an allusion to a contemporary comic. Such mocking resistance to attributions suggests the freedom of the totally autonomous artist to defy the art institution. But Rousseau's role becomes clearer too. For he also represents the polar opposite of the academic gaze (that is, of the perspectival space, chiaroscuro and classical subject): as do all the artists of '*l'art brut*' (schizophrenics etc.). Whereas Rousseau represents a response close to the distance from the art-world of the amateur painter, Duchamp's 'readymades' are founded on his astute feel for the needs of the art-world (including the demands for esoteric knowledge) which was conferred on him as a member of a family with generations of professional painters ('Duchamp was in the field like a fish in water' (1992: 343)). Rousseau, then, is the model for Bourdieu's handling of popular art.

Bourdieu's more recent work 'The Historical Genesis of the Pure Aesthetic' (1992 and 1993a: chap. 10) and 'The Genesis of the Eye' (in 1992) has extended the analysis of the 'ideology of the pure eye' or the 'aesthetic attitude'. What Bourdieu aims to show in these late works on culture is the essentialism and idealism of the dominant mode of reception. Against a static structuralism, he emphasises that the work can only be understood historically, arguing that this position does not entail a relativist aesthetic. Similarly, against the philosophically 'interactionist' aesthetics of Danto and Dickie, he argues that their correct emphasis on the autonomous power of gallery-owner and critic has also to be understood within specific objective conditions or historical limits.

Part of Bourdieu's irony is displayed in noting that recent philosophical analyses of art have adopted a nominalist position, hijacked from sociological symbolic interactionism. This claims that art-works are simply those labelled as art by members of the art-institution who have been authorised to perform acts of recognition, in part by the tactic of setting such objects within the framing of a certain space. Thus Danto argues that it is the gallery recognition of Warhol's *Brillo Pads* that permits his acrylics or silk-screens to become art. The explanation of the force of the art-world in being able to exert this impact on other agents Bourdieu derives from Durkheim's *The Elementary Forms of the Religious Life*. Where Durkheim had insisted against Kant that society creates the unconscious a priori, Bourdieu asks us to consider that history is the a priori. In other words, the aesthetic categories, considered as analytically separable from ethical meanings and empirical propositions, are conferred by the 'social group' or, owing to the absence of an academy in modernity, by specialised professionals, private gallery-owners or dealers, etc., who regulate canonicity or battles over value.

'The Historical Genesis of the Pure Aesthetic' is subtly arresting, however, because it shows that such autonomy is relatively recent and that it is *constrained within certain limits by the world of power*. Fifteenth-century Italian painting was organised around a mode of reception that was not yet premised on a purely disinterested taste. This is because art had not yet emerged as an institution, 'rationalised' around its one differentiating element, style. Consequently there is an extraordinary homology between the reception of the late medieval master-painter and that of popular art today.

It is paradoxical that art is less mystified when it has not yet become separated from supernatural religion, but this is Bourdieu's claim. For it is the critical discourse of modernity that has guaranteed literary value (as opposed to market value) only by attributing total timelessness and total universality to genuine works of art. Such overblown claims have their parallel in the aura of the artist. Whereas the fifteenth-century artist had economic needs in preserving a traditional family life, the modern artist is credited with an ascetic spirituality, which is devoid of all material interests. Ghirlandaio was concerned with the regularity and adequacy of his payment. The artistic economy was not yet a tabooed sphere, potentially capable of challenging the disinterested presentation of the artist.

Medieval contracts between artist and public were divergent from the modern in that the iconographical interpretation of the work was dependent on signs that were very widely diffused, in sermons, fairs and dances – like modern comic strips. According to Bourdieu, differences in interpretation were possible, but they were grounded in the lexicon or iconology used within the religiously based collective consciousness of the group and were common to artist and public. In contrast the autonomous artist is one whose signs are legible only to the few. The resulting fragmentation of the collective consciousness is the cost of artists' freedom in the choice of style and subject.

Bourdieu stresses the collective activity necessary to sustain the magical circle of belief in modern art: it is not just the role of artists but the rationales for their distinction created by museum curators, historians, teachers, etc., that are decisive. Critical discourses are sufficiently flexible and vague to accommodate extraordinary combinations of diverse and incompatible works. The concepts of art criticism have not been cleansed of their origin within a specific habitus.

Something strange has happened here. Artistic language has become part of an autonomous field of social relations premised on inclusion and exclusion, but it still retains the traces of its origins in a set of binary oppositions (heavy–light, brilliant–dull, original–conformist). These are – as we have seen – multivalent signs in relation to social class usage. They possess the *appearance* alone of neutrality. In reality it is the dominant social power which confers positive and negative connotations on these terms.

It is worth noting that Bourdieu aims to destroy essentialism without resorting to relativism. By locating a work within a particular period, its 'necessary' existence is revealed:

> But historicising them means not only (as one may think) retrieving them by reading that they have meaning solely through reference to a determined state of the field of struggle; it also means restoring to them necessity by removing them from indeterminacy (which stems from a false eternalisation). . . . The historicising of forms of thought offers the only real chance, however small, of escaping from history. (1993a: 263-4)

This is a provocative passage. Bourdieu is claiming that only a historical sociology can release art-works from their imprisonment within the class coffin of an Institution 'Art', an institution dominated by aestheticism and by the monopolisation for the elect of spiritual aesthetic grace. The objective meaning of the text can then be revealed and the work put to other purposes and practical uses, placed differently within the social relations of domination (such as struggles over class, environment and gender), etc.

In other words, historical sociology permits the work to be removed from its pedestal, where it touches the 'transcendent' or becomes the vehicle for weak Romantic abstractions about 'life', 'experience', etc. Instead it is situated through its artistic ancestry and its author's being in relation to time and space. This does not make writers or artists 'mouthpieces of myths' but makes possible the sort of appreciative return of the text to its generative cultural and social circuits. Through these means art and literature become not the vehicles of self-referential formal games operating as claims to distinction, but ways of thinking and feeling concerned with interventions in the world of action. Thus although he gives no hint of how this might occur, Bourdieu reveals clearly that he is an advocate of a changed mode of reception.

Critical issues in relation to Bourdieu's sociology of culture

There are three main areas that I wish to introduce in criticising Bourdieu's cultural theory. First, I want to raise a dissenting issue about Bourdieu's interpretation of Kant as a formalist. With some irony, Bourdieu labels his analysis of Kantian theory 'a vulgar critique of pure critiques of judgement' (1984: 485). He notes that for Kant art was the more pure the more it was segregated from an immediate or naive pleasure in certain categories of sense-data. In this sense it was a pleasure of a highly abstract and rationalist kind, premised on the denial of the senses and the privileging of intellectual capacities above all other modes of response. Bourdieu claims that such a separation of enjoyment from artistic pleasure could only be the consequence of a double repression, in which the self is distanced not only from the aristocracy but also from the people. Kant's own aesthetic philosophy, he suggests, possesses an elective affinity with his habitus as a professor and, by virtue of this, with membership of an economically powerless fraction of the dominant order.

He thus takes issue with the Kantian view that a judgement such as 'this is a good painting' can be simultaneously subjective and universal, or valid for everyone. Bourdieu's own field-work shows the enormous divergence of tastes and explains these in terms of the existence of different kinds of habitus. Why, then, did Kant want to insist on universalism? The argument that Bourdieu hints at is that the sense of the universal is itself derived from the peculiar power of the 'sacred'. In other words, it results from the impact of the 'conscience collective' or the respect for the group. By foregrounding the empirical discovery of clashes of taste, and the lower-class perception of their cultural inferiority, Bourdieu highlights his own powerful use of Durkheim's conscience collective or the false universalism of the aesthetic ideology.

This argument is one he returns to in a number of studies (1984, 1990c). I think it would be wrong to read Bourdieu as a postmodernist proposing a nihilist critique of the Enlightenment subject. Yet it is clear from his own evidence in *Photography* (1990c) that Kant's universal cannot simply be dissolved into the sublimated expression of individual self-interest. For example, Bourdieu shows that peasants and workers enjoy certain family portraits and photographs recording local celebrations. More relevantly, he states that they have a conditional aesthetic – a photograph of a dead soldier, for example, is not described simply as 'beautiful', that is, of universal aesthetic importance. Rather, they stress 'it could be used to show the horrors of war' (1990c: 86). Thus peasants and workers are making a distinction between a purely personal photograph (which might reasonably have no artistic value for anyone else) and powerful shots of the dead which would jolt the observer into a recognition of the cost of war. We can conclude that when working-class people reject a Mondrian, this does indeed raise certain difficulties with modernist critics' notion of a 'universal' aesthetic judgement which is held to exist as an analytical a priori – independent of any social codes or conventions. But Bourdieu's own argument depends on elaborating further the subordinate class's assumptions about a general interest, leaving us to conclude that his real target is not Kant but aestheticism and formalism. Against Bourdieu, it should be reiterated that the Kantian value of disinterestedness does not impose an aestheticist conception of art, since beauty as Kant conceives it does include 'resistance to evil' and the 'sensuous representation of the ends of humanity' (Kant, 1952: 77). There has been, of course, a twentieth-century purification of art and a consequent trend to the creation of a purely painterly 'second reality', but Kant could hardly be said to have anticipated this in his aesthetics. Bourdieu is certainly *right* to criticise Kant for his élitist exclusion of naive enjoyments of the pleasures of form, which were dismissed because of their dependence on additional 'charm' (sunsets etc.). However, despite some important assessments on the historical context of art, he has not proved the entire inconsistency of the Kantian problematic (see Crowther, 1994).

Secondly, Bourdieu has underestimated the unevenness of the trend to formalism in modernity. This argument will be developed more fully later. Here I want to suggest that there are particular difficulties with his division of culture into the field of *large-scale commercial production* and that of restricted production. I shall suggest that he has underestimated the capacity for work of artistic power to arise in the large-scale field. Bourdieu's conception of popular art is particularly disparaging and I shall challenge this.

Thirdly, I want to question the oversimplified conception of artists and writers. It is argued that this group comes from the dominated fraction of the dominant class and possesses a common habitus with consumers from this class. As such, the artist's drive to distinction invariably distances him or her from 'the people'. I shall argue that in certain cases artists can remain 'prophets' even if they seek symbolic domination.

The whole of Bourdieu's sociology is concerned with the emergence and explanation of the use of secular culture to buttress the ruling class as part of a conservative ideology. But the precise character of literature and art in this role is unclear. On the one hand, the formalism of the aesthetic gaze (the over-refined dandyism of technique, to use Arnold Bennett's phrase) seems to be vested in the restricted field as an attribute of museum curators, critics, etc. – especially the more patrician of these (1991: 95–6; 1993a: 261). On the other hand, Bourdieu seems to hold that it is an attribute of artists, who emphasise the aesthetic gaze in order to win a reputation (1980a: 266). It is this which is the artists' Achilles' heel, leading them in middle age to distance themselves from the public whose interests they formerly took up in order to satisfy their bourgeois customers.

There is in fact an unresolved tension in Bourdieu's theory here. He has two views of the artist. First, the artist is an austere and ascetic prophet-figure, as in both the theory and practice of Baudelaire (1992: 88–103). Secondly, given his dominant class habitus, the artist aims at a professional reputation which will ensure him the potential to resume a relatively privileged domestic life-style. This second view involves the artist playing a double game. He is going for a bohemian, anti-capitalist strategy but is hedging his bets by tailoring his painting etc. to the expressed wants of his bourgeois customers or patrons. In this way, exchange-value is never expelled from the bohemian Garden of Eden but slips in like a snake when the artist is most off-guard.[10].

Which is his final emphasis? I think that Bourdieu has been pushed into determinist and pessimistic conclusions. In these the texts are permanently allied to a hegemonic project. But perhaps it is necessary to look more closely at the specific contexts of reading and interpretative discussion (in the broadest sense). At certain points, possibly within transient groups, debate around texts tends to transform established structures rather than reinforce a call to order, as numerous ex-soldiers have documented on the role of Penguins in the Second World War. To rethink these issues is to pose the sort of questions that were raised about the 'Institution' of Literature in the 1960s and 1970s.

In this period, a number of writers – particularly on realism – argued that canonised Literature could not be regarded as immune from ideology (Bennett, 1981). For Eagleton, Baldick, Balibar and Macherey, and others, the argument was not so much about the texts themselves but about the relations into which they are put, some of which may serve to create ideological effects. There is evidently an identity of views between these arguments and those of Bourdieu above.

But Bourdieu is still unclear. We are left with a set of questions about modernity. In what contexts might artists be able to operate as genuine prophets even if they originate from the dominant class? Emphasis should be placed on the texts, and not on the personal dispositions of the authors. This is to restate the question raised by Benjamin, namely, at what historical moments and in what structural forces will the author be pushed to an aesthetics of politics as opposed to an aesthetic of style? It also raises the sort of issue touched on by Raymond Williams as to the 'anti-bourgeois character of much bourgeois cultural production' (1979: 155–6), and by Edward Thompson as to the placing of texts (for example, Shakespeare, Mrs Gaskell, Gillray, Cruikshank) within a popular radical tradition at certain points (1968: 809–10). Finally, it raises absorbing questions about the moments at which such anti-bourgeois artists are prepared to take the risks and discomforts of becoming austere prophetic figures.

In this context, the role of exile and internal or external emigration among writers has been especially emphasised (Eagleton, 1976: 133–4). This seems to me to merit more thorough research, just as does Bourdieu's similar but under-exploited category of 'cross-trajectories' (1989: 236). I might mention here the example of Rushdie as someone who has roots in the dominant class of a post-colonial society, but whose experience of migration has led him to articulate the experience of the subordinate masses. Rushdie writes of the poet 'bringing newness into the world' for this reason. We might use his own case to illuminate the trajectory through which this occurs (Rushdie: 1988: 272).

Bourdieu's tantalisingly brief comments on how a sociological analysis of production affects literary value reinforce these views, not least in his assessment of Flaubert's 'singular' achievement (1992: 9–14). For by removing the singularity of the creator in order to emphasise social relations, literary experience can be rediscovered

> at the end of the task of reconstructing the space in which the author finds himself encompassed and included as a point. To recognise this point in the literary space, which is also the point from which is formed a singular point of view *on* that space, is to be in a position to understand and to feel . . . the singularity of that position and of the person who occupies it, and the extraordinary effort which, at least in the particular case of Flaubert, was necessary to make it exist. (1996: xvii)

Notes

1. In sixteenth-century France, of course, the monarchical State and theological authorities used the threat of hanging to censor the reading of Protestant texts (Lefebvre and Martin, 1976: 310–12).
2. Bourdieu estimates that only 10 per cent of the French population were concerned with photographs as aesthetic objects in 1965 (1990c: 182).
3. Brubaker (1985) is an exception to this.
4. Willis's sensitive study of working-class nonconformists at school, mentioned by Bourdieu in *Language*, shows in much the same way that their culture valorises their exuberant laughter and patriarchal masculinity, rejecting the consumption patterns of the middle-class school conformists as effeminate (1977).
5. *Ancient Judaism*, on which Bourdieu draws, has a much richer historical analysis than *Economy and Society*, particularly in its explanation of the social relations of the prophets and the Jewish people. Could it be a *less* canonised text for this reason?
6. This was not unrelated, no doubt, to the fact that sales of bohemian artists were very low: Zeldin quotes the figures for *Les Fleurs du mal* (1857) as 1,300, while Verlaine's *Poètes maudits* (1884) sold even fewer (253 copies). However it should also be noted that not only did Zola have large sales, as Bourdieu acknowledges (594,000 copies for *Nana* (1871) and *L'Assommoir* (1876)), but some other bohemian writers, also now consecrated, have had high sales at the time of first publication. For example, Proust sold 449,000 copies of *Du Côté de chez Swann* (1913), thus equalling the achievement of the 'queen of romance', Mme de Ségur (Zeldin, 1977: 358–9). These differences are inadequately explained by Bourdieu's theory.
7. These readings of modernism are also a feature of Simmel's sociology. In the only reference to Simmel of which I am aware, Bourdieu stresses the closeness between his own concept of aesthetic attitude and Simmel's aesthetic disposition in which the interest in pure, contentless form derives from the experience of those who possess sufficient leisure to 'live to see' (1971: 1372–3).

8. Bourdieu is too polemical on Courbet at this point: his Realism should be seen as the outcome of combined relationships – his own class position and the political group to which he belonged as well as his position-taking in the movements of the artistic field.

9. This position-taking in the literary field has been closely described by Balibar and Macherey: 'The root of this constitutive repression is the objective status of literature as an historic ideological form, its relation to the class struggle. And the first and last commandment in its ideology is: "Thou shalt describe all forms of class struggle save that which determines thine own self" ' (1981: 86).

10. Bourdieu goes further and sometimes represents artists as particularly venal: 'One soon learns in conversations with these [gallery-owners] that, with a few illustrious exceptions seemingly designed to recall the ideal, painters and writers are deeply self-interested, calculating, obsessed with money and ready to do anything to succeed' (1980a: 266).

3

BOURDIEU, POSTMODERNISM, MODERNITY

In this and the next chapter, I shall locate Bourdieu's approach to the institution of art within key perspectives in the sociology of culture and cultural studies. His important contribution to the controversy over modernity provides the launching-point for a mapping exercise which seeks to explore the intertextual sources of his own thought about the sacralisation of culture. The aim is not only to elucidate his distinctive contribution but also to point to alternative paths that he has failed to develop. I shall start by focusing on the debate over postmodernism, identifying the strategic importance in *Distinction* but stressing also the need to locate this work in the light of his subsequent sociological history of modernism.

Bourdieu and the debate over modernity

After 1850, the experience of everyday life in a world increasingly moulded by the designs of a bourgeois patriarchy produced a new mentality in art. Bourdieu seeks to defamiliarise the complex divisions of artistic modernity, encoded within the clichéd couplet 'modern art'. The cultural field appears through this lens not as a peripheral object for study within the sociological hierarchy but rather as indispensable for understanding other social relations. Marx had the same perspective with respect to the broader cultural arena of belief, viewing the critique of religion in modernity as initiating the critique of all social relations. Similarly Trotsky had regarded Futurism as the modernist critique of the Aestheticist cult of beauty, which he pointed out was inextricably bound to the 'stagnant and smelly character of everyday life . . . produc[ing] that aesthetics' (1960: 145).

As I have shown, Bourdieu's central move is to characterise the experience of capitalism as engendering a complex inversion of the cosmos, in which the worldliness of the businessman is negated in the otherworldliness of the artist. Although in some respects he can be justly described as 'a Weberian lamb in Marxist wolf's clothing' (Nice, 1978: 30), it is especially in his concern to turn Foucault right way up, as Marx had earlier done to Hegel, that we can decode Bourdieu's theory as undertaken in the spirit of Marx. Like Foucault (1981b), Bourdieu wants to seize the classics – 'the gift of the dead' – from the 'sanctuary of History and the fetishised authors' to put them back into liberty (1992: 13). Unlike a Foucauldian approach, the lived experience or subjectivity of the author is not eliminated but is situated within a network of objective relations, especially those of the professional field, class and family. Such sociological work does not diminish the work of art, as conservative critics believe; rather it provides a rich accompaniment to it, which compensates for the earlier 'angelism' of the interest in pure form (1992: 15).

Since early modernism for Bourdieu is now 'a world we have lost', it is only by reassessing the artistic mode of existence, especially the symbiotic relations of the 'second bohemia' with the repressive brutality of the first dictatorship of the industrial bourgeoisie, that we can reconstitute that world. The persecution of Baudelaire, Flaubert, Lecomte de Lisle and others, together with the censorship and imprisonment of their publishers, represents the heroic moment of modernism which has now passed.[1] For the coming-into-being of autonomous art is an oppositional movement even though it declared itself to be about style or form. If the rupture of Flaubert and Baudelaire in literary history has to be understood as that of the *first avant-garde*, by using this benchmark we can see the entire ensemble of the modern relations of cultural legitimacy being set up in place, just as the first factories installed a new set of power divisions when craft authority was preserved elsewhere. In other words, the laws of modern art are only possible because of this break with realism. The art-world of *late modernism*, by contrast, has gravitated to a different position in relation to power. Objectively it serves to reproduce rather than to subvert the dominant class.

My contention is that Bourdieu's work is best understood as a sociological rebuttal of the history of much crude postmodernist thought. But it also marks clearly the *breaks* as well as the *dialectical continuities* of the present with the heroic period of modernism. In comparison with other recent French theorists such as Lyotard and Baudrillard, for Bourdieu the grand narratives of the first generation of Enlightenment thinkers are still unfinished: hence his indictment of the 'false radicalism' or inadequate social science of historical political movements which claim to authorise their action through the name of the subordinate class. Bourdieu does not 'dance lightheartedly upon the waters of difference' among the 'feline ironists and revellers in relativism' (Soper, 1991: 122).[2] But nor is it possible to see Bourdieu as simply 'against postmodernism', as though it merely encapsulated an *irrelevant* 'poverty of theory'. I shall briefly outline the theory of modernity in order to highlight the nature of Bourdieu's contribution. It should also be stressed that this construction of the debate suggests a free passage of ideas across national frontiers, while such circuits are still in practice uneven and subject to blockage.

It is necessary to distinguish the new social relations and distinctive culture of modernity and to probe the question of the links between the two. Debate has focused on the cultural coordinates of creativity, and – more specifically – on whether creativity in the late modern metropolis is doomed to exhaustion and decline (Anderson, 1984; Bürger, 1984; Orr, 1986). Anderson and Bürger have both argued that neomodernism is characterised by a culture which produces only artistic kitsch, in which the recycling of older ideas is prevalent. Modernism in this late epoch has thus been associated with the failure of the avant-garde and with an expectation of eternal cultural repetition of earlier cultural forms (Anderson, 1984; Orr, 1986). Indeed Ferry's *Homo Aestheticus* (1993) links contemporary avant-gardism to cultural poverty or 'cretinism'.

The merit of the modernity thesis as originally outlined by Berman (1983) is that it grasped imaginatively the wider dimensions of the change in traditional societies implicit in the drama of development. Emphasising the antagonistic class forces and the clash of modes of production, Berman's initial account nevertheless avoids economic reductionism in its presentation of cultural production within the varied experiences of urban modernity. This perceptive formulation hinges on three major epochs of modernity. First, from the sixteenth to eighteenth centuries, there is the *appearance of the new*, but without the vocabulary to explain it (it is prefigured, for example, in Rousseau's revolt against the artificiality of the court and the reaction to the tradition of the salon). Secondly, from 1790 to 1890 in Europe, Britain and America, there was a *simultaneous experience of the old world and the new*, together with the emergence of the idea of modernity and modernisation, especially in the thought of Marx, Nietzsche, Whitman and Baudelaire. These major theorists of modernity posited its dialectical character: they welcomed the modern world but recognised its contradictions. Although they possessed an exhilarating sense of disenchantment, summed up by Berman in Marx's phrase 'All that is solid melts into air', they noted also new forms of domination within modernity, not least the subjugation of aesthetic values to the law of the market. Thirdly, the twentieth-century experience is premised on *the expansion of modernism to the whole world* but also on the loss of faith in collective capacities to shape a progressive future, which Berman encapsulates as the 'flat totalisations' of the metropolis. Within this globalisation of capitalism, new modernist arts triumph in the periphery, as in the work of García Márquez, Fuentes or Vargas Llosa.

Parallel to the work of Bourdieu (1992), the structure of feeling of the urban modernists, with their secularisation, disdain for established authority and avid delight in the machine has been illuminatingly described both by Berman (1983) and by Frisby (1985). Succintly summarised by Baudelaire, modernity received its most lyrical (and regressive) paen of praise in the Italian Futurist Manifesto. Founded on the increasing supremacy of the new capitalist mode of production, with its ramifying exchange circuits and fragmented division of labour, the new metropolises of urban Europe established unprecedented forms of urban existence which turned lives upside down, not least in the architecture of the public sphere and in the new modes of communication (Schorske, 1961: chap. 2).[3] To this should be added the late nineteenth-century 'consumer revolution', especially in the city arcades with their 'exotic–chaotic' array of colonial commodities and domestically produced mass luxuries (Benjamin, 1973a; Featherstone, 1990;

Williams, 1982). Accompanying these changes in production and consumption was also a new conception of the cosmos, resulting from the displacement of the bourgeois understanding of the early modern Copernican universe by the uncertainty principle and the relativism of late modernity. Such a transition also generated a shift from the pursuit of work and pleasure in early capitalism, which had itself succeeded the feudal quest for religious happiness, to the ceaseless striving for 'excitement' in late modernity (Ferguson, 1990: 241–60).

Berman was thus the pioneer of a wider debate about modes of production which embraced the phenomena once classified as the 'cultural revolution' of capitalism (see, for example, Corrigan and Sayer, 1985). Along with the constant revolutionising of production, Berman explored other significant features of the post-Enlightenment bourgeois social order. Thus the geometrical structures of the new civic design of St Petersburg or the Haussmannisation of Paris and other city centres permitted also the easier imposition and policing of urban discipline. The consequent decline of the autonomous working-class dwellings in the medieval slums and the artisan trades carried out within them transformed the housing of the poor into dangerous enclosures and multiplied the tragic victims of development. Along with the blossoming of sociability in boulevards and cafés, the lonely figure of the poet or social investigator emerged, with his or her forensic and aesthetic inquiry into lower-class modes of life. Frisby has also brought to bear the insights of Benjamin, Simmel and Kracauer to expose the experience and meaning of the unparalleled extension of exchange and money. Thus direct knowledge of the rapid rise and falls of fortunes in the metropolis engendered a cool calculativeness on the part of city dwellers. For both dominant and subordinate classes, capitalist institutions created the co-existence of extremely rationalised, routine forms of life with their opposite, the adventure or the phantasmagoria, especially those visions of plenty which were stimulated by unprecedented commodities. The anonymity of the modern city facilitated also the transformations of gender relations implicit in the rise of 'new women'.

Frisby's account of modernity emphasises its new cultural forms. These arose most poignantly from the tragic sense of 'culture' as a reified and overwhelming force. Yet they were also apparent through the assembled objects of the newly constructed art galleries and arcades, which distilled a distinctive awareness of space and time, or through new popular literary genres such as the detective novel which played with the opacity of social relations (Moretti, 1983; Palmer, 1978).

The debate between Anderson and Berman renews older questions about the causes of cultural creativity, but this time in the context of modernism (Kroeber, 1963; Marx, 1973: 110–11; Sorokin, 1964). It seeks, in particular, to explain the ebbs and flows of modernist movements within the social locations of modern Western bourgeois societies. In a key essay responding to Berman's book, Anderson has christened the period from 1890 to 1930 the period of 'high modernism', the years of Kafka, Joyce, Musil, Braque,

Picasso and Matisse; of Cubism, Expressionism, Surrealism and Dadaism. Anderson suggests that the extraordinary flowering of creativity in these years depended not just on the social locations for modernity but on vital cultural coordinates. Three of these are central: the persistence of a monarchy or imperial power of an autocratic type; the institution of an academy with an official art, against which the avant-garde protested; and, finally, the adoption of socialism by the European working class (Anderson, 1984: 104). After the Second World War, these conditions crumbled, along with the disappearance of monarchies in Greece, Italy and the Austro-Hungarian empire, and the pre-capitalist, traditional worlds of which they were a part. When the juxtaposition of the older world with the new became less tense, the modernist movement it spawned lost its power and vigour. The avant-garde was linked no longer to a substantive rationality but rather to a demand for new shocks dominated solely by the 'tyranny of the calendar' (Anderson, 1984: 113). Modernism was now shown up as an empty category – by which Anderson means that it began to adapt to the calculative rationality or exchange-value which it once spurned (as an instance of such thought, see Bowness et al., 1964[4]). Consequently, the only sites in the present from which great art can emerge now are those of the global periphery, such as Latin America, where artists still confront the contrast in total social being between tradition and modernity.

Has metropolitan art lost the soil in which it once flourished? A similar argument is made by Orr, although he makes an exception of the neo-modernist flowering which occurred in the mid-1960s. Whereas Anderson holds that post-1930 (metropolitan) art has – despite exceptions – only weakened forms, Orr argues for a more significant revival of modernism through the works of Antonioni, Bergman, Godard, the Rolling Stones and the Beatles. Also attacking the determinism and pessimism of Anderson's case, Berman (1984) has argued that if the twentieth century has lost the grasp of potentiality as well as negation that the nineteenth-century thinkers possessed, there are still grounds for holding that great modernist work can be undertaken in the present. Moi (1985) has commented in similar terms on the *de facto* exclusion within the modernist canon of much significant work by women, despite the links at the philosophical level between the interest in the mind (of Surrealism, for example) and the multiple realities which have preoccupied women writers. The implication of her argument is that modernism is only now bearing fruit in this area. For all these reasons, we might want to qualify the monolithic image of cultural decline that Anderson has presented.

The subsequent cognitive mapping of postmodernist culture reveals certain distinctive elements of the claimed break with modernism (Jameson, 1991; Jencks, 1986; Lash and Urry, 1987).[5] First, there is the belief that cultural producers can no longer disclose the world because of the crisis of representation (Jameson, 1984). Only play on existing stereotypes is possible. In a world of simulacra and images, it is impossible to distinguish the authentic or real. Secondly, there is a crisis of creativity, so that the author is limited to pastiche or blank parody, in other words, to the recapitulation of earlier patterns of representation but without the earlier stable sense of ethics. Thirdly, postmodern culture lacks the consensus over time and the logical use of language that pervaded Enlightenment culture; for this reason, Jameson typifies it as schizophrenic (1983: 119–22). Fourthly, postmodernism occupies a different location from modernism, partly because of the canonisation of the latter. It entwines itself with the commercial messages or with best-selling cultural products that used to be kept apart from high culture. Pop art and punk music – both 'postmodernist' – are used to sell Levis. The suspicion of the market that characterised the sacred or auratic art of the period up to the 1960s is replaced by a playful acceptance of the commodity. In the most spectacular interface between nature and society, architecture, it is claimed by postmodernist historians that the new double-coded buildings – integrating the popular and the modernist – can even end deep-rooted social conflicts.[6] Networks of resistance against dominant discursive formations are celebrated as the surviving locations of critical thought, although these are restricted to limited local areas where the vernacular can reappear or to insulated interpretative communities where an identity of perspective can be maintained.

There are several types of critique that can be made of these theories (Callinicos, 1989; Dews, 1987; Harvey, 1989; Rose, 1991a). The 'fragile networks' of identity-formation (Habermas, 1987: 360) and the dissidence embedded in the new social movements are vulnerable to ideological volatility. They may turn into dark irrationalist traps heralding a return to the aestheticised politics of the 1930s (Eagleton, 1990: 396; Harvey, 1989: 304). Postmodernism overestimates the significance of subjectivist philosophies. It exaggerates the distinctiveness of its time. It fails to grasp the continued stratification of cultural consumption, in which the dominated class lack access to high culture, while it lacks any inkling of the power of cultural legitimacy. Even in terms of art, its claims are doubtful. Its double-coding and use of pastiche are not unique to this period. Double-coding is rather a feature of many earlier forms of art, as in the use of Renaissance images in the eighteenth century (Rose, 1991b). Further, it is based on misunderstanding of earlier cultural forms. For while there was an undoubted wariness of the kitsch of the culture industry, modernism by no means repudiated all popular art, but rather had what Huyssen has called a 'competitive pas-de-deux with mass culture' (1986: 24). Most importantly, the desire to de-sacralise art is common both to important groups of modernists and to postmodernism. The resulting confusion over periodisation has had a disabling effect on most postmodernists' categorisations: Le Corbusier's allegedly 'postmodern' Ronchamps chapel was built in 1925, Doctorow's *Ragtime* – also categorised in this way – was written in the 1940s, and while most writers date the move beyond modernism from the late sixties, others have identified the entire post-war culture as possessing these forms (for example, Gilbert and Gubar, 1988).

There is nevertheless undoubtedly a 'shift in sensibility' since the sixties, or a new structure of feeling (although less plausibly the 'transformation' claimed in the movement's self-conception (Jameson, 1983: 125)). Whether or not the cultural and social theories that make up postmodernism can be held to be consistent and whether or not it has any value, the phenomenon exists at the level of beliefs, with its own creative figures and with cultural critics who elaborate the rationales of its artists. As far as generalisation is possible, these highly heterogeneous cultural phenomena seem to me to be characteristic of a revival of earlier irrationalist forms of modernism, typified in the novels of Svevo (*The Confessions of Zeno* (1923)) or Céline (*Journey to the End of Night* (1932)), for example, rather than representing a distinctive new phase or a renewal of utopian thought.

The structural factors underlying the postmodern structure of feeling are undoubtedly the collapse of the post-war social-democratic 'consensus' resulting from the global restructuring of capitalism and the new international division of labour (Callinicos, 1989: 162–4). These have had an extraordinary impact on the struggle for educational capital, to which Bourdieu's 'school sickness' is a response. Together with the return to more exploitative, older methods of accumulation, these changes have resulted in a simultaneously greater competitiveness (for example, the fateful inter-city economic competitions underpinning the European 'cities of culture' razamatazz), the destruction of pre-capitalist enclaves throughout the sphere of work, and, lastly, the orchestration of new experiences of leisure, not least through the ideology of compulsory consumption (Sklair, 1991: 139–59). Developments such as the turn to holidays abroad on a mass basis and – of course – the Coca-Colaisation of the world have created a blandly homogeneous eclecticism, well summarised by Lyotard in his celebrated portrait of the 1990s bourgeois:

> Eclecticism is the degree zero of contemporary general culture: one wakens to reggae, watches a Western, eats MacDonald's foods for lunch and local cuisine for dinner, wears Paris perfume in Tokyo and retro clothes in Hong Kong. . . . (1987: 76)

Space and time have thus become dramatically compressed in the new global culture, underpinned by the exchanges of a transnational capitalist class (Harvey, 1989: 156).

In brief, a key motif in postmodernism has been the exhaustion of the avant-garde. A wider question is the continued existence of autonomous or two-dimensional forms of literature and art. Hence the pivotal importance of Habermas's critique of Derrida for his denial of the reality-disclosing character of literature (Habermas, 1987: 193–9), a denial, I suggest, which has its underlying explanation in the changing relationship of art to power.

The phenomenon of 'art embraced by the arms of power' most clearly marks the gulf from modernism's earlier location (Cockcroft, 1992; Crane, 1987; Zukin, 1982). This co-option of the avant-garde took place in the USA from the sixties of the Kennedy years, although it originated in the Cubist period (1907–12), when Americans were already buying French painting. Its arena was not just the auction-room and the museum, but the 'Gold Coast of lofts', the urban middle-class emulation of artists' practices of living in industrial warehouses (Zukin, 1988). Artists passed by a quantum leap from marginal figures to mainstream professionals, some of whom were now making a lucrative living off art (Featherstone, 1990: 17; Zukin, 1982: 435).[7] The ramifying effect of this was the domestication of bohemia in the 1970s and modernism's loss of its subcultural character. 'The irony in all of this is that the first time the U.S. had something resembling an "institution art" in the emphatic European sense', writes Huyssen, 'it was modernism itself, the kind of art whose purpose had always been to resist institutionalisation' (Huyssen, 1986: 193).

It is within this fractured debate on modernity and postmodernity that Bourdieu's *Les Règles de l'art* and *Distinction* offer a powerful alternative to existing theory. What Bourdieu has done is to provide an updated study of the changing structural position of modernist movements after High Modernism, on the lines of Macherey in France and of cultural materialism in Britain. It is by combining these approaches with the techniques and concepts first used in the historical studies of sects by Weber that he has introduced a fertile new analytical terrain. In the process he has produced the historical genesis of the artistic enclave which clarifies the very different relation to the field of power of the first avant-garde in the 1850s to comparable artistic groups – say, the Woosters – in the 1980s and 1990s. Bourdieu's theory identifies knowledge of legitimate art in the present period with the possession of social and economic power. But it has the important advantage over the critics of postmodernism of a much more detailed discussion of both the mechanisms of cultural legitimacy (consecration) and of the nature of the art-world itself.

For Bourdieu, the virtues of revolt and resistance in relation to artistic freedom are now forgotten or denied (1992: 76). Yet the decisive moment of modernism was the creation after 1848 of a world apart, separated from bourgeois salons and the market, in which art could be preserved by subterranean critique. Bourdieu is thus in agreement with Lukács, who writes of the 'crisis into which triumphant capitalism plunges the arts' after the failure of the 1848 revolution (1978: 148).

The world on the margins which these writers established was one diametrically opposed to the use of literature to make money, as in the case of contemporary Parisian 'cultural proletarians' (Marx, quoted in Prawer, 1976: 310). On the contrary, the work of art which was worthwhile was one that could not pay. Flaubert expresses this as a disdain for the crowd: 'When you don't address yourself to the crowd, it's fair enough that the crowd shouldn't pay you' (Bourdieu, 1992: 121). The perfection for which he worked created an apparent paradox: a search for a purity of form that would make the real appear real (unlike the Academy writers who wanted form to bring out the ideal) (1992: 142).

Bourdieu's originality lies less in linking the origins of modernist literature to the external determinants of the writers than in introducing the concept of artistic habitus, or learnt dispositions, through which artists expressed their social position in a distinctive artistic philosophy or set of meanings. Adorno had written in *Negative Dialectics* that 'dwelling in the core of the subject are the objective conditions' (quoted by Shulte-Sasse, in Bürger, 1984: xvii), and it is this insight which could be said to sum up Bourdieu's sense of artistic habitus too. The key difference he claims from earlier writers is that the objective conditions are not simply a product of external class position but are also shaped by the agents of the independent yet dominated world of art, with their commitments, alliances, competitive anxieties and interests (1993a: 286–7). Paramount among their concerns are also the interests of a more educated group. Their disdain for the social exclusivity of the dominant classes masks their retention of the privileges conferred by a superior education.

The 1850s avant-garde was one that was indeterminate or marginal in class terms. It lacked plebeian origins but could not identify securely with the aristocracy either. Although Villiers de l'Îsle Adam was the offspring of a very distinguished noble family, the others were sons of minor aristocrats from the regions (Théodore de Banville, Barbey d'Aurevilly and the Goncourts), of a colonial planter from Réunion (Leconte de Lisle), a top civil servant (and the nephew of a general) (Baudelaire), or from the liberal professions (Bouilhet, Fromentin and Flaubert). In five cases they had studied law (Flaubert, Théodore de Banville, Barbey d'Aurevilly, Baudelaire and Fromentin) (1992: 127). Their means of living came from rent and their expectations were of inheritances. It was precisely this stratum which valued cultural capital so highly.

Thus, for Bourdieu, the denial of the pyramidal construction of narrative both represents and heightens the break with the *collective consciousness* and sets Flaubert off, with his handful of readers, on their vertiginous path of lonely construction. Obliquely referring to the tragic world of Pascal, for whom God was present but always hidden, Bourdieu suggests that modernism has a similar conception of the hidden quality of the ethical law which it expresses in its works.

It is from these modernists, together with Zola, that the new public sphere takes shape. It has its own economic ethic and its own economic order, its own work ethic and its own status order. From this region there gradually emerges the new charismatic role of the artist, or, in Bourdieu's terms, the *transubstantiation of the artist*. Within the avant-garde, literature develops not just by incorporating the work of earlier writers, but by embracing the thought of the advanced scientific thinkers of the epoch. Bourdieu cites the role of Cuvier, Darwin and Lamarck for Flaubert (1992: 147), with whom might be compared Barbara Hepworth and the constructivist Circle's adoption of Einstein and Maxwell (Martin et al., 1971: 245).

The mid-1880s marks *the maturation of the avant-garde*. New laws now structure the literary field. Although they are responses to a specific epoch, the rules acquire the character of timeless ahistorical necessities. The dualist structure by means of which art signals its distance both from the market and from naive taste is now condensed into the new rule that the accumulation of symbolic profits is inversely related to the accumulation of economic profits, *the rule of artistic disinterest*. By the late nineteenth century a new hierarchy of genres will be founded on this assumption, with poetry acquiring precedence over the novel and drama. The novel itself is segmented in a pyramid of esteem, starting at the top with the psychological novel but then marked by the pre-eminence of the naturalist novel over the novel of manners, and, most notably, over the regional popular and the industrial novel: a hierarchy in which the last four subordinate genres are excluded from the category of 'literary' altogether. The social capital possessed by the readers also has its impact on the work's artistic status: the higher the readers' social capital, the more likely that the work will be greeted enthusiastically. Whether the avant-garde fosters a committed or pure art is dependent on the nature of the historical period. Here two principles determine the specific character of the modernist movement: first, the external class forces, such as a shift away from trade unions on the part of the working class or the turn to spiritual issues on the part of the bourgeoisie; and, secondly, the *dialectics of consecration*, in which a new group bids for dominance against a more established group of authors within the literary field. The emergence of the psychological novel at the end of the nineteenth century, for example, required both such developments. Bourdieu refers to this as *the laws of transformation and conservation*.

While each movement comes into being with a sense of its own distinctiveness – even of constituting a whole new world of art – certain underlying regularities can be detected through the discourses of the mature avant-garde. Of these, three principles of new artistic practices stand out: the constancy of change; the rigour and strenuousness of artists' actions; and the order which art creates within the chaos of the world. All these put a premium on cultural capital. Such a stress on the continued importance of education fits neatly with parallel research on the crisis in French secondary and university education after 1880, and, especially, on the fears of an unemployed educated stratum (Ringer, 1992: 86, 127–40). For the underlying interest of the avant-garde is to separate themselves from the uneducated, both from the intellectual lumpen-proletariat and from the best-selling writer or artist. Avant-garde art gains its poignant conception of its own radical struggle less from any committed character it demands from its members than from the sheer weight of the existing educational system. Consequently, the cost of the new rules of art was that art became progressively less popular. Lukács (1978: 201) states that Molière's maidservant might have been consulted over his endings (just as Lenin's cook was to be able to run the ship of state) but that not even the ascetic Tolstoy's peasants could help with his novels, despite their realism. Bourdieu has even erected modernism's exclusive qualities into a structural trait. What he calls the 'production of belief' in modernism is based on its *permanent distance from workers' and petty-bourgeois taste*.

When the consecration of modernists extends to their reception in the ordinary educational system – schools, museums, etc. – then the final stage of modernism has taken place. The key historical change is the new phenomenon of *collective* belief. In other words, the high market-price of Impressionist and other modernist paintings can no longer be explained simply in terms of the law of value, that is, the cost of the work is related to the cost of producing a worker (the painter) with the appropriate skills. Hence Bourdieu argues that the material value only represents the *outer husk* of art. Its *inner kernel* is collective veneration of spirituality and genius. While the great liquidity of wealth in the modern period has facilitated the soaring prices of art-works as commodities, the underlying process is the operation of the consecration process. The fetishism of economists veils the fact that it is collective belief which creates the creator:

> In contrast to fabricated objects with a weak or nugatory symbolic import (undoubtedly increasingly rare in the era of *design*), the work of art, like religious goods or services, amulets or various sacraments, receives value only from collective belief as collective misrecognition, collectively produced and reproduced. (1996: 172)

Bourdieu is undoubtedly right that such collective beliefs in the art heritage serve as the fiduciary guarantee of value, but it might also be asked whether art has not turned now into a stable (global) store of value, at a time when nationalised currencies are too volatile to serve this function.

Several conditions of the avant-garde art of early modernism have now changed. There has been a decline in numbers of those who are supported by allowances and can sustain themselves without selling their work; even the existence of state benefits has in the long term only a marginal impact in this respect. The high prices of modernist works have rebounded on the claimed 'disinterestedness' of the artist, showing that art is not always inimical to bourgeois levels of income (1984: 231–2; 1992: 211). Finally – and most strikingly – there has been a change in the response of the dominant class to artists: since the haute bourgeoisie has long ceased being rigorously self-denying and thrifty, it is art that has become the main claim to a nobler existence (1993a: 44; Huyssen, 1986, chap. 10). Secularisation means that in a period of widespread religious disillusionment for scientific reasons, art can be offered as a source of spiritual grace (hence the importance of its claim to universal value). Secondly, artistic distinction and the taste for difficult works provide profits of distinction or symbolic capital. Closely related to educational capital (measured by educational achievements plus time), this is a form of capital which results from the possession of a habitus closely linked to the scholastic skills of parents and to the artists' distance from material necessity.

Bourdieu's model of social ageing implies that what now separates the 'commercial' from the 'professional' is the *interval of time* that is imposed between labour and reward for the latter (1992: 211; see also Sanguineti, 1973). Thus bohemia as a location of subversion loses its power and becomes ineffective: dissidence is authorised by change for its own sake.

Transmitted through the 'cultivated disposition', art has now become part of the dominant class's consumption. It follows that it can no longer be seen as an enclave culture or an 'Iona island' of retreat from advanced capitalism, as Adorno had viewed it (1996, also in Bloch et al., 1977: 188–9).[8] The shock of the new in Bourdieu is precisely to register this historical change in the objective relations of social space. The empirical study of reception thus permits a social unmasking of the relations of culture which raises new hypotheses about social interests, including those of socialist intellectuals.

Bourdieu's work is devoid of the anti-humanist melancholy which has so permeated the thought of Foucault and Lyotard. Bourdieu writes of art and consumption like many of those who have associated themselves with postmodernism but he sets these spheres within a totalising perspective. In my view, a *critical subtext* can still be decoded within his work. His apparent perspectivism is merely a stage of the analytical process and therefore not vulnerable to the type of attack that Habermas has levelled so brilliantly against Bataille, Foucault and Derrida (Habermas, 1987).

Lash makes an interesting claim, despite Bourdieu's protestations to the contrary (see Bourdieu and Wacquant, 1992: 155), that there is a postmodern core to Bourdieu's ideas (Lash, 1990: 239). I have stressed so far that Bourdieu does indeed argue for historical development in the nature of bourgeois society, but (unlike, say, Foucault) he has linked the new consumption regime catering to sexual desire and the aesthetic to market realities. However, it is wrong to absorb Bourdieu into the postmodernist fold because he has not sought to identify a total cultural change from the epoch of modernism. I am unpersuaded by the case made by Lash for two reasons: first, because it misinterprets Bourdieu's view of class and, secondly, because it mistakenly claims that Bourdieu's mapping of the cultural field has established a logic of 'de-differentiation' (Lash, 1990: 263), in which the recent conversion of high art into commodities has accompanied the growing consumption of mixed popular and high arts by consumers. Bourdieu does not propose that the discourses of high culture have been fundamentally weakened. The reverse is true: there is a constant re-division of the field – as old 'mass' culture such as 'science fiction' or 'cinema' breaks up into art and (mere) entertainment – but the stratification of culture is as deep-rooted as ever.

For some curious reason, the selling-point for *Distinction* as an imported good has been the section on the new petty bourgeoisie. It is this class which Lash also claimed earlier to be the bearer of a brave new postmodern world (Lash and Urry, 1987). However, Lash's subsequent designation of the 'service class's' affinities with postmodernism (1990: 251) suffers from imprecision and even from a certain violence of abstraction. He conflates two class fractions that Bourdieu is careful to separate. While in *Distinction* Bourdieu does indeed refer to the 'new' petty bourgeoisie (as against the 'old' artisan and shopkeeping groups and the 'executant' petty bourgeoisie of clerks and junior management), he has always clearly separated this from the '*noblesse d'état*', which has had a growing importance in the changed mode of bourgeois reproduction since the war, and which is composed of politicians, the military, the judiciary and senior public administrators. Lash, on the other hand, premises his cultural shift on a vaguely defined group of 'yuppies' or '*bas clergé*', who possess a greater volume of cultural than economic capital and whose consumption of middlebrow as well as avant-garde works is viewed as an augury of the future (Lash, 1990: 293). But he fails to recognise that throughout the period of modernism there have been groups with higher cultural than economic capital. Moreover, in contrast to his view of massive de-differentiation, other studies of cultural reception have found crucial aspects of readership segregation and stratification that are broadly similar to Bourdieu's analysis. As a case in point, only a tiny fraction of women in my own sample used *both* formulaic mass literature *and* modernist or critical realist 'high' literature (Fowler, 1991: 124).[9]

As Bourdieu has consistently argued, there has *always* been a wider audience (taken from the petty bourgeoisie and industrial bourgeoisie) for the most accessible and securely consecrated works of high culture throughout the whole period of modern art. What is more, the commodification of symbolic goods through the dealer/publisher and critic network has *always* existed (in misrecognised forms) throughout the period too. It can be conceded that the post-1960s expansion of the education sector has extended the public for canonised writers. But, despite this, the habitus for cultural production and reception is surely very different in the case of *each* of the new strata (new petty bourgeoisie, new mandarins and the new entrepreneurial élites of the business school model (Bourdieu, 1989)). Lash fails to recognise this because he continually reverts to a mechanistic notion of habitus. This is devoid of Bourdieu's much more powerful and subtle conception of time.[10]

Art in the arms of power: the crisis in working-class reproduction

For Bourdieu (1984), aestheticism is the dominant *masculine* disposition of our time, in sharp contrast to the ethical response to the aesthetic which still characterises women. Such an assessment in terms of style alone unites two groups with a taste for luxury: the haute bourgeoisie and the new petty bourgeoisie. Often adopting a radical 'countercultural' aesthetics which is exemplified in new artistic goods, the rejection of ascetic self-denial distinguishes the new from the old petty bourgeoisie. Such a shift to fun and aestheticism, which liberates the body as a site of pleasure, can be partly explained by commercial interests:

> It may even be wondered if the ethic of liberation is not in the process of supplying the economy with the perfect consumer whom economic theory has always dreamed of. . . . (1984: 371)

The cult of art is intensified by the discrepancy between *subjective* radicalism and *objective* wealth, but also by political disappointment (1984: 366).

In Bourdieu's view, 'lazy positivists' forget that it is the nature of the conflicts over power which determines the competitions within social space, especially through establishing the parameters of positions within the various fields – the rules of art, the rules of the market, etc. (1984: 94). What is important in this context is the way Bourdieu describes the link between distinction in literature and rewards in the material world. The 'gentle violence' of literary missionary work aspires to democratise the cultural heritage, offering it to all (1984: 229). But such front-stage democratisation is often combined with a back-stage demand for a favourable conversion rate. By these means, high scholastic capital is cashed in for high levels of material capital. Certainly, the general interest of the dominant class requires universalistic educational selection as the main mechanism for the competitive struggle. However, given the weakness of trade unions, a new mode of domination has been institutionalised in the metropolitan countries. This new mode depends on consumption as well as intensified educational struggle, and,

> substituting seduction for repression, public relations for policing, advertising for authority, the velvet glove for the iron fist, pursues the symbolic integration of the dominated classes by imposing needs rather than inculcating norms. (1984: 154)

The consequence is a profound attack on the remaining forms of social solidarity. Endlessly delayed entry into labour markets and continuous life-long education, coupled with cooling-out mechanisms for rejection, serve to depoliticise frustration. They mask awareness of failure as anything other than a personal loss of honour:

> Whereas the old system tended to produce clearly demarcated social entities which left little room for social fantasy . . . the new system of structural instability in the representation of social identity and its legitimate aspirations tends to shift agents from the terrain of social crisis and critique to the terrain of personal crisis and critique. (1984: 156)[11]

In other words, Bourdieu's distance from postmodernism lies in his continued retention of an objectivist understanding. He consequently repudiates what Lyotard has called 'temporary epistemological contracts'. For behind his explanation in terms of group differences of position-taking in cultural and other forms of consumption, there exists a back-stage struggle for the possession of power and the capacity to shape the future: the first is grasped subjectively by agents in terms of binary oppositions ('original', 'common', etc.); the second is illuminated by the causal analyses familiar in historical materialism or realism. Moreover, *taste* leads us often to refuse what we can't have (*amor fati*) just as women traditionally have prided themselves on their refusals of egoism. But a scientific constructivist sociology can also show that there may well be limits to the objective processes that create the magic of turning frustrations into subjective taste or damaged identities. When expectations are out of kilter, taste results in *hatred of destiny*. It is with this possibility that a *break with tacit acceptance* can occur. In one pregnant passage of *Distinction*, Bourdieu describes a scenario of accelerating social fragmentation:

> Everything suggests that an abrupt slump in objective chances in relation to subjective aspirations is likely to produce a break in the tacit acceptance which the dominated classes previously granted to the dominant goals, and so to make possible a genuine inversion of values. (1984: 168)

I have argued that Bourdieu's sociology has given an important place to a theory of literature and art and their changing historical role. The next chapter will begin the job of locating the key intellectual traditions behind Bourdieu's own work. While by no means a complete survey of the thinkers on whom he has drawn, it demonstrates the significant historical materialist, poststructuralist and interactionist influences which have shaped his sociology of literature and art.

Notes

1. The heroic movement was definitively over by the 1871 Commune when these aging writers repudiated the Communards (Lidsky, 1970: 45). Flaubert, who was 50, had already written that 'Politics is dead, just like theology. It's lasted 300 years and that's enough' (1869) (1970: 34). Lidsky, cited by Bourdieu, provides an important analysis of responses to the workers' movement in terms of the proximity to Paris and the age of the writer (1970: 42–4).

2. 'I am inspired by a scientific conviction which is not fashionable today, since one is post-modern. . . . This scentific conviction leads me to think that, if one grasped the social mechanisms [preventing a real scientific internationalism,] this is not in itself sufficient to master them, but one increases the chances of mastering them, inasmuch as these mechanisms rest on misrecognition' (1990d: 2). In the same lecture, Bourdieu argues that the interests of certain minor intellectuals have obscured the close links between the historical and social critique of rationalism (from Durkheim to Foucault) and the neo-Kantian rationalism of Habermas (1990d: 7). His continued use of the term 'rational' testifies to his underlying acceptance of Habermas's view (1987) that the project of modernity has not been completed.

3. Schorske notes that the building of the new cultural monuments of Vienna contributed to the emergence of an 'aristocracy of the spirit' (1961: 45).

4. 'Naturally, the bitterness dies and the fugitive comes back in triumph: the routine is built into the institution. But underground the search for the genuinely unacceptable, the despicable and the disgusting begins over again. It is a process of action and reaction, the instability of imaginative art that has been institutionalised. It is a truer and crueller basis for the academy than any of the upholstered aesthetics of other times' (Bowness et al., 1964: 18).

5. Postmodernism is used by Jameson (1983) to cover the work of Greenaway, Lynch, Warhol, Venturi, Pynchon; Crowther (1993) discusses German artists like Kiefer and Baselitz; while Harvey also analyses *Blade Runner* under this category.

6. 'Monta, Watanabe, Shirai . . . Izogaki and Takayama are using travesty as a kind of mirror-image genre of cultural confusion, and if it's practised long enough it may have the unintended consequence of uniting a fragmented society' (Jencks, 1986: 73).

7. In this respect, Zukin's excellent study of the American field of art is important in that it possesses a two-pronged empirical strategy – it explores initially the changes in the housing markets which facilitated the successive transformation of industrial warehouses, by artists and the bourgeoisie, in a movement that created an extended group of patrons for modern art outside the public galleries; simultaneously, it examines how the tax mechanisms facilitated private ownership of paintings and thus increased prices by extending the size of the collecting public: these two elements changed the market structures for painting by increasing the number of artists who made a lucrative professional career out of the restricted field of art. It

would be desirable to have more empirical analyses of corporate art ownership and its effects in the same period.

8. The legitimation of the avant-garde is measured by the acceptance of abstract expressionism, especially by teachers and other professionals (Bourdieu, 1984: 94–5).

9. Even assuming formulaic mass culture is not typical of mass culture, this suggests only that the field of large-scale production may be becoming more complex in terms of the status of different genres, authors and publishers, not that there is a fundamental 'redifferentiation' or abandonment of the high–low distinction and its pervasive social effects. I would add, however, that among the readers of serious writing, there were an important group of women who had cultural capital but working-class backgrounds (Fowler, 1991: 170). Bourdieu's theory does not account for them (see also Lamont, 1992).

10. In my view, Bourdieu is immune from Habermas's (1987) criticism of poststructuralism as a relativist and irrationalist form of thought. Of course, Bourdieu emphasises that in the modern world (including the artistic field) reason is still often cloaked in myth. But, unlike the case of Derrida (say), Bourdieu does retain the notion of art as possessing a critical, world-disclosing character, as we have seen in relation to Flaubert and Baudelaire. Thus his attack on the institutionalised role of canonical art – and its commercialised 'industrial art' twin – has to be connected to his account of the way the habitus operates, with its socialised dependence on binary oppositions. In the absence of reflexive awareness, art historians themselves maintain these elements of myth since their critical vocabulary lacks rigour (indeed, concepts such as soigné, rare, etc. change historically and owe their linguistic provenance to the nobility). Habermas writes that the 'disclosures of power theory get caught up in the dilemma of a self-enclosed critique of reason that has become total . . . . Hence [there is] no clarity about what it means to pursue a critique of ideology that attacks its own foundations' (1987: 96). But Bourdieu's thought could not be a similar target for Habermas. Indeed, Bourdieu's appeal to a reflexive sociology as a self-monitoring tradition reads very much like Habermas's own communicative reason: 'The first person who can turn back upon himself in a performative attitude from the angle of vision of a second person, can recapitulate the acts . . . just carried out'. (Habermas, 1987: 297; cf. Bourdieu, 1994a: 14–17). In brief, I prefer to read Bourdieu as concerned to use some of the tools of mythological analysis to elucidate the character of contemporary (rational) ideoogical critique. This would all have been easier were he to have been less ironical – and in particular, were he to strengthen further the political implications of his scientific studies. One occasion when he *does* elaborate on this is when he develops the notion of 'heroic' or 'autonomous' work in cultural production and criticism as against 'heteronomous' 'media-intellectuals' (1992: postscriptum, 1996; Rigby, 1993). One aim of Part II is to highlight such aspects of Bourdieu's rational pedagogical project.

11. Compare Durkheim on the structural forces creating individuation (1989: 252).

4

THE HISTORICAL GENESIS OF BOURDIEU'S CULTURAL THEORY

Dialectical materialism and genetic structuralism

Despite the rules of the game in which distinction is achieved through the denial of predecessors, Bourdieu himself is in a line of descent from Lukács, Goldmann and Benjamin. The theory of practice developed by Bourdieu is dedicated to the classical aims of social criticism, especially the Enlightenment critique of magic. In this respect, it extends Marx's analysis of capitalist society, with its fundamental concern for demystification and its insistence that 'the real is the relational'. Despite Bourdieu's methodological refusal to engage in prediction of the future, there is an important continuity with some of the guiding ideas of the 'Hegelian' work of Lukács.

In 1923, Lukács inventively combined Marx with elements of Weber to produce a wider account of the development of capitalist society. Bourdieu, too, like Lukács, aims to criticise the 'eternal' laws of economics in order to get behind the 'given' order. Lukács had been distinctive not just in penetrating behind the outward appearances of the 'economic set-up', to their essential form, but in uncovering other linked forms of reification, which he derives from Max Weber, especially the law and bureaucracy. Lukács had developed from Weber's theory of the rationalised worlds of art, politics, etc., a theory of their effect on the working class. Within this, Lukács had deployed Weber's emphasis on the multiple characters of dispossession in bourgeois society, in a way which now seems to resemble very closely Bourdieu's problematic of taste:

> [i]f the proletariat finds the economic inhumanity to which it is subjected easier to understand than the political and the political easier than the cultural, then all these separations point to the still unconquered power of capitalist forms of life in the proletariat itself. (Lukács, 1968: 77)

The outcomes of such compartmentalised development are precisely the subject of Bourdieu's method of objectification, but often via survey techniques. His constructivist sociology will reveal the disinheritance of which Lukács writes.

However, the theoretical class consciousness which Lukács so problematically 'imputed' to the working class and which vies with its actual 'empirical psychological consciousness' has in Bourdieu become the *social scientists'* theory of practice. Such scientific practice retains the Lukácsian warning to reject all dualisms (subjective/objective etc.), in order to build a post-Feuerbachian theory of humans who act in the world self-consciously. Bourdieu's form of practice also has its 'rational utopianism' (cast in the logic: 'If you want *x* then *y*' (1993b: 48, 25)), but this has been profoundly affected by the character of working-class reproduction. For, in Bourdieu, the empirical-psychological consciousness of the working class has been expressed historically in a popular culture which is overwhelmingly defensive, colonised, carnivalesque (1984: 491): it thus appears weak in transformative powers.

Everyone knows that Lukács' later aesthetic theory presents a more simplistic model of social development, which is then linked to literary forms. His concern is not to attribute the writer to a class of origin or, indeed, to a class destination for its works, but to specify the conditions in which literature flowers and significant form emerges. His conception of literary realism, whether that of Shakespeare or Balzac, depends on the linked ideas of an 'extensive totality', or the representation of all significant social milieux, and an 'intensive totality', or the representation of social types, depicted as individuated figures through their antagonistic world-views. Lukács' argument was that critical realism retained the consciousness of the whole community through the values of their representative, the writer, as in the instances of Dickens, Stendhal and Tolstoy. Their forms are all potentially popular in the sense that their understanding of the social is complex and dialectical. They penetrate beneath the everyday given world to reveal the underlying forms of conflict and estrangement; indeed, it is this which distinguishes these works from their uncritical twins (1969). For Lukács, these works are not mere reflections. The novelist could only construct his/her subject adequately when he/she belongs to the public sphere and is thus in touch with collective consciousness. Naturalism, with its mechanistic elimination of subjectivity, as well as the entire tradition of literary modernism ('subjectivism') were dismissed on the weak grounds that their techniques failed to fit the rules of classical realism.

For Bourdieu, in contrast, modernist movements preserved literature from the threats of both power and the market. But there was a cost for such movements and the cost gives Bourdieu's work a certain Lukácsian resonance. For bohemian modernism loses its closeness to the roots of popular action and to a communal form of collective consciousness. *It is this which permits an anti-capitalist, anti-academic art to gradually come to play the role of legitimating the class it opposes*. Granted, Bourdieu issues his strictures against Lukács' 'short-circuited' theory of literature, which neglected the professional and avant-garde structures behind the modernist permanent revolution (1993a: 140). Yet, especially in his work on reception, *Distinction*, it could be said that Bourdieu expresses in some ways 'the revenge of the Lukácsian'. In other words, he adopts the same empirical problematic as Lukács, but in very different historical circumstances. This is not to say that Bourdieu rejects modernism as Lukács did, nor does he concern himself much with a normative aesthetics. It *is* to say, rather, that through sociological empirical analysis he comes to an assessment of its role which is discomforting to those who would like to believe that modernism is still a revolutionary weapon.

Further, in constructing rules for the analysis of literature Bourdieu has designated his approach the 'genetic' sociology of culture, recalling the 'genetic structuralism' of Goldmann, Piaget and Durkheim, as well as Lukács. Of these, Bourdieu appears only to use Goldmann as the butt for his criticism (1992: 284–6), levelling against him an attack for producing a reductive sociology of literature, which is impaired by analytical short-circuits.

While this is justified in the case of his theory of the novel, there is still a profound debt owed by Bourdieu to Goldmann. This will be apparent to anyone who knows *The Hidden God* (1964a), for it is precisely in *this* work that Goldmann has explored *the internal field of writing* which is fundamental to his interpretation of the Pascal and Racine texts. Moreover, this internal field *overlapped* with the field of religious thought and practice, just as literature has overlapped with politics before and after 1850. Since Bourdieu has stated emphatically that 'the sociology of culture is the sociology of religion of our time' (1993c: 147), it is unthinkable that he did not grasp the fertile uses to which Goldmann put his study of the relations between Jansenist theology, the field of power and the field of literature. Despite his disclaimers, my view is that it is in fact *this* work which is the model for Bourdieu's own approach to Flaubert and the 'second bohemia'.

Goldmann's problem was to explain the emergence in French seventeenth-century thought of Racine, the main architect of French tragic drama, and Pascal, the pioneer of the mathematics of the roulette wheel (for gambling in this world) and the theological wager on the existence of God (for the next) (1964a: 91). What united these creative developments was a *tragic vision* (1964a: 26, 34). In Pascal's *Pensées* this took the form of the *paradoxes* of a hidden God, one whose existence *appears to be denied* by the character of the world, yet who retains an *ultimate* power (1964a: 36–8). Such a simultaneously present and absent God is, in terms of epistemology, the source of a divine revelation; in terms of morality, the guarantor of a rigorous piety, and in terms of political practice, the purpose of a radical flight from the world. Pascal's philosophical position was founded at once on the heroism of gambling, the denial of rationalism and the demand for abstention from all civic political involvement. Racine's *Phèdre* similarly excludes the possibility of any *compromise with the world* (1964a: 376–9).

What experiences in the field of power might create the terrain favourable for such a theological perspective? Goldmann argues that there were a series of royal measures that created fundamental differences in the relationships of fractions of the dominant class. As absolutism developed, with its peasant base, it displaced the class of the recently ennobled group of legal professionals – the *noblesse de robe* – and replaced their administrative role by the 'intendants', a class fraction that was more bureaucratic in ethos, lacking the autonomy conferred on the *noblesse de robe* by their legal training. A further subordinate dynamic was the political castration of the feudal aristocracy, whose domestication at Court and ban on military praxis led them also to a sense of enforced marginality (1964a: 26). Here, then, we have the combined forces of two groups whose objective relegation from influence was matched by their subjective sense of decline.

It was the experience of declining class fractions that was the decisive moulding force of Jansenism (1964a: 105). However, Jansenism itself possessed different ideological wings and Pascal and Racine took an internal trajectory from one to the other between 1637 and 1677. The Convent of Port-Royal was the initial setting for the hegemony of the Barcos circle, an extreme wing which argued that the test of salvation was the retreat from the world into the Convent itself (1964a: 157). This group was superseded as the dominant ideological influence within Jansenism by the less extreme followers of Arnauld, whose centrism generated an epistemology with a limited rationalism in relation to the 'factual sphere' and a minor role for ethics (1964a: 393). Unlike Pascal, the Jansenists as a community moved from the extreme to the moderate position. This softening of ideological stance can be decoded from the shift from *Britannicus*, *Andromaque* and *Phèdre* to the Arnauld-influenced intellectual stance of *Esther* and *Athalie* (1964a: 149).

Both Goldmann and Bourdieu argue that the biographical method is radically unsuited to explain literary texts. What is at stake, instead, is the existence of a series of homologies or structural equivalences between fields that in the seventeenth century were only beginning to be autonomous. Goldmann maps the changes in the chances for economic rewards on the part of a recently ennobled group and the parallel decline in their political power. Together, these create the social habitus of tragedy.

Despite differences in conceptualising desire and the body, Goldmann's portrayal of the ideological world at Port-Royal is recognisable in Bourdieu's later delineation of Parisian bohemia. The revolutionary theological world of Jansenist Catholicism becomes the reverse world of dissent. Goldmann's modalities of opposition are recalled even in Bourdieu's choice of language. He writes of the new bohemian field as 'most favourable to a critical perception . . . criss-crossed with *paradoxes*' (1992: 100; my italics), of the *paradoxical* economy (1992: 123), and of Baudelaire as a purer revolutionary than Flaubert, just as Goldmann had contrasted Barcos with Arnauld, revealed paradoxes, and so forth (1964a: 114, 116).

It is true that Goldmann does not consider the specific conditions for literary production and the role of education within them. In this limited sense, he is guilty – as Bourdieu argues – of a short-circuited explanation (1993c: 140). As later Bourdieusian historians have shown, seventeenth-century France also saw the birth of the distinctive institutions of classical literature. The founding of academies and the multiplication of salons alongside them created the arena for new kinds of literary conflict (for example, between the Ancients and the Moderns or between the new linguistic purists versus the court nobility) (Heinich, 1987; Viala, 1985: 31–3, 173). Freedom in the Academy was only 'distant and limited' (Viala, 1985: 175), but it was already of enormous strategic significance if a writer was able to gain a wide public. It certainly adds another dimension to Goldmann's study to grasp that Pascal and Racine were also Academicians, salon members and recipients of literary honours (Viala, 1985: annexe 2). Pascal, particularly, appears as a transitional figure: an Academician who was also the author of the illicitly published *Provinciales*. His use of imaginary communications between writer and reader in the letter form created an extraordinary vehicle for ideas that acquired a new readership from the bourgeoisie and nobility of both genders who made up the bookbuyers of the emergent market (Viala, 1985: 174).

But the existence of further mediating prisms through the founding of the Academy and the spread of market distribution does not serve to refute Goldmann. His detection of the structural homology between power, theology and literature still stands. Such classic explorations of world-view still retain considerable explanatory weight in Bourdieu's conception of the forces shaping the habitus of thinkers.

Benjamin's 'illuminative flashes' and Bourdieu's socio-analysis

Bourdieu periodically quotes Benjamin. Indeed, it is Benjamin's writing that provides the 'dialectical images' for Bourdieu's more empirical approach.[1] From the urban landscapes of modernity, Benjamin sketches out the new patterns of cultural production and reception. His work on reception, especially, has been decisive for Bourdieu.

For Benjamin, the community role of literature in pre-literate societies, in which a story was common to a whole group of storytellers, has as its opposite the fetishism of the artist's signature in the twentieth century. Equally, the simple multi-functional aesthetic of unnamed T'ang potters contrasts with the mixture of idealised spiritual drives and repressed economic interests of their twentieth-century collectors. It is this profoundly historical view of the variety of artistic institutions which gives Benjamin's approach its power. Bourdieu converts Benjamin's aphorisms into theories which are tested through both historical and quantitative methods of research.

Benjamin's cryptic notes on reception illuminate the phenomenon of the re-sacralisation of literature which preoccupies Bourdieu. His ironic comments on the 'pre-history' and the 'after-history' of a work of art suggest precisely a social theory of the production and the consumption of literature.

> For a dialectical historian, these works incorporate both their pre-history and their after-history – an after-history by virtue of which their pre-history too can be seen to undergo constant change. They teach him how their function can outlast their creator, can leave his intentions behind; how its reception by the artists' contemporaries forms part of the effect that the work of art has on us ourselves today, and how this effect derives from our encounter not just with the work, but with the history that brought the work down to us. (Benjamin, 1979: 351)

The peculiar role of time in this passage enriches Bourdieu's inheritance from phenomenology. He also observes the re-interpretation of the pre-history of artworks and, especially, the sequestration for other purposes of consecrated radical texts (Bourdieu, 1993a: 256).

Benjamin's essay on oral narratives, 'The Storyteller' (in 1973b), also fits closely with Bourdieu. For although the work of art has not yet been secularised completely in pre-capitalist societies – so that its aura springs from this closeness to the religious life of the community – it is also a less elevated form of communication than the aesthetic in bourgeois society. The circle around the storyteller ensures that the story is not mystified as is the work of the genius from the Renaissance on. It springs out of common experience and can be adapted to social needs. In this way it is remote from art in modernity, which derives its authenticity from its uniqueness and its authority from its distance from the spectator. Bourdieu similarly emphasises the communal role – often of a quite practical kind – served by the bard or poet in tribal Kabylia, especially the importance of conveying to the young the 'noble past' : 'this past is not experienced as such, that is as something left behind and situated some distance back in the temporal series, but as being lived again in the presence of the collective memory' (1961: 95). In striking opposition to the West, Kabylian cultural apprenticeship serves 'to impose an impersonal form of thought on personal feeling. In these formulas is expressed a whole philosophy of dignity, resignation, and self-control' (1961: 96). The Kabylian poet encodes in his work several layers of meaning for different audiences, including the esoteric and the more accessible.

Benjamin's storyteller has his or her modern counterpart in the figures of both collector and author. Both of these have been profoundly affected by the bourgeois division between mental and manual labour, expressed in the opposition between genius and anonymous drudge (Benjamin, 1979: 359). For this reason, Benjamin views the European future as potentially lying with a displacement of the art institution itself, either on the model of the Soviet newspapers, which he reported as relying heavily on readers' letters, or by developing the popular arts to respond to the masses' interests in defamiliarising shocks. As I have shown, Bourdieu has similarly identified the 'invention of the artist' and the dispossession of the masses which accompanied it, although his analysis is devoid of any countervailing structures that might prefigure a different future.[2]

The decline of aura has become a cliché of contemporary thought, but it has been wrenched from Benjamin's bleaker view of the re-sacralisation of art:

> [T]he distorted nature of art in class society produces forms which objectively 'mock ... the masses' ... despite the subjective views of the artists. (quoted in Buck-Morss, 1989: 69)

Importantly, however, although Bourdieu quotes Benjamin on the magical qualities conferred by the artist's signature (1993c: 148), he neglects the fact that for Benjamin avant-gardes may temporarily possess the tools for an active disenchantment. Thus, for Benjamin, the intervention of the surrealists involved the alternation of shock devices and memory triggers to counter capitalism's resort to mythicising irrationalism. Hoping to wake Europe from the collective dream in which it slept (1979: 225–9), the surrealists thus served revolution by using the 'image sphere' to create a '*profane* illumination'. Benjamin viewed such artistic practices as breaking the contemplative approach to art, 'short-circuit[ing] the bourgeois historical-literary apparatus' (quoted in Buck-Morss, 1989: 57) and destroying the seductive use of art as a 'pendant' for 'snobbery' (1979: 234).

There are other echoes of Benjamin. Is it a coincidence that photography has a parallel place in both writers' perspective? For neither Benjamin nor Bourdieu is twentieth-century photography itself a consecrated genre (Benjamin, 1979: 192; Bourdieu, 1990c: 65).[3] Bourdieu writes of it as a 'middlebrow art' that therefore cannot enhance the dignity of the collector (1990c: 68–70). But studies of camera clubs show that those who do invest in it are typically lower professionals or politically conscious workers. As in Benjamin's active sense of the author as producer, their passionate interests lead them to wrench the form from the formalism of their teachers, combining the latters' technical knowledge with their own set of visual values.

It is also Benjamin who provides the crucial link between the fragments of modernity and consumption in recent French theory. The subterranean shocks of modernism, Benjamin hoped, would destroy 'commodity phantasmagoria'. But this could only be grasped by recognising the allure of the new order of consumption, not moralising about it. For Benjamin, the aesthetic desire for the beautiful commodity, which had first taken shape in the Parisian arcades, linked individuals together as members of a *mass* rather than a *class*. The same kind of exhortation to production that fits the industrial worker for maximum productivity begins to be developed for exhortations to consumption. It is partly in this seduction of the market that the tragedy of culture consists (Benjamin, 1973a: 166). Similarly, in *Distinction*, the department-store is 'the poor man's gallery' (1984: 565). If the working class still predominantly expresses the traditional tastes of necessity – glitz and cheapness – the new petty bourgeoisie develops its aesthetic sense through the pleasures of consumption.

Finally, it is perhaps Benjamin who originates recent conceptions of the canon. Recalling Bourdieu's *Les Règles de l'art*, it is no accident that Benjamin defined Baudelaire as a 'secret agent' against his own class. For both theorists (as well as Simmel), the fundamental concern is to show the paradoxical alienation produced by the canon: the 'cultural treasures that are piled up on humanity's back' (Benjamin, 1979: 361). Thus Benjamin: 'we are instructed in the reading of Baudelaire precisely through bourgeois society, and indeed, already long since *not by its most progressive elements*' (cited in Buck-Morss, 1989: 55; my italics). For him, as for Bourdieu later, the consecration of the 'secret agent' means that difficult feats of analytical subtlety are needed to recover the original meaning of the avant-garde. It was Benjamin who said that the 'bourgeois literary and historical apparatus' only 'preserved cultural objects from oblivion at the cost of their revolutionary use-value' (Buck-Morss,1989: 128, 55). The consequent reappraisal of the subjective experience of the metropolis is that Benjamin came to see revolution as only the emergency brake on the locomotive of history. Bourdieu seeks to strip history of any residual historicism, his only trace of Benjamin's prophetic Marxism being his cryptic allusions to 'rational' forms of structural transformation (1993c: 48).

Foucault: the Bourdieusian critique

There seems to be considerable disagreement over the degree to which Bourdieu has been influenced by poststructuralists such as Foucault. My view is that there are certainly elements of convergence, but that Bourdieu's conception of relative autonomy attributes more importance to material and political struggles than Foucault does. It is true that Bourdieu's criticism of authorship, his analysis of practice and his notion of position-takings within a set of possibilities of a given cultural field sometimes have an uncanny resemblance to the thought of Foucault. Both also have started from the assumption that the Enlightenment conception of ideological mystification obscures the taken-for-granted representations through which humans apprehend the world, which are overwhelmingly collective in character and the product of socialisation. Such elementary classifications structure the universe by means of categories of time, space, law, nature, etc.: when internalised, they produce what Foucault (1989) calls the 'never-said' and Bourdieu (1990b) calls 'doxa': unquestioned social conceptions which acquire the force of nature. Paradoxically, the rationalist quest to destroy ideological mystification develops in part through the continued use of this unquestioned stock of knowledge.

Thus, when Foucault introduces his conception of 'episteme' or the 'field of discourses', he says that his archaeological project is to 'depresentify things' so as

> to conjure up their rich, heavy, immediate plenitude, which we usually regard as the primitive law of a discourse that has become divorced from it through error, oblivion, illusion. . . . (1989: 48)

A discursive formation takes on a reified or material form, rather like Althusser's ideological practices. Clinical discourse, for example, is determined not merely by a set of interpretative rules or descriptions but also by 'institutional regulations, teaching models' (1989: 33).

Bourdieu shares many of these assumptions when he approaches the areas of both gender and aesthetic discourses. That is, he is principally interested in doxic attitudes towards high and low and the invention of the artist. The equivalents to Foucault's *The Archaeology of Knowledge* (1989) and the epistemic regimes of *The Order of Things* (1970) can be detected in Bourdieu's early and enduring concern with the 'historical genesis' of the modern cultural field. Whereas Bourdieu (1990a) perceives such taken-for-granted doxa leaving their effects on incorporated and reified history, Foucault had hauntingly described discursive formations as 'one great text'. A closer view suggests that there are other marked resemblances: between Foucault's attack on authorship (1981b) and Bourdieu's strictures against the charismatic artist or between Bourdieu's emphasis on artistic 'habitus' and Foucault's 'intersecting discourses' in art. In other words, both attack a mystical, or atomistic, view of individuality which depends on the philosophy of consciousness, much as Durkheim did in the early years of the twentieth century (Lukes, 1973: 488). Nor is this quite all. It is also strikingly evident that the structuralist concept of 'reverse discourse', produced under the pressure points of different relations to power, is also present in Bourdieu's thought. Bohemianism comes into being as the 'world upside-down' of political economy, much as, for Foucault, gay and queer politics valorise homosexuality. This is why Bourdieu resists the concept of popular art, which seems like another such inversion:

> [T]o speak of a popular aesthetic is to create a misleading reverse ethnocentrism, since such a popular aesthetic is remote from the cult of beauty for beauty's sake and the sort of experiences which condition this. (1971: 1373)

He clarifies this again recently when he argues that it is only 'do-gooders of the people's cause' who nominate popular art, since this process rests upon the profoundly mistaken assessment of popular works in the light of an alien discourse of distinction (1994a: 153–4).

These points of alignment should not veil the very real differences between the two. It is difficult to see how Foucault's power microcosms are mapped on to more causally effective social structures, in terms of the concentrated power of the State or dominant class. Moreover, his disarming treatment of each discursive formation 'as a sort of great uniform text' reveals the true limits of his aspirations to develop a *sociology* as opposed to an interpretative study. His 'materiality' is only spoken or written materiality.

Bourdieu's break with structuralism was premised on seeing individual agents as actively struggling with their conditions of life in capitalist agriculture or domestic production, and it is in the context of these direct experiences of nature, labour and property that Kabylians, and others, make and transmit meanings. Foucault's *Order*, by contrast, delineates incompatible epistemes but proposes no clear material realities within social structures to which these correspond.

Current debates on the sacralisation of art

By borrowing from the classical sociology of religion (priests, prophets, heretics, etc.), Bourdieu has reinvigorated analytically the study of the field of literature and art.[4] His genetic theory of the sacralisation of art within a pure aesthetic is both paralleled by other studies of the wider field (Bürger,

1984; DiMaggio, 1986; Levine, 1988) and enhances them. Sacralisation is particularly apparent in the period since the late nineteenth century, as writers on America have revealed, when the ring-fencing of cultural activities which were once communally shared went hand-in-hand with the consecration of artists. However, it will be argued that Bourdieu's concern to detail the dynamics of the high–low division has failed to consider adequately the nature of popular art and has obscured the 'prophetic' moments of the European avant-garde.

Bourdieu's historical account of the 'rules of art' neglects any distinctions between *modernism* and the *avant-garde*. Yet the avant-garde cannot be seen simply as those who, at any given date, staked all on their originality (Nora, 1967: 56). Rather, they were artists who wanted to challenge the fundamental structures of the art institution, that is, the entire bourgeois 'rationalisation' of art (Weber). For the avant-garde, ending the artificial gulf between art and life requires abandoning art's sensuous existence as playful pleasure or a holiday from the rules, since this can only be won at the cost of conformity to domination and quantitative rationality elsewhere (Bürger, 1984). An art that is re-incorporated into everyday life denies two kinds of apartness, that of the uniquely creative genius and that of the passive public. Thus Duchamp's readymade signed urinal did not merely reveal the fetish of the signature and the role of critics in conferring the label 'art' to the art-world. It was also emblematic of the avant-garde's demystification of genius as the purely 'individual creation of unique works'. Breton similarly intended that his poetry would be extended by the audience, who would take up the baton of artistic production communally. That the 'neutral' art institution, like a juggernaut, crushed their critiques whilst simultaneously co-opting them posthumously should not obscure the subjective reality of the avant-garde moment (see Bürger, 1984: 13).

Yet Bourdieu takes the disinterestedness of the avant-garde as evidence only of a strategy of distinction. He reads their dedication to destroying the separation between art and 'life' as an empty gesture, or, rather, an occupation of the high moral ground which has become part and parcel of the artistic habitus. Instead, the modern artist's concerns are fundamentally centred on his/her *reputation*. Duchamp is, for him, an exemplary case: supremely at home in the artistic world as the offspring of a line of painters, every move he made was that of a 'fish *in* water'. Thus for Bourdieu, the stakes of the game make the search for artistic recognition paramount over all other ends, not least the political.

But, against this, the avant-garde also represents a type of sectarian movement. It looks chiliastically to the end of the bourgeois world, even if the weapons it brings to bear on this are often those only of artistic technique.[5] In this context, it is notable that the history of Surrealism has become rewritten to obscure the fusion of independent revolutionary thought with the Freudian science of the mind in its artefacts and happenings. Of course, like sectarian movements' accommodation to the temporal world, the failure of the avant-gardes has retrospectively displaced their art, returning it once again to the museums of the legitimate and autonomous tradition. By this token, too, some celebrated modernist movements, such as Italian Futurism, bear only a superficial resemblance to the avant-garde proper. For while Futurism's criticisms of 'museum-art' bear a striking resemblance to many other avant-garde manifestos, the movement was also characterised by divergent elements, not least its militarism, belief in the submission of women, active cultivation of reactionary political regimes and its strangely uncritical 'modernolatry' (Castelnuovo and Ginzburg, 1981: 72), which left unquestioned the context of artistic activities. Yet, despite these difficulties, it is still necessary to *classify the types of modernism* in terms of these artists' subjective 'missions' or world visions. We cannot just rely on the dominant (legitimate) reception of their texts or the movements' unintended social consequences.[6]

By focusing closely only on the birth of modernism after 1848, Bourdieu fails to assess fully the nature of twentieth-century avant-gardism. Due to his concern to 'bend the stick the other way', his provocative accounts of Dadaism and Surrealism stress only the professional and economic interests of artists within the autonomous art-world. In this respect, he effectively dismisses the *ideal interests* of artists and their subjective reasons or commitment for doing as they do. In particular, his vague innuendoes about artists' 'interests' confusingly conflate their economic interest in having enough materially to be able to work with a quite different interest in economic *accumulation*.

Bourdieu needs to go beyond the first, heroic modernism to explain the nature of later avant-gardes more fully. In the case of Scottish Art Nouveau, for example, an avant-gardist moment occurred between 1890 and 1901, as the group moved from the enclave of Symbolism and Decadence associated with Aestheticism to act as a progressive spearhead aiming to dissolve the boundary between art and life (Eadie, 1990). For this brief period, a group of Glasgow artists around the architect Charles Rennie Mackintosh rejected the view that art should serve merely as a romantic 'other' to the instrumental logic of capitalism and envisaged its rational development beyond a narrow formalist concern for beauty. The key components of the visual ideology of Scottish Art Nouveau stressed the need to go beyond not just the art–science distinction but the entire art–life distinction as well. The question of mechanised design illustrates this:

> [M]achine-made goods did not have to be plain or ugly: . . . machine techniques did not violate integrity of design. Under Mackintosh, the Glasgow Art Nouveau movement signalled the attempt to rationalise art and to integrate it with objective society at the same time as it emphasised individuality, creativity, spontaneity, and experimentation. . . . (Eadie, 1990: 25)

Bourdieu neglects analysis of the conditions for movements *of this type* to emerge (although, paradoxically, the patronage of a specific fraction of the nouveau riche *bourgeoisie* is crucial in this instance). Of course, explanation is also necessary of the *transitory* moment of Mackintosh's flowering as an architect and of the extraordinary burst of group activity around him. But, symptomatically, Bourdieu fails to identify the sources for the *continuous* re-emergence within capitalism of such group disinterestedness. Instead, he focuses on the invidious quest for recognition and even for (long-term) economic rewards. But – to take the sect analogy further – it is only by deploying in the cultural field the type of analysis that Troeltsch (1931) and Niebuhr (1957: 20–1) applied to radical movements for religious transformations of the world that we can end the dualism of fatalistic materialism (Bourdieu) and idealising avant-garde culture (Bürger). At the very least, it is necessary to classify the features which made some movements more easily recuperable than others.

Finally, in Bourdieu's argument, the concern for popular art – or 'cultural communism' – is yet another intellectual 'illusion' contributing to this phenomenon (1993c: 11). Symptomatically, if, for some writers, Brecht is an exemplary materialist, for Bourdieu he is not materialist enough. For Brecht fails to see that his programme for a popular art might simply figure, objectively, as a guarantee of his own symbolic capital. Far from becoming part of popular culture, Brecht's 'political theatre' is merely part of the same 'socialist opiate' that intellectuals enjoy (1984: 452).

Bourdieu is in danger at this juncture of committing 'the intentionalist fallacy', a reductive analysis of texts in terms of their author's motives (in the case of Brechtian plays, to be understood cynically in terms of a self-serving delusion). This is not to deny that the texts themselves merit reading in terms of the social and literary conditions of their birth. But Bourdieu's analysis reveals more about Brecht's fashionable revival in the 1970s than about his reception in the inter-war years. In particular, Bourdieu disregards the historical significance of an earlier 'radical canon' or oppositional cultural tradition amongst working-class trade unionists. For this case, Willett's account of the extensive democratic movement for a 'new civilisation', which developed in Germany in the second half of the 1920s, shows that the figures of Brecht, Grosz, Heartfeld, Piscator and Masereel played a significant role (1979: 91–111).

If 'Brecht' figures in this way merely as an author to be unmasked, it is because Bourdieu is himself weak on certain aspects of the cultural field. This includes popular art (see chapters 6 and 7) but also the artistic developments that have taken place on the global periphery or within the European 'regions', which partially counter the ethnocentrism and class exclusiveness found in the literary and artistic establishment. Indeed, it seems to me that these voices from the periphery might confirm Bourdieu's ethnography of the metropolis precisely by their cultural distance from its institution of art. I do not want to idealise these developments. Recent work by Durand (1989) suggests that some of the same sociological dynamics that Bourdieu has isolated in Parisian modernism now have their counterparts in the Third World, as in the use of culture as capital and its transformation into economic capital in Brazil since the 1960s. However within some post-colonial or anti-colonial discourses, it *is* possible to discern writers who articulate the experience of the disenfranchised or subaltern masses and whose readership is derived from *all the literate*. Within this category an important group of writers could be described – somewhat brutally – as 'hybrid' in the sense that exposure to the imperatives of migration has profoundly affected their world-view (Bhabha, 1993). Such writers are often working in areas where the break of the literary field between restricted and expanded production is only embryonic, as in the cases of Arguedas (Peru), or Poniatowska (Mexico), or, in the 1960s, Neruda's poetry. Here, writing stands in a close relation to earlier anti-Spanish cultures of resistance, encompassing traces of community popular arts, not unlike the older epic forms. These contrapuntal narratives (Said, 1993: 258–65) have some unexpected parallels with the early eighteenth-century English novel; they possess popular energies which have wrested development of the form from the monopolising guardians of high culture (see also Bhabha, 1993: chaps 9 and 11; Spivak, 1988: chaps 12 and 14).

The dynamic of consecration outside France

Earlier critics, from Coleridge to the Leavises, wrote of the consecration or sacralisation of art and literature. But Bourdieu's systematic and defamiliarising application of religious language *is* distinctive, from his view of the museum as a collection of ceremonial objects to his account of the legitimate art-institution. In his view, this has always incorporated anti-academic critiques, much as the Catholic Church once responded to popular movements by taking over elements of their culture. What he has not done, however, is to enquire fully into the historical origins and coordinates of similar processes of sacralisation outside France. In this area, recent work done in the United States on the split of American culture into high and popular arts is very valuable (Becker, 1982; DiMaggio, 1986; Levine, 1988) although it lacks the more systematic framework of class reproduction and cultural legitimation provided by Bourdieu.

Levine's *Highbrow/Lowbrow* (1988) provides sustained evidence for the thesis that in America the division between high and low is as recent as the second half of the nineteenth century and that it has to be related to the dynamic of capitalism. His archival case-studies on the reception of Shakespeare and opera show the democratic nature of audiences in the eighteenth and the first part of the nineteenth centuries. Thus, the theatres in the first half of the nineteenth century were like early twentieth-century cinemas, drawing a representative range of occupations, including prostitutes and the *habitués* of gambling saloons, miners and farmers (1988: 21). Going to a Shakespeare play was not an obligation undertaken for the sake of status or respectability. Rather, Shakespearian drama was presented to audiences which were often boisterous and spontaneous in their responses to both actors and the acts represented (1988: 23). In keeping with Bourdieu's view of popular culture, participation by the audience meant that the texts were not sacrosanct, but Shakespeare was not understood by the lower classes simply as oratory and narrative action, but in terms of dramatic or poetic artistry. The historical records suggest that the moral conflicts, ambitions and political clashes were as clear to the lower-class sections as to the élite. Sophisticated and frequent burlesques of Shakespeare and the allusions to his plays in political speeches presupposed a common understanding of Shakespearian drama: 'Shakespeare was part and parcel of nineteenth century discourse' (1988: 37).

The turning-point at which American popular culture began to take a separate path from that of the wealthy gentry can be located in the bitter Astor Place riots of 1849, which left 22 dead. Theatregoers and a crowd of 10,000 fought over divergent class styles in drama and especially over the merits of aristocratic or more robust, democratic interpretations in the acting of *Macbeth* (1988: 63–5).

The loss of popular involvement in Shakespeare is linked by Levine to the decline of melodrama and oratory, the presence of larger numbers of non-English-speaking migrants and the organisation of theatres by entrepreneurs who assumed a cultural hierarchy (1988: 46-7, 79). The consequences of this decline were momentous:

> By the turn of the century, Shakespeare had been converted from a popular playwright whose dramas were the property of those who flocked to see them, into a sacred author who had to be protected from ignorant audiences . . . . (1988: 72)

Developments in art and opera (Levine) and the organisation of the symphony orchestra (DiMaggio, 1986) reveal the same pattern, with the collapse in spontaneous popular support and the consequent need to bolster audiences. The late nineteenth century reveals a whole series of musical organisations – from Souza's brass band to the Boston Symphony Orchestra – couching the language of their invitations to audiences with appeals to a strict sense of order rather than incitements to enjoyment. This disciplining or 'taming' of the audience took on similar forms in the development of the élite provision of culture elsewhere: plumbers' overalls, for example, became out-of-place in the first New York museum. It was accompanied by the loss of autonomous control by musicians with the growth of new professional managements under overall direction from civic bourgeois élites. The outcome was a bifurcation of high and low culture – a classification of taste which was to become a taken-for-granted assumption in the construction and segregation of public territories:

> When we look at Boston before 1850 we see a culture defined by the pulpit, the lectern and a collection of artistic efforts, amateurish by modern standards, in which effort was rarely made to distinguish between art and entertainment, or between commerce and culture . . . . By 1910, high and popular culture were encountered far less frequently in the same settings. (DiMaggio, 1986: 195)

Such segregation and the accompanying rise of cultural entrepreneurship had as its bottom line the creation of class closure. 'Art' was ring-fenced from the market, while the appointment of professionals (musicians, art historians, etc.) provided initial support for the creation of difficult new forms, accompanied by lengthy time intervals in acceptance. The consequence was a classification in which the 'dignified parts' of the culture were separated from the rest. It thus became impossible to envisage in Boston by the turn of the century the chorus of 10,000 and the orchestra of 1,000 that had celebrated the end of the Civil War. Art instead became the terrain of incompatible currents of a class closure and democratising missions to the people (see also, on Britain, Baldick, 1983).

The studies of Levine and DiMaggio are essential evidence of how a secular high culture replaced the Protestant Ethic as the basis for cultural legitimation. But their evidence needs further genetic explanation. The high–low division cannot be isolated from the decline of craft and the rationalisation of work (Taylorism, Fordism, etc.). These produced a belief in the stupidity or bestialisation of the manual worker (Palmer, 1975; Sohn-Rethel, 1978), akin to what Bourdieu has called the 'racism' of class (1994a: 178). Moreover, the psychic investment in the high–low division can be understood when culture became a means of class closure and mobility through the 1920s application of IQ tests to migrants and the use of meritocratic recruitment in the labour market (Lipuma, 1993: 27-8). In brief, these powerful studies of the disinheritance of a people from their culture need to be placed within a more sophisticated assessment of educational practice and reproduction, such as those provided by Bourdieu and his colleagues.

Perhaps perversely, it is within the debate on the sacralisation of culture that I would place Howard Becker's work. Bourdieu (1988c) welcomed the collapse of the 'academic temple' of structural-functionalism and thus also its demolition agents, of whom could be mentioned Goffman (on whom he wrote an obituary), Gouldner (who also pioneered a reflexive social theory) and Becker. Becker's book *Art-Worlds* (1982) has been a source rich in phenomenological insight to which Bourdieu (1993a) has paid tribute.

Its radical departure lay in Becker's refusal to classify culture into 'high' and 'low'. Instead, Becker considered cultural production in light of professional and craft work. This gives his style and subject its debunking quality, departing from the 'high seriousness' of bourgeois attitudes to art (Bloch, 1986). Two moves create this effect. First, it challenges the undersocialised individuality of the great author by stressing perspectives from the sociology of occupations: notions of support-personnel,[7] teamwork and division of labour, co-operative activities, transmitted skill rules, etc. Becker suggests that the same practices are at issue in the popular as the high arts: even Emily Dickinson needed a supportive audience, to which she appealed by using the conventions of psalm-rhythms. This then causes him to regard art-worlds as composed of several different, non-competing universes, principally between art and craft, art and folk art, art and naive production. The key questions for Becker concern how subjects perceive their worlds, using scripts but also transforming their scripts. Having had his baptism of fire in deviancy theory, Becker thus aims to restore meaning to the subjects of art-worlds. Since Bourdieu's break with structuralism derived from its passive view of agents, this represents a point of confluence between the two.

Crucially, then, Becker pioneered a theory of the art institution which was later adopted in the field of aesthetics. The fertile new insights of phenomenology concerned the ways in which objects came to be *labelled* art, that is, *exhibited in the 'sacred' space of the gallery*. For Becker, this is a process predicated on conflict: even within the field of 'integrated professionals', specific art-works require a rationale from reviewers and critics before they can be accepted and are even then placed adversarially against other producers. Consequently, the toughest questions for Becker are to explain why certain movements fail to gain artistic legitimacy (why jazz but not stereography in the visual arts?)[8] or, in terms of artistic producers, why some maverick use of conventions may ultimately be recognised as pioneering while others are viewed as too transgressive and fail to acquire backers.

Bourdieu (1992, 1993a) is deeply indebted to the new ways of theorising subjective experience that the interactionist perspective provided, especially in its explorations into the magic of labelling or 'nominating' objects as art. Becker's *weaknesses* lay in mapping the micro art-worlds onto the field of power: for example, in explaining his own finding that conflicts may arise between museum publics and curators on the composition of contemporary collections. Bourdieu's much clearer conception of how the restricted art-world relates to the possession of economic and cultural capital gives him an extraordinary advantage, since he is able to show how reified social structures profoundly influence agents historically through their habitus (1980c: 13).[9] In Bourdieusian work on museums, clashes of artistic perception and evaluation are explored in relation to class habitus and the amounts of educational, social and economic capital that each agent brings to bear on his or her experience. Thus Bourdieu complains justifiably that Becker's musicians, film-directors and maverick sculptors act as if marooned in their desert island art-worlds, stripped of the structures influencing their interpretations (1992: 288). It is almost as though – save for the use of conventions – the artist is a *tabula rasa*.

Yet the balance is not all in his favour. Becker's tactics are calculated to distance readers from their complicity with the legitimate high–low division. His radicalised conception of professional skills and support networks is applied equally to (popular) film and poetry. In contrast, Bourdieu's refusal to theorise any existing popular art suggests that he is still partly enchanted by the aesthetic ideology he wishes to deconstruct.

Becker has countered the tendency to economic reductionism in the Marxist sociology of art, but regrettably replaces it with a one-sided stress on group lived experience which bypasses such objective relations. Yet there are, in turn, elements of Becker's phenomenological approach which have been grossly neglected by Bourdieu. Becker gathers rich examples of art being produced in the maelstrom of clubs and pubs and film studios of the modern city, in other words emerging from the commercial, large-scale field. Except for a fleeting consideration of recuperation, Bourdieu has no category for the 'canonisation of art from a popular base' (1975: 17; 1993a: 39). In contrast, Benjamin's insistence, in his work on Art Nouveau, that their posters were 'the commodity of a commodity' (Eadie, 1990: 34) as well as Medvedev and Bakhtin's literary theory (1978) suggest the importance of this pattern.

Taking the example of the visual arts alone, a historical sociology of modernity indicates that there are at least four crucial ways in which the restricted and expanded fields have become permeable. First, simple *crossovers* occur, as in the case of Picasso and Braque, who used painters' varnishes and popular newspapers for their collages and so 'made a thinkers' art out of workers' artifices' (Varnedoe and Gopnik, 1990: 36). A similar use was made of graffiti by Dubuffet and of comics by Miró. Comics, especially, powerfully affected the Surrealist mainstream (Varnedoe and Gopnik, 1990: 85, 173). Secondly, developments in the popular field are taken up from the sphere of lower-class culture and later '*trickle down*' to popular culture once more in a wheel movement, as in the instance when the Cubists' use of found materials, exploited by the Russian Futurists, subsequently spread to become the 'official public language of a nation' (Varnedoe and Gopnik, 1990: 52). Thirdly, there are forms which are developed by the *same* artists in *both popular arts and in the 'citadel of the avant-garde'*, as in the Kinder-Kids comic strips for the Hearst papers drawn by Feininger, using caricatural figures which were adapted to quite different political and formal effects in his contemporary Expressionist paintings. Picasso's comic strips for *L'Humanité* are another example (Varnedoe and Gopnik, 1990: 166–7, 181). Finally, *modernist styles can be extended in popular media*, as in the delicately linear Art Nouveau comic strips painted by Winsor McCay (Varnedoe and Gopnik, 1990: 162). Such instances counter Bourdieu's general assumption that modernism and popular genres exist in hermetically sealed fields. They reveal also the originality and intensity which have sometimes emerged in sites quite cut off from the recondite imagery of the academic and modernist traditions.

Within this chapter, I have hoped to elucidate Bourdieu's inheritance from those thinkers who have had most impact on him in terms of cultural theory. In developing his own arguments about the art institution, I have argued that Bourdieu's sociology is a powerful disenchantment of the magical mechanisms associated with legitimate culture. It is weaker at exploring the subjective experience of the construction of new art-forms and new social scripts. In the context of modernity, I have suggested that Bourdieu needs to distinguish further between avant-garde and other modernist movements.

Finally, I have suggested that Bourdieu has not entirely succeeded in extricating his own approach from the aesthetic formalism he attacks, especially in the reification of the distinction between the restricted and extended cultural fields. If Bourdieu is right that there is no popular *aesthetic*, the claim that there is no popular art is contestable (1984: 395), as I shall argue in chapter 6. Moreover, the crossovers between low culture and the avant-garde are much more numerous and complex than he has suggested. In this respect the phenomenological approach to the arts proposed by Becker has certain important advantages over Bourdieu's hermeneutic explorations of artists' strategies. The remaining chapters seek to deepen understanding of Bourdieu's principal theories of culture, while also providing test-cases in which their validity can be assessed.

Notes

1. The connection is directly apparent through Bourdieu's quotation from Benjamin, but also through the similarities in their substantive views of the historical genesis of modern art.

2. *Free Exchange*, however, does theorise such social structures and the role of the critical artist (Bourdieu and Haake, 1995: 108).

3. This position has been outdated by subsequent events which all lead one to suppose that photography has been partially consecrated since the 1960s when Bourdieu was writing.

4. Bourdieu's study may have its derivation from Trotsky as well as Weber. Trotsky imports from religion the model of writers as prophets ('Art, don't you see, means prophecy' (1960: 168)), influential critics as 'priests of the bourgeois literary tradition' (1960: 130) and of 'canonisation within school textbooks' (1960: 128). Cultural production, for Trotsky, was especially the contribution of an intelligentsia, crushed by Tsarism, who, needing support from the lower strata, 'tried to prove to the people that it was thinking only of them, lived only for them and that it loved them "terribly" ' (1960: 168). Foreshadowing Bourdieu's critique of popular art, Trotsky criticises the wishful populism of Proletkult, which sought the hothouse growth of working-class art rather than accepting that new developments in art can only emerge when the material conditions for them have come into being.

5. Often, but not always: the death of the poet, John Cornford and active service of Orwell in Spain are well known. Breton's censored speech on freedom in Haiti in 1945 triggered a revolution (Lewis, 1988: 163–4).

6. On this point, see Carey (1992), who explores the conception of the mass, suburbia and women in the writings of British avant-gardes. He notes especially the retention of élitist ideas in the novels of D.H. Lawrence and Wyndham Lewis, in comparison with a middlebrow writer such as Arnold Bennett.

7. Not only, for example, did Sonya Tolstoy write seven fair copies of *War and Peace*, but Tolstoy's reading of her own diaries about marriage came to fruition in the complex presentation of female protagonists in his novels (Smoluchowski, 1987: 68).

8. On this, he suggests that stereography never shifted to the 'autonomous sphere' because it 'failed to change its imagery and machinery rapidly enough to avoid the stigma, deadly in a style-conscious society, of being out of date' (1982: 349).

9. These derive especially, but not entirely, from the field of power: other, more delimited fields, such as those of religion, law, etc., also deposit their structuring structures on the habitus.

PART II

CRITICAL INVESTIGATIONS

5

BOURDIEU AND MODERN ART: THE CASE OF IMPRESSIONISM

There are several reasons why a study of Bourdieu's cultural theory should assess his work on Impressionism. First, it is clear that Bourdieu deploys this example to develop a sociological explanation of the *birth of the autonomous artist* analogous to the earlier birth of the capitalist entrepreneur. Bourdieu explains the free art of modernism by revealing structures and perceptions which derive from both the field of power and the field of culture. He explores especially the key moment in the nineteenth century when deskilling or the increasingly fragmented division of labour highlighted the 'hyper-skilling' of the artist. This was also the moment for the vindication of the rights of genius, to justify artists who had failed in market terms. The new conception of genius in France, from the 1850s, equated artistic commitment with *non*-economic goals (1971: 1350). Yet in Bourdieu's tragic view, the main struggle against the bourgeois order in the name of that art was destined to be conducted by the members of the dominant class themselves and to be carried out in terms of a struggle for significant form (1971).

Formal achievement as the only guarantee of genuine art is signified, first, in the authentic artist's experience of suffering, which itself offers proof of talent, and, secondly, in resignation in the face of the work's impenetrability by the uneducated 'popular gaze'. In order to show the interest of Impressionism, we need to pause for a moment on the 'invention of the life of the artist'. Initially (in 1975a), Bourdieu explains the fundamental elements of the artistic habitus as consisting in a state of indeterminacy which is linked to the aesthetic disposition. But this indeterminacy within the image of the artist presupposes a repudiation of the collective consciousness (including its bourgeois and popular dimensions), such that the artist is 'without hearth or home, without law or faith' (1975a: 70). This is the intellectual precondition for the ethos of the artist – he is empowered by this rootlessness and secularism, which, in exposing him to solitude, also make him the 'sovereign Berkeleian observer' (1975a: 70).

There are further preconditions, for the artist's career is structurally linked to a material experience which Bourdieu believes has its origin in the inheritance patterns and personalities of the dominant class. Put more strongly, the dedication to an artistic life is a response to the social experience of insecurity among bourgeois and aristocratic young men, either second sons or, in the initial instance, deprived of their anticipated inheritance. The commitment to art can then be read as an expression of sour grapes in which a negative state, the necessity of poverty, is transformed positively into a virtue, temporary material dispossession into a special kind of seeing. This *ressentiment*, which consists in 'making a virtue of a necessity', figures as a frequent Bourdieusian motif and is in his view deeply symptomatic of the cunning of class reason.[1]

The main psychological parameters of the bohemian artist are now established. They lie in a double negation, the rejection of the work of capital valorisation in the bourgeois vocation and the denial of the latter's claims to moral legitimacy:

> [A]esthetic disinterestedness has its origins in practical roots, the indeterminacy of artistic life – in indeterminacy submitted to as a destiny, the chosen curse from failure. (1975a: 69)

The consequence is the emergence of a new art-world, outside the field of power, for which the artist positively elects.

These general ideas are first fleshed out on the visual arts in Bourdieu's essay on Manet and his Impressionist followers. This article was followed by *Les Règles de l'art* (1992), in which Manet appears as part of the modernist 'Holy Trinity', along with Flaubert and Baudelaire. Yet, unlike the other two, Manet is viewed only in terms of his formal innovations.[2] This chapter will therefore approach Bourdieu's study of Manet and Impressionism to pinpoint certain symptomatic weaknesses in his account of movements of artistic modernity. I want to show that Bourdieu has provided a method for the sociological study of art but that his writing on Manet and early Impressionism has misinterpreted its character. Far from being the first major milestone on the route to the depoliticised painterly qualities of abstract art, Impressionism – at least until the mid-1870s – depicted the new spaces and types of urban modernity. It demythologised the spectacle of leisure and liberated consumption from its traditional centres. In so doing, it showed the tensions as well as the freedoms of the new social strata of the Second Empire. Its visual codes detected the first traces of the split, later to be so pronounced within the modern personality, between the *consuming self* and the *producing self*.

Bourdieu's treatment of the new autonomy of art is an explicit attempt to stir the reader from a clichéd understanding of history. It presents us with bohemia as a world in reverse, but this time contrasted with the Academy as the basis for organising all national artistic activities. In this way, Bourdieu wishes to rescue Manet from the condescension of a posterity that no longer finds scandalous the scandal he created amongst his first critics. When, as in *Distinction*, studies of contemporary reception show that the bourgeoisie now feels a close affinity for the art of the Impressionists (1984: 292), Bourdieu wants to show that at its genesis things were different: the ideological structures of Impressionism and the bourgeoisie appeared neither elective nor in affinity.

To revitalise the historical grasp of the field, Bourdieu's strategy is to sidetrack the now over-familiar Marxist concepts of artistic proletarianisation, alienation and development through changes in artistic forces of production. Instead, Bourdieu approaches the symbolic revolution of Manet as an artistic *Reformation*, that is to say, the shift from one 'Church' with a priesthood that monopolises orthodoxy to a state of competing cults. This is a fundamental change in the organisation of artistic legitimacy or what Bourdieu calls the 'production of belief' – the equivalent in ideological terms to the departure of a nation's banking system from the gold standard. The Durkheimian language of nomos (a regulated existence) and anomie (lack of regulation) is introduced to help construct the stakes involved in artistic change. On this account, the achievement of the pinnacle of a 'timeless and universal' appeal is a competitive trophy shared by both academicians and modernists. The difference is that in the restructured field the artist ceases to be 'the high-level civil servant of Art' (1993a: 243).

Both the Academy and the avant-garde are adapted to a succession of artistic styles, but only within modern art is the artist totally independent in relation to the State. Like the monk bound by the Rule of St Benedict or the priest controlled through the papal hierarchy, the artist within the academic system is forced to submit himself (women were excluded) to the authority of the State, which is exercised through Salon juries, provision of prizes and a system of commissions. As a civic delegate, he must depend on its 'hieratic' (sacred) power to consecrate his work. This alone gives the painter his authorisation and justifies his high fees. In bohemia, in contrast, the production of belief via the acquisition of a reputation is a process stripped of the security offered by official competitive success.

A word is necessary about the Academy to supplement Bourdieu's remarks. This institution had been imported into France in 1648 using the Italian Academy as its model, permitting a key distinction to be made between the practitioners of liberal arts and mere guild workers or craftspeople (White and White, 1965: chap. 1). Reorganised in 1663, it achieved a systematic and bureaucratised form of control over the arts, an exchange in which professionalism was the artist's stake and conformity to State validation its price. Anthony Blunt labelled the French Academy as 'the closest and most complete State control ever exercised before the present century' (1970: 322): his complicity with Stalinism made him perhaps the only Western art historian truly qualified to judge such command systems of the artistic economy. It became compulsory not only to submit to the French State's hierarchy of genres but to attend mandatory art theory classes, thus rupturing the bonds that had earlier drawn art to craft through a shared emphasis on practice. France thus acquired 'the most fully developed form of academic training known in Europe' (Blunt, 1970: 324). In the initial years of the new Academy 'all were orthodox and there were no heretics' (1970: 325).

Yet by 1863 the Academic system was in tatters. Bourdieu describes this as the bankruptcy of the fiduciary capital of the State artistic culture, that is, of the system through which

> the State, rather like a central bank, creates the creators guaranteeing the credit or fiduciary currency represented by the title of duly-accredited painter. (1993a: 251)

From the 1880s the Academy ceased to control the École des Beaux Arts. The tones in which Bourdieu describes this are in terms of the educational crisis faced by another type of *homo academicus* – that of students and university staff in 1968. What emerged from these challenges and changes was a collective conversion to a new structure of exhibition and distribution based on the critic–dealer system (Bourdieu, 1993a; White and White, 1965). From that time on there is the emergence of a 'new eye', the spectator of modernity. 'Manet dooms the academic eye' (Bourdieu, 1993a: 248), and in doing so creates a 'new world'.

Manet is the revolutionary within this academic world (1994a: 148–9). He massively subverts the institution of art by refusing submission to its sacred authority. To this hieratic art, born from the moral career of discipline and order of the priestly hierarchy, Manet's art possesses the upstart originality of one who appears to lack rigour. In a brilliant perspectival gaze, Bourdieu thus renews the potential for a historical understanding of Manet using an interpretative study of contemporary reviews. He foregrounds, first, the view of the threatened academicians and subsequently that of the Manet circle.

The *priestly type* of academic eye demands total fidelity to the set of prescribed noble subjects and to the normative set of techniques for bringing off artistic form. Although not enforcing the degree of stereotyping imposed on Indian temple sculptors, the mid-nineteenth-century Academy demanded absolute conformity to a variety of rules. These required that formal considerations of colour and line should in all cases be subordinated to the moral presentation of the subject. Within this, a legitimate portrayal of the social hierarchy was prescribed, with the hero elevated above the mundane figures of banker, peasant, etc. Specific techniques were also debarred, such as brushwork revealing individual strokes. Taken together, State bureaucratisation of art had created an apparatus calculated to enhance narrative readability for the allegorical subject of the painting (Bourdieu, 1993a: 245). There had already been a dilution of control over the arts in the nineteenth century, leading to a struggle between the 'inner gaze' (as in eighteenth-century art, especially that of Watteau) and the externality of the 'academic gaze' (as demonstrated in the Revolution's Classical style, David, etc., and the history painting of the Second Empire). These style wars were linked to a struggle between classes over cultural reception: while the restored aristocracy favoured the refined elegance of Watteau, the *nouveau riche* bourgeoisie of Louis-Philippe's and Louis Napoleon's regimes chose the discreetly eroticised classicism of Orientalism or the post-classical pastiche of the *juste milieu*, dominated by an eclecticism of form and a similar hotchpotch of ideas.

Bourdieu's study of contemporary reviews shows that Manet's Salon submissions were ridiculed by his academic detractors as incompetent, but also iconoclastic, paintings. Jean Clay has amplified this by revealing that much of the moral outrage at *The Execution of Maximilian* (1867) was provoked by reading the painting as a type of formal play. A series of dramatic contrasts in the interlarded strata of whites, for example, served to diminish the simplicity of the subject Manet had drawn from newspaper reports and thus disrupted the expected response. Manet's originality lies in 'suspending images in a new way' or 'recycling' old images:

> Manet treats the artistic heritage the way Benjamin's *flâneur* handles merchandise. The Louvre is a *passage*, a market stand, where the painter strikes his bargain. (Clay, 1985: 3)

In abandoning classicism in his paintings of racing, Clay argues that Manet conveys the horses' speed by new devices, such as 'unfinished' lines of hatching. However, unlike Bourdieu, Clay also argues that this artistic anomie – which always falls short of the degree zero of painterly dismemberment – was matched by Manet's interest in *social meanings* and, in particular, in the qualities of modernity.

For Bourdieu, the essence of newness in art was the attack on the hegemony of literary or narrative values so as to remove the appearance of *natural necessity* in the choice of means of representation (1993a: 247). Thus the painterly constructivism evident in Manet's sketchy brushstrokes or the tonal weight of his patches of colour is the consequence of the anti-illusionistic demystification of the artistic prophet. As in a Brechtian gaze at classicist certainties, the 'new eye' promotes the conflict over style to a political act: one which in itself destroys the taken-for-granted classifications rooted in the rules of form. For regulation is always linked to the *sense of order* imposed by the academic artist as a delegate of the State. He is right, surely, that such art was a crucial part of the cantilevered support structures for a much wider set of representations which had once extended from bottom to pinnacle so as to legitimate the whole regime of Louis-Philippe.

Bourdieu uses his hermeneutic skills to take, successively, the position of the invaders and the defenders of the established cultural field of nineteenth-century French art. The full heterodoxy of Manet and the Impressionists can only be grasped by reading these aesthetic duels as struggles over the purpose of painting. For these defenders (and some others) the new art represents a failure to signify. It possesses a cold objectivism which is in itself an attack on the intricate order of the classical cosmology and especially on the salience of the traditional moral order within the ideal mythical or historical composition. Then, by a dazzling shift of position, Bourdieu discloses the opposite perspective: the new art's defence of a symbolic revolution in which artistic conventions become a matter of free inquiry. There is a deeper structural opposition here that Bourdieu has noted in passing elsewhere: the opposition between the logic of an artistic practice closely tied up with power and that of the experimental artist (1980b: 29).[3] Thus in order to understand the significance of events which led from the 1863 Salon des Refusés to the end of the École des Beaux Arts' control over teaching in the 1880s, we have to see it as the decline of a monopolistic group with its own professional interests. But not just that: the end of the academic monopoly denied the dominant class and the State a law-like, official consensus over the representations of the real, just as the end of the sumptuary laws of feudalism meant the end of a fixed, traditional style of life. This opened up art as a new sphere of collective insecurity as painters struggled to earn recognition as artists. Insecurity is heightened by dependence on the operation of the market but it is not explicable by the market alone:

> From now on no one can claim to be an absolute holder of the *nomos* even if everyone else has claims to the title. The constitution is, in the true sense of the word, an institutionalisation of anomie. This is a truly far-reaching revolution, at least in the realm of the new art in the making, it abolishes all references to an ultimate authority capable of acting as a court of appeal: the monotheism of the central nomothete gives way to a plurality of competing cults with multiple uncertain goals. (Bourdieu, 1993a: 252–3)

Here is Bourdieu's key presentation of the cultural field of Impressionism. The significance of Manet in particular and the Impressionists as a group is that they inaugurated the modern freedom of the arts, located within 'the restricted field of cultural production'. Especially important for Bourdieu is that this new painting was founded not just on the rejection of bourgeois art but on the rejection of a social art founded on Realism.

This is an arresting analysis of the old nomos and of its transformation. But it has a teleological view of Manet: it reads his paintings as the first stop on the autonomous path to Abstract Expressionism. In this respect, Bourdieu interprets Manet and the Impressionists as dominated by a 'truth to media' which itself derived from a symbolic revolution (Bourdieu, 1992: 160; 1994a: 148–9). On this view, Manet is emblematic of a new specialisation in art. Like the scientist in physics, he has broken with the normative ways of seeing. His triumphs are necessarily esoteric. For whereas in artistic revolutions, it is those who have most 'artistic capital' (that is, are most artistically well endowed with skills and knowledge) who engineer change, in political revolutions, it is those with least social and economic capital who back transformations. However, I want to argue, first, that Manet is *not* just revolutionary by innovating new means of production. He is also revolutionary in the choice of subject and its meaning. Secondly, while Bourdieu is correct in seeing the emergent organisations of art as a new anomie (that is, a new narrowing of the sphere of control by the collective consciousness), he has failed to explore the ways in which this artistic de-regulation both reflected and represented the economic anomie of the new consumer industries (Durkheim, 1989: 254–8).

Bourdieu is right that Manet and Impressionism have to be understood in terms of positions taken up within the autonomous field, and in part as a movement of renewal springing from a critical response to the older, established generation of Realists. He just doesn't carry this far enough.

In other words, if Realism had a rural subject, Impressionism had an urban focus. If Realism depicted work, Impressionism depicted leisure. But leisure now – unlike seventeenth-century Dutch painting – is marked unmistakably by high capitalism and its transformation of everyday life. Consequently Impressionism enters into the historical moment of organised commercial culture, in order to produce from it the general, or, to use Baudelaire's more familiar words, 'La modernité, c'est le transitoire, le fugitif, le contingent, la moitié de l'art dont l'autre moitié est l'éternel et l'immuable' (cited in Frisby, 1985: 14). It captures that moment in which classes begin to mix in a new urban setting and in which sociability bursts out of the bounds of family and Church.

Bourdieu's reading of Manet and the genesis of the modern avant-garde is the dominant modernist one. It stresses the formal dimension of Manet's work, explaining his artistic rupture precisely by his mastery of the whole field (that is, the reworking of the old). Thus, just as Heisenberg and Bohr spearheaded new paradigms, Manet is viewed as a professional, whose painterly concerns sprung from the new paradigm emerging with the crisis of Academic authority. The crisis itself is created by an unprecedented change: a small number of authorised painters in Paris became engulfed by a flood of painters trying to live off art. (One historical study has revealed that 3,000 painters lived in Paris by 1863 with 200,000 reputable canvases presented to the Salon jury each year (White and White, 1965: 83)). In tones tellingly close to Durkheim's (materialist) explanation of the new division of labour of capitalism as the consequence of increased population, Bourdieu situates the birth of modernism in the new division of artistic labour. From now on there will be a restricted field with appeal to the educated viewer, sectioned off from an expanded field, containing both bourgeois best-selling art (Horace Vernet etc.) and social art (for example, that of Courbet or Ribot). The aesthetic disposition of the educated public creates the 'fresh eye' that supports a new world. For this reason Bourdieu suggests that contemporary critics utterly misconceived the projects of both Manet and Whistler when they insisted on reading *narratives* into paintings such as Manet's *The Absinthe Drinker* (1859) or Whistler's *Girl in White* (1862). Manet created, says Bourdieu, 'the unbearable lack of meaning' (1993a: 249) in which there is a rupture with the readability of myth or the old history-centred painting. They refused to accept that by breaking with Renaissance perspective and objectivism, these artists were instituting a new mode of representation, which was based on optical effects and dictated by the subjective ordering of the perception of the outside world. For the academic painters' depiction of the ideal, of a set of public values, had now disappeared. Where previously, as in the medieval world, art had been a kind of comic strip, available for everyone and reinforcing political–moral values, now its underlying unity beneath its diversity of subject was its form. The purest expression of this is the ideology of Aestheticism, in which beauty for beauty's sake becomes the complement of work for work's sake (1971: 1373).

The artistic revolutionaries' position-taking is also supported by the changed material structures of the field. The new paradigm is grounded on the market-price and on the critic–dealer system. On this structural terrain artists designated themselves as beings despised and rejected of men, sensing, like Flaubert, that 'the blood of Christ quickens in us' (cited in Grana, 1964: 125). In brief, this conception of artistic ideology is Bourdieu's equivalent to Foucault's category of 'author'.

Bourdieu's formalist interpretation of Manet does have some resonance. It is immediately clear by seeing, amongst Impressionists, in a Realist painting such as Sège's *In the Chartres Countryside* (1884) how much the abandonment of perspective, naturalistic colour-values and the spontaneity of sketchy brushstrokes have subsequently become routine. Despite this, my view is that Bourdieu's own historical genesis of Manet and anomie is in itself insufficiently historical. In drawing on Durkheim's analysis of anomie in *The Division of Labour*, Bourdieu discovers that the redivision of the artistic field creates a differentiation so wide between commercial artists and the avant-garde that these seem almost like different species, afterwards highlighted by the late nineteenth-century segmentation between 'highbrow' and 'lowbrow' taste.

But this subsequent problematic should not be used to impose a classification of the events of Manet's life from the 1850s until the 1880s. Bourdieu's interpretative mapping of the field of visual arts at this point is itself sometimes weakened by the same binary opposition between form and function that he wants to explore as an ideological classification. Rather, Manet in particular and the Impressionists in general failed to gain a public understanding of their work because they wanted to do things which were often the work of popular genres. They were exploring the nature of the new social relations. To put it at its most bland, painting, for them, needed a fresh iconography. This is concerned with the nature of modern existence, and especially with the experience of the 'new social strata' whose entry into the spectacular arena of modern consumption was being initiated.

Bohemia and the artistic field

Manet and, later, the Impressionists were inhabitants of the new world of bohemia. Bohemian cultural production became fused with the various secular cultures of this-worldly rejection founded under the impact of Romanticism, such as the 1830s Suicide Club (Grana, 1964: 79–80).

The bohemian public sphere of the metropolis had to be constantly renewed. The intense experience of powerlessness of the young corresponded to their repudiation of the market. As they became older, a combination of the adoption of a professional identity and the impact of greater economic needs as they acquired wives, mistresses and children provoked an accommodation to the market. Bourdieu notes that this period of maturity was typically marked by a more ascetic work-discipline in a pale reflection of the vocational exigencies and specialisation demanded outside bohemia by the market. Corroboration for this can also be found in the regularity and frequency of the output of these painters (White and White, 1965: chap. 4).

This process was completed in the Impressionist world by the 1880s. By this time the painters were getting older but, more importantly, they had been repudiated by the unconsecrated avant-garde of the 1880s, the Symbolists. Labelling the Impressionists collectively as *ouvriers* (workers), the latter founded their precarious artistic existence on the inner experience of the isolated self (Gamboni, 1989: 52). Indeed, the group ethos of the Impressionists may have been particularly strong because the art-world was in a process of restructuring *after* the collapse of the academic system but *before* the extension of the dealer system made paintings into ordinary commodities (signalled by Durand-Ruel's first mass purchase of low-priced Manets in 1870) (Hamilton, 1954: 155). Thus the anonymous co-operative world of Impressionism's 'Société des Indépendents' represented this transitional 'time of the societies' within the public sphere, before the economic impact of the dealer-collectors broke up this guild-like solidarity (Gamboni, 1989: 51). In this connection, it is interesting that the Impressionists took on the collective title '*les intransigeants*' in the 1870s, following the attack by Spanish anarchists on the Spanish Government. Mallarmé's comment on the movement's visual simplification aligns it surprisingly with the nature of popular artistic motifs: Impressionism, for him, possessed the 'eyes of the "energetic modern worker" ' (Eisenman, 1992: 193).

Bourdieu asks us to deconstruct the artistic text by supplementing the classic Marxist and psychoanalytic approaches with studies in the art-institution itself. Schematically, then, analysis of the Impressionists should include the following dimensions:

First, the artists' *position in the cultural field* (high or low, that is, restricted or expanded (commercial) production). These artists' actions have the effect of separating the generations within the avant-garde. In terms of Manet and Impressionism, such positions vary, reflecting Manet's earlier date of birth and his consequent stronger orientation to the Salon, to which he always sent his paintings. The Impressionists, however, sought independent means of exhibiting their work in the Second Empire, both in the State Salon des Refusés and beyond the auspices of the State. Here it is worth recalling the strength of hostility to these painters in the nineteenth century (Hamilton,1954: 1), which must surely be linked to the subterranean culture through which they sought to sustain their deviance.

Secondly, the *position in terms of class or class fraction*. In this respect, the Impressionists were a mixed group: Manet, who was the son of a magistrate and whose mother's father had been a powerful diplomat, possessed the habitus closest of all the artists to the haute bourgeoisie; Degas was the son of the owner of a finance house whose business went bankrupt in this period – which did not prevent him acquiring a substantial inheritance; Monet was the son of a successful shop-keeper; and Renoir was the child of a tailor and a laundress, the only working-class member of the group. Bazille and Sisley are described as middle class, as – later – was Cézanne, whose father was a small tradesman and later a banker; Pissarro, like Monet, had lower-middle-class origins (White and White, 1965: 112).[4]

Thirdly, the *trajectory of the family within the class* from which they come. For example, Mallarmé's turn to Symbolism is understood as a concern for pure art that chimes in with the bitter experience of the declining aristocracy and their powerlessness to control economic events (1993a: 57).

Finally, the *position of the artist within the family*: the psychoanalytic dimension, as presented in detail in Sartre's *The Family Idiot* (1981).

This method allows Bourdieu to explore the artist's social relations, especially his/her cultural authority and its unanticipated material benefits. It contrasts with the residual idealism of the current author debate. But it has omissions that I shall now clarify. I want to argue *against* this interpretation of Manet's art as a formalist modernism. The recent turnabout in Manet studies has cast doubt on this, as have new studies of Impressionism. However, before I introduce this point, I want to refer briefly to Realism: indeed Bourdieu himself recommends that we consider the ideas shared in common and not just the points of differentiation between two styles.

Realism

Bourdieu writes little about Realism, merely, as we have seen, distinguishing the first, Realist moment of plebeian intellectuals from the second bohemia, which he sees as the cradle of modernism. However, he notes the persistence of a Realist group of 'proletaroid intellectuals' within the second bohemia (Bourdieu, 1992: 92) led by its theoretician, Champfleury, and including Courbet, Bonvin and Gautier among its members (1992: 110). The Realist school persisted into the 1870s and 1880s, at which point they took the title 'Naturalist'.[5] There were major differences within the Realist school at the level of cultural politics, for example between the uncompromisingly oppositional art of Courbet and the State-commissionied works of the many Realists who were close to propaganda in their depictions – Bonhommé's portrayals of the extraordinary *The Factories at Le Creusot* (1855) or the *Workshop with Mechanical Sieves at the Factory of La Vieille Montagne* (1859) with their contented workers (Weisberg, 1980: 74, 76). But in general, Realists produced paintings that had an uneasy tension between their depiction of the whole nation as undergoing major change and their sympathetic depiction of the victims of that change: see, for example, the work of Meissonier, Antoine Leleux and Teissert, all of whom showed in the Realist Salon of 1850–1. In fact, both Realism and Manet's circle constituted a break with the Academy, but they possessed different responses to capitalist modernity.

The Realists broke with the supremacy of myth and history painting in the academic tradition so as to paint lower-class subjects, especially peasants and the rural bourgeoisie . They relied upon methods that used sketches or painting in *plein air*, cut off from the usual conventions of the studio and often drawing on popular images (Schapiro, 1978: 49–53; Weisberg, 1980: 6–7). Courbet especially represented the nature of rural life and work to very diverse groups, from the metropolitan crowds of all classes for the annual Salons to rural fair-goers (Clark, 1982a: 85; Frascina et al., 1993: 78–9). His subjects were derived particularly from the social conflicts that came to their peak in the 1848 February Revolution and which permeated his later work. Such tensions produced a crisis in the country as small landowners became dispossessed by usurious capitalists. In his painting, Courbet, already alive to traditional poverty and to the demanding rhythms of agricultural labour, began to reveal the strange paradox of charity being given by beggars to starving peasants, and, highlighting the reappearance of Jews as convenient scapegoats in the country areas, portrayed himself (as an artist) in the person of the wandering Jew. Bourdieu's historical periodisation of bohemia obscures the fact that Courbet's painting continued throughout that point of 'rupture' of the nomos which is dated with Manet.

Millet, despite his competence with classical conventions, also developed a new iconography of modern life. Taking his family from the Paris cholera scare in the 1830s, he settled in Barbizon, a village in the first open arable land beyond the forest of Fontainebleau. Here his painting took on a progressively starker portrayal of images of country labourers, displacing the organicist illusions of the pastoral code with its basically harmonious character of rural life. There is a world of difference between the landscapes of Theodore Rousseau, with their images of a nurturing and healing nature, and the Realism of Millet. Predictably, the reviews of his most significant paintings of rural work (*The Sower* (1850; 1851), *Women Gathering Faggots* (1850–1), *Harvesters Resting* (1853), *The Diggers* (1855), *Man with a Hoe* (1859–62)) make it clear that the dominant class did not find Millet's representations of rural life to its taste. In the 1850s, Millet was considered increasingly troublesome, even, like Courbet, a socialist (Clark, 1982b: 81).

Daumier should also be mentioned at this point, in terms of his development of an art of satire and political caricature. Especially in his drawings, he delineated the marginal groups of wanderers and the hunted performers known as *saltimbanques*, who transgressed the rigid controls of public entertainment of 1853 by singing at rural fairs and in the poorest inner-city districts of Paris.

Thus it was not the art commissioned by the Bureau des Beaux Arts that was important in the period after the 1848 Revolution. Rather, it was the art of more overtly *reactionary* painters like Millet, whose experience led them to create public painting out of their private world. As Clark points out:

> Millet's subject-matter became dangerous, the one bone left in the gullet of the Empire, the one class not to get its pickings from the economic boom. (Clark, 1982b: 81)

In being positioned close to those criminalised by the new laws against wood-gathering, who were passing from peasantry to an impoverished semi-proletarianised existence, Millet was able to draw on a series of motifs from Michaelangelo and Renaissance art in a new way. Clark notes the distinctiveness of this ability:

> How strange an ability this is! Or perhaps it is stranger that no other artist had it, and that art in the nineteenth century showed everything of modern life except those who lived it. . . . Daumier and Millet . . . are in improbable contact with the commonplace. (1982b: 122)

A recent Foucauldian study has questioned the distinctive anti-bourgeois character of Millet's painting and thus implicitly challenged the interpretation above (Green, 1990). Nicholas Green has argued that Barbizon artists aided the development of 'nature tourism', which had its origins in the area in the 1840s. No doubt, but there was a telling time-gap between the key works of Millet from 1846 to the mid-1850s and the development of an artists' colony in the 1860s, with its later influx of urban bourgeois into the area. Indeed, Green himself shows that the population remained the same between 1846 and 1856 (1990: 296, 305). There is a more crucial point at stake. As Marx suggested, there has always been a Romantic anti-urban response to bourgeois society. However, the simplistic attempt on the part of Foucauldians to produce a single metropolitan vision – a uni-dimensional ruralism – begs too many pressing historical questions concerning the nature of the underlying alignments involved. For the moment of the 1840s, it is clear that the discontents of the Louis-Philippe monarchy and its financial aristocracy produced a composite form of peasant and bourgeois protest which surfaced in the February Revolution but spectacularly decomposed after. Schapiro (1978) has shown that the movement of Realism associated with Courbet, Champfleury, Buchon and Dupont had a quite different set of spectators (including peasants) and a quite different set of sources from later movements of art. An interest in arts outside the high academic tradition led these professional painters to immerse themselves with naive cultures, derived both from folk-songs and from the long tradition of anti-clerical, anti-feudal popular protest found in cheap engravings. Within their art, images of work played a crucial radical political role. As Schapiro pointed out:

> In the forties and fifties, the mere representation of labour on the scale of the *Stone-breakers* and *Knife-grinders* was politically suggestive. (1978: 51)

To summarise: I am arguing that within Realism there had already emerged a vital break with academic conventions that is uncharted by Bourdieu: the flouting of the dominance of history painting so as to engage with the painting of modern life. This art was still constrained by the rules, juries and exhibitions of the Salon. Manet's painting was a vital step in the development that led to the ending of the academic monopoly. But it was not because he instituted a revolution at the level of form alone. Rather it was because he also continued the Realists' fascination with contemporary experience, although now, as in the case of Baudelaire, who mediated between the social and modernist bohemias, there was to be a turn to the 'artificiality' of the city.

Manet and, later, the Impressionists are the first subculture to be concerned with the expansion of the commodity into the market for personal needs, which Marx calls 'Department II'. In particular, Impressionism was interested in depicting the new leisure–pleasure economy, the 'colonisation of everyday life' with sites of 'spectacular consumption' (Clark, 1985: 9). The 1850s was not the first time at which consumption had become fashionable for the bourgeoisie. The Orléanist monarchy had also seen the emergence of promenades along the boulevardes, the arcades and chic shopping. However, this first metropolitan gaze had gone hand-in-hand with an artistic preference for landscape; consumption and environmental anxieties about disease preoccupied an urban stratum that assuaged its anxieties with the suburb, the country house and the 'spectacle of nature' (Green, 1990).

Manet and the Impressionists possessed a metropolitan gaze as well, but one that was turned inward on the city itself, and on the distinctive institutions of that re-made popular culture of the Second Empire. Baudelaire stressed that a poet should always 'avoid those places where the rich and joyous congregate and should feel drawn to everything "feeble, destitute, orphaned and abandoned" ' (cited in Grana, 1964: 136). The Impressionists also were pulled to these *paradis artificiels* of the metropolis with their multiple and mysterious cultures re-ordered by capitalism and money. Drawing on such new subjects and breaking with the old iconographies of revolution was the only feasible strategy when the threat of censorship and jail awaited those who crossed permissible limits in the Second Empire. Nor was the threat an empty one: Manet's friend Richepin was jailed for satirical literature which Manet himself had illustrated (Kasl, 1985: 50).

The new interest in sites of spectacular consumption is epitomised in the ballets, the music at the Tuileries, the bar at the Folies Bergères, the newly opened *cafés-concerts*, the racecourses and the expanding seaside resorts. Rosalind Williams has described these untraditional social relations as creating a democratisation of luxury. Many more people, she writes, were to

> experiment with discretionary consumption, to become familiar with its intellectual and sensual pleasures and with its consequences of envy, vanity and ennui . . . the consumer revolution becomes far more than a rise in economic statistics or available goods. It is more like the Copernican revolution, the overthrow of one world picture by another; the replacement of the cramped, heliocentric world of consumption by a vast, centreless universe. (Williams, 1982: 57)

Bourdieu raids Durkheim and criminologists' theories of anomie to describe the new painting of Manet, but he has perhaps overlooked in this context Durkheim's use of anomie as a deregulation of traditional life-styles with new consumption patterns. He himself has ignored how close to Marx is Durkheim's interest in the anomie created by new markets. For it is also anomie that is a consequence of the commodity battering down all resistance to it (Marx, n.d.: 53). In other words, it is not enough to describe Louis Napoleon's regime as profits without precedents (as Bourdieu does), for it was also associated with two interlinked phenomena: the revolution in consumption and the emergence of the department store. Oddly, although Durkheim had characterised modernity as an epoch in which desire in general is loosened from its restraints, this theme is also strangely absent in Bourdieu. And yet artists' acquisition of freedom had surely also exposed them to the effects of both that anomie and the 'cold wind of egoism', of which Durkheim wrote that it 'freezes their hearts and weakens their spirits' (quoted in Lukes, 1973: 195). To this, Durkheim had linked the high rate of suicide among 'men of letters', second only to those for entrepreneurs. Marx had explained how artists were unusual in having to create a need for artistic meaning, that is, to create the demand for the goods they produce (1973: 92). Durkheim is surely right about the consequences:

> Now he may assume to have the whole world as his customer, how could passions accept their former confinement? . . . Reality seems valueless by comparison with the dreams of fevered imaginations; reality is therefore abandoned, but so too is possibility abandoned when it in turn becomes reality. . . . (1989: 255–6; 256–7)

Nor can it be presumed that the bohemian rejection of commercialism entirely protected artists themselves from the effects of the expanded consumption of art, with the world market centred on Paris. Bourdieu fails to consider precisely how the anomie of art was also tied to this new leisure–pleasure economy:

> A thirst arises for novelties, unfamiliar pleasures, nameless sensations. (Durkheim, 1989: 256)

It is this thirst that the painters were also to investigate.

The rise of the department store, new life-styles and Impressionism

The department stores that arose in Paris, New York and London, like the 1867 and later Expositions, were the show-cases of international trade and colonialism (see Miller, 1981: chap. 2; Williams, 1982: 62). They collected together the ingredients of new life-styles in an exotic–chaotic mode (Williams, 1982: 69) which catered to 'the theatre of dreams' (Ferguson, 1990: 68). Ancestors of today's glitterati, the customers discovered that the new mass consumption:

> displayed a novel and crucial juxtaposition of imagination and merchandise, of dreams and commerce, of collective consciousness and economic fact. In mass

Switzerland', lawns, an artificial lake fed by new artesian wells and 400,000 new trees (Herbert, 1988: 145).

It is this *socially constructed nature reserve* in the city that is the scene of many Impressionist paintings, from Manet's *Concert in the Tuileries* (1862), to Berthe Morisot's *Summer's Day* (1879), Monet's *Monceau Park* (1878) and various representations of chic picnics from Manet's bizarre *Déjeuner sur l'herbe* (1863) to Monet's identically titled portrayal of a similar elegant and organised occasion (1865–6). Renoir's *Skaters in the Bois de Boulogne* (1868) and *The Swing* (1877) are portrayals of unself-consciously alluring young women in this urban pastoral. Through these park portrayals, Renoir provided utopian images which he codified into a wider critique of Academic painting and rationalised industry in his ideas for a 'Society of Irregulars'. Many of his paintings are representations of sociability and a joyful sensuality which fit with the wish-fulfilments of popular culture: see, for example, his *Dance at the Moulin de la Galette* (1876).

The *cafés-concerts*

Just as a vibrant music-hall culture emerged in London after the ebbing of Chartist hopes in the 1840s, so commercial bars and cafés sprang up in Paris after 1848, in which working-class singers, especially women, performed to crowds of men or couples, some desultory in their interest in the singer, some in rapt attention. Their number grew from perhaps two dozen (1860) to nearly 200 in the 1880s (Herbert, 1988: 82). Clark has shown that while this popular performance was not part of the old artisan tavern society that had earlier championed socialism, it was still coarse and vigorous, with lyrics that fell foul of the political proprieties or the bourgeois sexual delicacies of the Second Empire (Clark, 1985: 306–10). Over 2,200 cafés and *cafés-concerts* were closed by the anti-Commune junta, which attributed considerable power to the oppositional democratic ideas of the singers (Herbert, 1988: 87).

The *cafés-concerts* were mixed in their customers, in ways that were still strangely new. They contained not just plebeian prostitutes, the '*prolétaire d'amour*', like the absinthe drinker painted by Degas (*Absinthe* (1876)), but also 'counter-jumpers' (the respectable shop assistants) and clerks, both groups being members of 'the new social strata' or petty bourgeoisie. A sizeable minority of observant members of the bourgeoisie also broke with the conventions of good society to go, aloof from each other in their collective pursuit of urban authenticity (Herbert, 1988: 91). The paintings of the cafés emphasised the directness, sensuality and break with decorum that prevailed, stressing the lack of distance between the half-dressed performers and the audience through the use of non-Western framing devices and collapsed space (See Manet's *Café-Concert* (1878), Degas's *The Glove* (1878) and *At the Ambassadors'* (1877).

consumption the needs of the imagination play as large a role as the needs of the body. Both are exploited by commerce, which appeals to consumers by inviting them into a fantasy world of pleasure, comfort and amusement. (Williams, 1982: 12)

By the 1880s, Paris was to become the pioneer city of the new visual idiom of public imagination, the advertising poster (Varnedoe and Gopnik, 1990). This extraordinary change in the circulation of commodities created by the increased dependence on the universal market, went hand-in-hand with the needs of factory-owners for non-traditional retailing outlets such as Samaritaine (1869), or Bon Marché (by 1877 the world's biggest trading establishment), which could respond with the *coaxing of demand* by the proprietor.

The new form of shop was marked by the standardisation of prices, and the loss of the personal dimension expressed in haggling. It created shopping as a form of leisured search for the ultimate dream-commodity, since it ended the traditional obligation to buy on entry. The great shops created their own worlds. Idealised graphic portrayals of the act of consumption of their clothes, food and other goods diffused images of bourgeois family life on an unprecedented scale. Yet, paradoxically: 'Consumption itself became a substitute for being bourgeois' (Miller, 1981: 184–5). Moreover, the rhythm of buying was now increasingly orchestrated by the shops' own timescale of seasons and cultural events. A whole cycle of communal meals, Christmas parties and musical soirées was initiated in these semi-public semi-private spaces. The department stores were even intricately linked to new leisure activities, such as cycling, via the sale of equipment, as well as originating their own new pathology, kleptomania (Miller, 1981: 201).

I want to argue, following Clark, that Impressionism was the imaginative representation of the new 'urban idylls' that had thus emerged for the first time in Paris, the city of modernity. In this respect, the key aspect of Impressionism is its unmasking of the character of urban experience. Unlike Realism, it did not explore the world of work (a powerful exception is Monet's *The Coal-dockers* (1875). Thus Monet painted the industrial area of suburban Argenteuil but only under snow, disguised, while his portrayals of the recently constructed Gare St Lazare show *trains but no drivers*. However, as we shall see, it was a form of painting that was concerned with the oblique impact of industry on the new *rural* sites of hectic weekend amusement. And in the paintings of Manet and Degas, especially, some of the conflicts and tensions of modernity are laid bare.

Impressionism's depiction of the bourgeoisie at leisure also encapsulates some of the working class's aspirations towards free time. The new kinds of mass market goods (clothes, holidays, etc.) were luxuries and adornments that in themselves expressed aesthetic needs and which should be seen as shared by both bourgeoisie and working class. Working-class culture was founded on a double negation, provoking the desire to escape work as the *degradation* of labour but also to assert, against dominant culture, the *dignity* of labour. As Green puts it, paraphrasing Jacques Rancière's study of workers' dreams, *La Nuit des prolétaires*:

> Dressing, speaking, thinking not like waged labour was paradoxically integral to 'being' working class. (Green, 1990: 7)

Impressionism, then, is a focal point for exploring the rise of the 'society of the spectacle', that is, a qualitative leap forward in consumption in which images or visual depictions have a crucial role to play. The Situationists in the 1960s explored the ways in which a popular culture intertwined with consumption had been fostered by the newer media:

> The spectacle is the moment when the commodity has achieved the total occupation of social life . . . the world one sees is its world. . . . At this point in the 'second industrial revolution', alienated consumption becomes for the masses a supplementary duty to alienated production. (Debord, 1977: para. 42)

Impressionism is the first register of the *allurements* of the new mass production and the money-economy.

I want to emphasise that in the unprecedented social relations of modernity, Impressionism was not simply relaying bourgeois discourses or ideologies about leisure. But nor was it wholly negative towards urban modernity, as so many modernist artists were to become by the 1890s.[6] I suggest rather that Impressionism was an ironical and critical discourse, not least through its juxtaposition of the old with new, often ugly modern objects so as to undermine any simple romantic myths, for example those of the countryside. More importantly, I want to accept that in Manet especially there is a kind of demystifying modernism. This has the effect of accentuating social contradictions. In other words, the role of *flâneur* that Manet adopts makes him into an active figure, unmasking the 'mysteries of the city'. In contrast, Bourdieu's view of Manet's practice as an artist restricts his transformative impact to that of innovation in form.

I am anxious about Bourdieu's polarisation of popular culture and art. The art of the Academy had obtained a popular audience as well as an élite one, even if the academic hierarchy of artistic genres represented the last flourish of a feudal world-view (White and White, 1965: 79–80). However ambivalent his ultimate stance towards the fetishism of (high) culture, I think Bourdieu reads back into Impressionism the *total detachment* from the culture industry which was the product of a later period.[7] This dates particularly from the 1880s following the sacralisation of high culture (Levine, 1988: 132). Bourdieu reifies and imposes an over-rigid classification on a fluid field. Instead, I prefer the idea of seeing Impressionism rather as a 'subculture of resistance', which shared the modernists' initial interest in a 'brokerage between high and low', especially those forms of popular entertainment and leisure which were the only areas left unconstrained in a repressed social order (Crow,1985: 258).[8] It is the fascination of the Impressionists with the new popular cultures emerging in the 1850s which alone explains why Manet made drawings from the photographs of nudes, at that time seen as pornographic (Clay, 1985: 30). It is this absorption which

can explain why he and his friends frequented and painted the *cafés-concerts* where working-class women sung contemporary songs, often with an insouciance and subversive humour that caused the censor to swoop. Manet's impulse to mix class signifiers by imitating the speech and walk of Parisian urchins shows this receptivity quite starkly, too, however unsustained and self-conscious (Crow, 1985: 248). The same desire both to explore scientifically and to celebrate vitality can explain Degas's attraction to the ballet, which – although once a court art – was the social equivalent in 1860s Paris to disco-dancing now.

In what ways did the Impressionists reveal the meaning of modernity? I shall chart the subjects they chose and then discuss the distinctive character of their representations. Partly because of constraints of space, I shall focus on questions of content, but I do not want to deny Bourdieu's argument that there were massive changes in technique, including the abandonment of the Renaissance use of perspective. The artistic rupture created by Manet certainly existed, but it occurred because he developed a way of showing together the objective outer world of the metropolis and the inner world through which it was experienced (Hanson, 1977: 134; Shiff, 1992: 187). In this new fusion, Manet and the Impressionists transcended the classifications of the period: they combined elements of Realism – up to then restricted to the representation of lower-class life – and symbolism – seen at that date as the images of dreams (Hanson, 1977: 134).

Street fashion

The Impressionists did not paint Parisian department stores. Yet it is the shop-owners' positive view of consumption as a kind of permanent fair that also emerges in their view of the fashionable middle class strolling through the urban parks, the cafés and out in the new boulevards: see, for example, Caillebotte's *Paris Street, Rainy Weather* (1877) and Renoir's *The Umbrellas* (1881–6). Manet's *The World Fair* (1867) is indicative of his response to urban crowds, those spaces where confrontation with the stranger may provoke a transient sense of unity followed by loss, to which Baudelaire drew the painter of modern life.

The parks

Louis Napoleon ordered new green places, partly for their own sake, partly for their political expediency as a safety-valve. 'Nature' marched hand-in-hand with modern industry. The new parks were literally man-made; the Buttes Chaumont were converted from the old place of execution into a terrain of controlled urban walks and family entertainment; a fake mountainous landscape was arranged with a concrete-based lake, waterfalls and a grotto with fake stalactites in 1867. The much-extended Bois de Boulogne had an ersatz 'American savannah' and 'mountains and valleys from

Race-tracks

Longchamps, in the Bois de Boulogne, was built in the last third of the century and racing became a key pleasure site of modernity, not just among the returned aristocrats but among the new entrepreneurs and industrialists. It was an especially Anglicised sport (Le Jockey Club etc.) which was the counterpart in leisure of the English investment of capital into the rail network and much new industry. This also provoked the attention of Manet and especially Degas, whose experimental painting of racehorses and their jockeys developed a formal innovativeness that was particularly attuned to the presentation of speed and of the competition: '[Degas's] jockeys', writes Herbert,

> are lurid entertainers who jostle one another in dense packs . . . they prepare for the competition which Degas's society said was the essence of progress. His genius is to have created pictures that render the strains that underlay this 'progress'. Instead of a whole body, or a whole scene, with its traditional unities, we are parts. We have to understand the relationship between them and this reconstruction becomes our mode of comprehension. . . . Degas's dynamism with its choppy rhythms and abrupt shifts looks forward to the twentieth century's thirst for motion. (1988: 169–70)

Boating

The countryside was a place of retreat, even if only for a day. As I have already hinted, the landscape genre itself is a product of bourgeois culture, and indeed our ideas about the countryside are shaped by urban realities: 'it is the material and cultural fabric of the metropolis which is seen to set the terms for the social production of the countryside' (Green, 1990: 11).

The Impressionists helped to crystallise and diffuse this new structure of feeling. They painted in the new down-river beauty spots that spawned artists' colonies as the vanguard of weekend trippers, villages such as Chatou, Croissy, Bougival (La Grenouillère), or the small industrial town also on the Seine, Argenteuil, now accessible by rail for the petty bourgeoisie. In terms of technique, these depictions of reflections and the way light releases the prismatic potential of water were as extraordinary as Turner's earlier Impressionist treatment of seas in England (see, for example, both Monet's and Renoir's paintings of *Sailboats at Argenteuil* (1874)). But perhaps just as epoch-making was the break with the élitism of the romantic gaze and with the disdainful appeal to high culture implicit in the patrician derision of popular enjoyments. Instead Manet, Pissarro and Seurat register, but only obliquely, the imposition of new labour-processes and an enhanced time discipline by their inclusion of images of factory chimneys. In Manet especially, the tensions of the brief weekend are evident even in the throes of enjoyment: see, for example, his touchingly over-dressed and anxious young Parisienne, with her partner on an outing in a hired pleasure craft (*Argenteuil, Boating* (1874)). Seurat's juxtaposition of an industrial landscape with stiff youths, half-dressed in work-clothes, provides the clearest contrast between industrial life and the brief moments of leisure (*A Bathing Place at Asnières* (1883–4)).

The holiday

The modern institution of the seaside holiday with its ersatz architecture appears in many of the Impressionists' paintings. The town is imported, so to speak, along with the Parisian holiday-makers in their decorous fashions. Degas clarifies the whole social base of bourgeois fashion and, incidentally, the academic convention of the nude by revealing in one Gauguin-like study the unaffected sensuality of country girls swimming naked (*Peasant Girls Bathing in the Sea at Dusk* (1875–6)). We have to understand, then, an opposition between their naked spontaneity and the stiff formality of the urban bourgeois visitors in his other paintings of the beach, in which a utopian impulse makes the girls the site of hopes to shed the constraints of bourgeois lives. Manet in Normandy also simultaneously explored new subjects with an economical and direct style. Shifting from his stereotyped 'romantic gaze' – fishing boats, moonlit skies, beaches with exotic local fishermen – he experimented with sketchily painted family groups on the beach in town-clothes, shown pursuing their rituals of pleasure: the whole visitors' substructure discreetly hidden (*The Beach at Boulogne* (1869)).

It is perhaps Monet who most clearly opened up an ironic perspective on the new social relations of the seaside. His numerous holiday paintings coolly record the stiff separation of these bourgeois family members, the emblems of nationality in the flags everywhere, penetrating and intermingling with the sought-for 'nature', the casino eclipsing the church in his view of the promenade at Sainte-Adresse, as though to highlight the arbitrary fortunes created by the new speculative commercial ventures. Within such an ironic mode, from the 1860s to the mid-1870s, Impressionism created the seaside for its subject:

> [The] world of vacation hedonism. . . . Morisot shared with Manet, Monet and Renoir the invention of a colouristic language that rose from the study of leisure and outdoors light, those paired circumstances that proved so vital to early modern art. (Herbert, 1988: 284)

It was only at the end of his life that Monet came to paint the depopulated landscapes of the Normandy coast, along with his turn to water-lilies, and to stress in these beach scenes the ravaging destruction of an angry sea. It is as though there was now a gulf between nature and the human world that was lacking before.

Ballet

The retrieval of ballet from its degraded status after the 1789 Revolution was a late nineteenth-century invention. Ballet was thus a more unstable art-form than it is now. This was because of the association between the disclosed legs (that is, the uninhibited sexuality) and the vitality of the dancers which linked them to the lower classes. When Morisot, Renoir, Cassatt and Degas painted the ballet, they were displaying a world of working-class performers. Degas dedicated half of his whole output to studies of dancers. He was particularly concerned to unmask the real social relations of the girl workers, who often came from the poorest part of Paris, and whose labour might be the support of a whole family. He shows them not just in the public view, but also in rehearsal, looking exhausted as they sit waiting around. They often became prey to the predatory gaze of the bourgeois men, such as the Jockey Club members, who were prepared to transgress respectability by going into the backstage world. The girls are often with their mothers, whose role appears to be to strike a good bargain for the girl in terms of marriage or lovers. It was only subsequently, in the late 1870s, that lower-middle-class girls entered ballet, and much later for girls with social or other capital.

This may explain the nature of Degas's portrayals of the dancers. Certainly he broke in a quite revolutionary way with the whole set of academic conventions for depicting women, and, especially, with the classical poses obligatory for the nude. A sculpted study of a woman shows her standing awkwardly examining her foot; a pastel represents a girl whose upper torso is bent double between her legs. Especially in his maquettes and his larger sculpture, Degas portrays his dancers taken unawares, poses in which the women's faces are often almost abstract, as though their main significance is their manual labour-power. Marx had described the mechanisation of assembly-line workers as producing a form of automatisation; similarly, ballet for Degas leads to the robotisation of the dancers, their bodies disciplined into the repetitive patterns (Herbert, 1988: 128; Kracauer, 1975). Thus, on the one hand, in Degas's cynical materialism, race-horses and ballet-dancers are merely interchangeable instances of trained flesh. On the other hand, his admiration for their skill and grace is evident in his sculpture of a '*petit rat*', *The Little Fourteen-year-old Dancer*. His sonnet to her acknowledges that she has produced a strange beauty from the mixture of ethnic groups and the poverty of the harshest urban areas. In this case, Degas's artistic honesty pushes him in directions at odds with the prevalent racism of class and ethnocentrism, attitudes with which he himself dabbled, as is evident in his reading of Lombroso's criminology. Testimony of the latter are his pastels of delinquent boys at the law-courts, with the same Mongolian faces as the little dancer.

Bridges

Finally, I want to stress how much the emblems of modernity in Impressionism which would have repelled their first public have lost their shock value for us: the massive geometrical ironwork of Caillebotte's *Le Pont de L'Europe* (1876), for example, bravely takes up half the picture's space.

Monet uses new bridges to destroy the romantic view of the pure country and the traditional character of rural pastimes. *The Railroad Bridge, Argenteuil* (1873–4) indicates this, being used to frame small leisure sailing boats. Rather than an unfortunate intrusion into the picturesque, the uncompromising concrete bridge and revolutionary communications implicit in the train it bears are revealed as the condition for the bourgeois leisure of yachting.

Manet as the catalyst for Impressionism

As Bourdieu realises, the career of Manet poses the question of formalism especially sharply. Yet the recent turnaround in Manet studies has balanced his revolutions in *form* with reappraisals of the *meanings* of his works.

Despite the brilliance of his typification of bohemia, Bourdieu understates its precise significance for Manet as the location of stigmatised groups. Manet painted various pictures of bohemians in his early work: *Les 'Saltimbanques'* (drawing 1861), *The Water-Drinkers* (drawing, 1862), *The Old Musician* (1862) and *Gypsy with a Cigarette* (1862). Further work has now shown that the artist did not just associate himself with bohemia as a refusal of the ascetic work ethic of the bourgeoisie. In fact Manet was valorising the image of gypsies in a quite oppositional manner, for gypsies had historically been associated with the stigma of outcasts, seen as Jews or their associates, child and animal thieves, by the rural peasantry, and as pariahs by authorities (Brown, 1978: 31). The gypsies who had encamped triumphantly on the Champs-Élysées during the 1848 Revolution had been recently evicted:

> During the events of 1848, the *saltimbanque* fair that sprang up on the Champs-Élysées . . . was regarded as a metaphoric democratic city where everyone was accepted . . . . (Brown, 1978: 53)

Manet championed the gypsies as their quarters in Little Poland in Paris, shared by artists, were being transformed by reconstruction under Louis Napoleon. A strict penal code now condemned gypsies to be transported if they broke the laws limiting their immigration and restricting them to town boundaries (Brown, 1978: 39, 41). Manet in *The Old Musician* (1862) identified the artist – or himself – with a gypsy fiddler. In doing so, he aligned the life of the artist with an illegal and degraded outsider, more like the migrant workers of post-war Europe. Such transgressive realism also linked the artist to the *saltimbanque*'s tradition of socio-political satire and to the sensuality and female independence of gypsy women (Brown, 1978: 444):

> *The Old Musician*'s depiction of the gypsy/artist is probably a tangible indication of the degree to which Manet himself has internalised feelings of marginality. . . . it is this 'cool' quality that helps to define Manet's modernism. (Brown, 1978: 525, 527)

Bourdieu (1993a) refers to Couture's rejection of *The Absinthe Drinker* (1859), quoting the hostility of Manet's teacher to its muddy colours. Yet this is another Manet self-portrait, serving not only as a pastiche of Velasquez but also as a sharp counter-image to current caricatures of Parisian 'types'. By showing the working class's need to get drunk, Manet's painting was 'providing language in which to speak about the marginal parts of Second Empire society' (Lajer-Burcharth, 1985: 25).

It is possible just to read this as an early rebellion to be quickly supplanted by the pleasures of the elegant *flâneur* later on. Yet this underplays the continuity in Manet's liberal Republicanism, a radical position for the period. Manet's *The Execution of Maximilian* (of 1867), of which the lithograph was censored, shows the Mexican Juárist army killing the French puppet-ruler Maximilian in uniforms made to resemble those of the French. It is therefore best interpreted as a critique of French colonial adventuring (Hanson, 1977: 115–16). What is more, Manet's portrayals of *Civil War* and *The Barricade after the Commune* (both 1871) contained coded attacks on the Mac-Mahon Presidency for the deaths of Communards (Baas, 1985). It is commonly agreed that Manet's lithographer hid the stone on which they were engraved to avoid repression.

It is plausible that the same bitter critique led Manet to the earliest version of *The Rue Mosnier Decked Out in Flags* (1877), with its crippled veteran – possibly a Communard – contrasted savagely with the flags flying for the State-imposed holiday (Kasl, 1985: 56–7). Finally, the 1881 portrayal of the exiled journalist, Oliver Paine, a liberal critic of the Third Republic, reveals the continuities in Manet's public concerns at the end of his life (Hanson, 1977). All these works invite a re-evaluation of the painter. The portrait of the artist as a formalist dandy needs to be replaced by a view of Manet not as animated exclusively by political concerns, but as an artist whose concern with contradiction and social tensions discloses consistently radical interests (Hanson, 1977: 126).

Perhaps the best summary of Manet's response to the painting of modern life is by Clark. He argues that the Impressionist circle (including Manet) saw modern society as no longer about social classification (or estates), but about freedom and individuals. But, in the 1860s and 1870s, their use of irony permitted disclosure of the ambiguity of modernity, and especially of the continued impact of the material structures of class within the spectacle of consumption.

The most clear-cut case for this view is the painting *Olympia* (1863). Contemporary critics were outraged by Manet's remake of the *Venus of Urbino* by Titian. In a content analysis of the reviews, Clark revealed that only six of these saw the picture as about class and prostitution. Instead, the reviews deplored the omen of the morgue she was thought to represent, the dirty, coal colour of her outline, her india-rubber skin, her ugliness.

Clark suggests that what the critics repudiated was a figure who refused to stay in a known and familiar place, as did the conventional courtesan or the mistress; instead, Olympia is emblematic of the vast army of around 120,000 prostitutes in Paris, many of whom were unregistered (1984: 105). He reads money as liberating the working-class girl from submission to her clients.

Manet flouts with a new realism all the academic rules that made the nude sexless and innocent. The painting disturbs because class is imprinted on her body:

> Desire was the property now – the deliberate production – of the female subject herself. It was there in her gaze, her consciousness of being looked at for sexual reasons and paid accordingly. . . . (Clark, 1984: 131)

It might be added to this compelling characterisation that the painting gains poignancy when it is seen as a representation of a working-class woman whose composure and luxury is heightened by the spontaneous compliance of her black servant. Senegal had become a French colony in 1858; Morocco a French protectorate in 1860. In choosing in 1862 to lay bare so clearly the new patterns of ethnic division within the lower class, Manet was perhaps prefiguring the subtle social consequences of imperial power with its capacity to incorporate all strata around a fictive national community.

As Bourdieu comments, Manet was the transitional figure in the restructuring of the cultural field which took place from the 1850s (1993a). By the 1880s, Manet and the Impressionists had become more *adapted* to the art market. If, through the nineteenth century, Paris had become a European city of culture, by the end of the century, it was the centre of a global market for art (White and White, 1965: 8, chap. 3). The critic–dealer system that had emerged in the interstices of the Academy in response to the new bourgeois public had – by the late 1880s – undermined it and created a new unregulated network of consumption. But it also created a structure in which high material rewards went to those who made their names in 'this commerce which was not commerce' (Bourdieu, 1993a: 39). At the end of their lives, the Impressionists earned the salaries of other middle-class professionals. Durand-Ruel, for example, sold his 35 Manets for 800,000 francs (White and White, 1965: 126) and gave 5,850 francs for the *Bar at the Folies Bergères* (1882) (Hamilton, 1954: 271). Although Manet died too young to make money out of art, Monet, Pissarro and Renoir, after 30 years of poverty, were making substantial incomes, Degas was comfortably off and only Sisley of the original group was lacking a middle-class income. Perhaps also they were adapting to the culture of those who bought them.

The argument of this chapter has been that it is not sufficient to approach Manet simply in terms of his 'barbarous' or misunderstood style. Certainly, given the significance of academic brushwork as artistic currency in the 1850s, Manet's 'weakness' in this respect represented a radical departure from ruling conventions, as also did his 'failure' to constrain his colours within the linear construction of pictorial space and to organise figures within that space convincingly. This may indeed have been due in part to inadequate technique (for example, the figure of the woman in the backgound in *Déjeuner* had provoked much debate on this score). However, as Zola's review made crystal clear, stylistic innovation alone was not important. What was also apparent was a new sense of realism. Castagnary, the Realist critic, might have attacked Manet for not sufficiently addressing 'society as it is', but it remains true that Manet's painting both opened up new spaces – the theatre and the boulevard rather than the cathedral and the palace – and depicted new personalities, through whom the subjective experience of modernity was conveyed. In other words, with Manet we have ignoble subjects, ignoble styles and even ignoble pastiche.

As much as Courbet's, Manet's painting was 'a dance with ideology', made more effective by its artistic allusions – his new themes of consumption and leisure, middle-class idylls and fears. It is this disruptive power that lies behind his political liberalism, his 'madness'. In this sense I argue that Manet cannot simply be seen, with Bourdieu, as the painter who abandoned 'finish', destroyed solidity, disrupted perspective conventions and introduced blocks of black: rather these changes in signifier occurred because the relations he depicted were simultaneously cut free of tradition, and provided graphic representations of the new impact of money and class.

Women and the new anomie in art

I have already touched on the change in conceptions of women as they entered into the realm of commodities in an independent, individualistic way. This opens up the question of male domination in the art-world of Impressionism, and about this Bourdieu is curiously silent. He has not explored adequately how the new way of seeing in Impressionism channelled into art the new leisure, consumption and popular cultural spheres. If he had done so he would have noted that the 'new eye' was still a 'male eye', that it is no accident that he writes of charismatic prophets and not of prophetesses. If we are going to link art to power, it is not just class origin and family position but also gender divisions which should be analysed in relation to the restricted and expanded field of art production.

Manet and Impressionism developed an art which interrogated taken-for-granted categories of bourgeois reason. Manet's appropriation of the bohemian as the image of the artist reveals the undermining of eighteenth-century certainties, including the bourgeoisie's perceived distance from the 'other' – children, primitives and madmen (Ferguson, 1990: chap. 1). But this did not extend to the last of the Enlightenment 'others': women. They remained distanced from the new principles of Impressionist art in key aspects of cultural practice.

It is surprising that Bourdieu does not theorise the inhospitable space of the first avant-garde to women more systematically. For understanding their omission from traditional art histories does not mean merely putting the women back in, discovering a hidden heritage lost in auction rooms or even a subculture with subterranean connections. It means, rather, perceiving how the whole field of cultural production is structured in such a way as to marginalise women artists. This occurs through the basic categories of traditional art history, the monograph and *catalogue raisonné*, which celebrate the single creative individual, the division between art and craft, and the privileging of certain forms of art over other types of artistic expression.

Bourdieu's insistence on the historical genesis of the work of art is incomplete unless it also extends this same treatment to the work of women producers. Bourdieu has hardly started to chart the precise cultural expressions through which male domination became a second nature even within the artists' world-in-reverse.

Bohemian space had no clear boundaries. Contrary to the implication of nostalgic artistic tourism (Mark Twain's San Francisco etc.), the Impressionists were not enclosed within an exotic enclave. Rather they colonised certain public spaces, some of which became identified with bohemian ideas, such as the Café Guerbois, others of which retained their own social worlds. Bourdieu gives us a very good idea of this when he charts onto a Paris city map the social worlds of *L'Éducation sentimentale*: (1975a: 86; 1993a: 149). These imaginary locations, like that of the artist, traverse very different class and moral areas. In terms of the public spaces of the metropolis, it is clear that, for bourgeois or aristocratic women, parks, cafés, bars, nightclubs and boulevards could only be experienced within a couple. Thus, unless, like Bonheur, you obtained a licence to disguise sexual identity with trousers, it was impossible to wander observantly. Thus as painters, women were excluded from much of the new leisure–pleasure economy. We need to discover what contradictions existed within the roles of artists and women that were distinctive to their gender. Bourdieu's category of habitus and artistic habitus as the internal disposition corresponding to external social position can provide us with a crucial tool for this purpose, suggesting why so many women painters were unable (in the nineteenth century) to become as strongly innovative as were a minority of the male painters. His *Les Règles de l'art* alerts us to divisions between regional or naive artists as against metropolitan professional artists. But it needs to be expanded to account for the ways in which artists both are moulded by gender positioning and represent it. Recent work has suggested some useful leads to follow here.

In the Second Empire women painters were doubly marginalised. First, there were social constructions of artistic genius that denied women the solitary heretic role that Bourdieu identifies with the birth of artistic anomie (Battersby, 1989). Secondly, there were repressive restrictions on women that meant they were precluded from adopting the role of 'invisible man' or *flâneur* while also being constrained to experience themselves as quintessential consumers. The new department stores created the first link between women and consumption, invoking the customer as a bourgeois woman in advertisements (Bowlby, 1985: 20–1) or playing on female daydreams in décor, as in the adornment of the whole of Bon Marché in bridal white for the spring sales (Miller, 1981: 168).

Bowlby notes the new aestheticisation of industry through which department stores wooed specifically female customers:

> The dominant ideology of feminine subjectivity in the late nineteenth century perfectly fitted women to receive the advances of the seductive commodity offering to enhance her womanly attractions. Seducer and seduced, possessor and

> possessed of one another, women and commodities flaunt their images at one another in an amorous regard. . . . (1985: 32)

These new incitements to fantasy and to consumption as play became difficult for a woman artist to combine with *serious production*.

It is true that the women in some respects benefited from the decline of the Academy and its institutionalised patriarchy: the emergence of independent studios in which women painters could be taught meant an unprecedented increase in the numbers of women painters in Paris.[9] (Some of the new distribution arrangements also favoured them: women painters appreciated the juryless Salons of the Independents from 1848 (Frascina et al., 1993: 239; Weisberg, 1980: 316)). The demise of the Academic hierarchy of genres also potentially benefited women since those subjects with the highest prestige (for example, history-painting) were often contrasted with the more feminine low-prestige subjects such as still life (the artist hero of Zola's *The Masterpiece* (1886) speaks of the depiction of a carrot being pregnant with revolution (1993: 40)). Yet the prohibition of the life class and hence the nude continued for women. The emergence of the new division of the artistic field did little to reduce the salience of gender in restricting the access of women to modern painting, and we shall see why.

A fundamental principle of exclusion was provided by the invention of the life of the artist as that of a suffering Christ or prophetic figure, premised as these were on the principle of genius. This form of secular self-annihilation and rebirth was not available to women (Battersby, 1989). In both Kantian and Romantic aesthetics, the genius was distinguished from the mere craftsman by his possession of the knowledge of artistic rules, coupled with his uniqueness of vision. Women could serve as muses to draw out male qualities of vision but they could not themselves take on this lonely and magisterial role. Edmond de Goncourt inverted the essentialist conception which precluded women's equivalence with men in art: 'there are no women of genius, and . . . if they manifest it, it is by some trick of nature, in the sense that *they are men*' (quoted in Frascina et al., 1993: 231).

The women Impressionists had to negotiate this barrier. For some, an effective marriage bar meant that they gave up painting even if talented (Edmé Morisot) (Parker and Pollock, 1981: 43). Others viewed their work less as the public and professional activity identified with male artists than as one that they combined with domesticity and especially the management of the bourgeois household (for example, Berthe Morisot). It is noteworthy that none of the women Impressionists had to live off art, as Bonheur had done in the 1840s and as the working-class artists' model, Suzanne Valadon, was to do in the 1880s. It is the consequent lack of self-image as pioneering bohemians that may well explain why painters like Berthe Morisot or Cassatt, however strong and subtle in developing light palettes and sketchy brushstrokes, failed to develop the experimental drive of Manet, Seurat and some of Monet's work. Their distinctive angle of vision led them to a domestic Realism, with less distanced representations of the female or child subject, but not to the epoch-making new subjects represented by *Déjeuner*

(1863), or the *Bar at the Folies Bergères* (1882) or Monet's *The Railway Station at St Lazare* (1877). Not surprisingly, their own portrayal by their fellow male Impressionists indicates the relatively hidden character of their work. Manet's paintings of Berthe Morisot never depict her painting; rather she is shown as part of a family group (*The Balcony* (1869)), as a well-dressed girl sitting in leisure in a comfortable interior or as a figure made austere by grief (*Portrait of Berthe Morisot with Hat, in Mourning* (1874)). Even his painting of a woman artist at work, Eva Gonzalez, denies her any vivid subjective experience of her acts as a painter: she appears in evening dress delicately touching up a canvas, with her face averted.

Such differences in artistic trajectory and habitus for men and women had their origin in the exclusion of women from the bourgeois public space. Joan Landes has pointed out that the term for a public man (*homme publique*) means one who has a creditable, disinterested commitment to the social and to an anticipatory future. *Une fille publique*, on the other hand, is a prostitute (1988: 3). Thus the public sphere did not – even in an imaginary unity – transcend gender interests (1988: 56-7). While the French Revolution's Constitutional Assembly under the Girondins had permitted women the right to work, to the vote, to crèches, to divorce, the Jacobins had rescinded these freedoms. The Napoleonic Code had finally put the nail into the coffin, refusing women access to the vote and to independent professional careers. In brief, 'Marianne' in Delacroix's famous image of the 1830 Revolution, suggested only a figurative image of the nation as female and not that the emancipation of women was to be tied to bourgeois and popular demands.

In particular, the sphere of consumption liberated men for a whole new way of seeing, but this was not the case for women. Respectable women were denied access to many of the new sites of modernity, sites which were always available to the 'lions' of the Jockey Club. Clark was the first to show the Impressionists 'trespassing' on such popular or *risqué* spaces, but a gender perspective on the women Impressionists is only unevenly offered. The subjects of Impressionism are revealingly totted up by Pollock in a table entitled the 'erotic territories of modernity', which graphically differentiates between the 'ladies' portrayed in the parks and theatre *loges* by both male and female painters (Cassatt and Morisot) and the 'fallen women' of the backstage theatre, the cafés, the *folies* and the brothels, who were the subjects of Manet, Guys, Degas and, to a lesser extent, Renoir but *none* of the women (Pollock, 1988b: 73).[10]

These women painters nevertheless possessed a distinctive iconography. Their paintings betray their restrictions, for we can see how the angle of vision creates enclosures (balustrades, verandas, fences) within which their female subjects are placed (see, for example, Berthe Morisot's *The Harbour at L'Orient* (1869) or her *On the Balcony* (1872) (Pollock, 1988b: chap. 3)). Even without these motifs, other pictorial devices have created similar effects. Pollock suggests that the compression of space is a frequent element of Cassatt's work, as in the seclusion of the figure of a woman behind a tapestry frame in *Woman With Tapestry Frame* (1879), thus creating a visual homology for the highly constrained experience of bourgeois women within domestic crafts and indeed their social confinement. Further, the changed angle of vision transforms what is seen, so as to heighten empathy. Children are represented from a point parallel with their own height: a woman's face is shown averted, retaining some of its privacy, rather than full face and dominated by the artistic eye. Women workers, such as the wet-nurses painted by Morisot and Cassatt, are presented more as part of a community of women caring for children than as exotic or erotic subjects. Even where the emphasis is on women's appearance and dress, as in Cassatt's paintings, the subjects appear more contemplative than in many portrayals by male painters.

The eighteenth- and nineteenth-century public sphere was construed as the expression of the universal interests of humankind in rational communication. However, the other new institutions of the bourgeois world intruded into the public sphere, turning its clubs, philosophical societies and institutes into the narrower domain of the middle class rather than the working class; the male rather than the female (Habermas, 1987; Landes, 1988). Despite its oppositional ethic and its repudiation of class apartheid, bohemian society turns out to have a similar false universality at its heart, for it concealed a set of social conditions effectively excluding women. Although he has a perceptive awareness of the gap between rhetoric and interests, Bourdieu fails to convey fully the rich yet ambivalent sectional worlds of the metropolis.

Conclusion

Bourdieu's perspective on Impressionism takes very much the conventional view of Impressionism as a revolution in form, even while it provides an analysis of its historical genesis. I have suggested that this fails to take account of the artists' interests in new types of bourgeois and popular culture. However, it *is* permissible to accept Bourdieu's concern for the attenuated place of objective representation within Impressionist art, but only at a much later date, certainly not earlier than the mid-1870s (see Frascina et al., 1993).

The new autonomous art of late Impressionism and post-Impressionism gradually forgoes Pissarro's peasant, Caillebotte's narrative interests in his subjects (which came to seem old-fashioned and redundant) and Manet's sharp critical awareness of the social realities of the metropolis through the percipience of the *flâneur*. A similar point can be made about Monet. By the 1880s a gulf between the natural and the human worlds had opened up. Monet now paints angry seas and deserted beaches as though to point to the revenge of the elements on the social. It is this deepened disenchantment of the world, associated too early by Bourdieu with Manet's 'fresh eye', which now precipitates the singular interest in the 'permanent revolution' of form. In other words, Bourdieu's weakness, in terms of Impressionism, is his failure to show its early character and the potential for the restricted field to develop artistically in several different trajectories, each profoundly affected by the nature of the specific period and the constituents of the avant-garde. Despite these omissions, Bourdieu's analysis provides the important parameters of a new sociological history of the development of capitalism, the class nature of the avant-garde and the critic–dealer system. For critics such as Greenberg, by contrast, artistic autonomy is presented as an aesthetic imperative, as an embattled and lonely modernist remnant struggles with historicist certainty in a perpetual conflict against kitsch (1961).

Bourdieu has written on numerous occasions of the battle over social classifications implicit in changes in representations. His emphasis on the conflicts within linguistic signs – 'in revolutionary situations common words take on different meanings' (1991: 40 and n.29, 264) – could easily be extended to the study of Manet and the Impressionists. Moreover, he never reduces representations to mere superstructural insignificance but considers them a part of every action, an element of society in the mind. Yet, for all this, Bourdieu still views Impressionism as a group of painters unduly obsessed with the effects of light and with the desire to impress on the spectator the conventional nature of colour. He has neglected the fact that Manet and the earlier Impressionists were extending the scope of Realism to include the utopian moments of everyday life and that they possessed a subcultural outlook, linking their resistance to other forms. This does not imply that they were always successful – *Olympia*, for example, cannot quite solve the contradictions inscribed in its contours (Clark, 1980: 39) – but they did provide an ironic, distanced perspective on social relations within a regime that had a 'protofascist' character. Concerned to prick the inflated bubble of the cult of art, Bourdieu removes these elements from view.

Notes

1. The material roots of this bohemian ethic are explained as a cultural investment in suffering, much as Weber expanded on Marx's account of religion to pinpoint the appearance of a theodicy of bad fortune among the Israelites. Jewish belief in a special contract with God became more firmly held the more they were tested by the misfortunes of exile and diaspora (Weber, 1952).

2. Bourdieu contends that Clark's interpretation of Manet has 'bent the stick too far in the opposite direction' (private interview, May 1993).

3. One of the implications of these nineteenth-century French conflicts over painting is that the 1930s duel between Lukács and Brecht bears certain analogies with them. See the Conclusion to this volume.

4. A marginal member, Louis Forain, whose father was a craftsman, was unable to develop anything other than a clichéd, ironic gaze at the bourgeoisie, possibly because immediate economic necessity required him to earn his living as a newspaper caricaturist (Reff and Valdès-Forain, 1995).

5. A recent writer on realism, Weisberg, regards the difference between the two as elusive (1980: 16–18).

6. In this sense we might compare Impressionism with eighteenth- and nineteenth-century thinkers such as Goethe and Marx who develop a dialectical view of modernity, seeing it as possessing positive and negative elements (Berman, 1983).

7. In this context, it is noteworthy that Impressionists first appeared as the 'Anonymous Society of Painters, Sculptors and Engravers, etc.' in an exhibition at the studios of the photographer, Nadar – and photography was certainly not canonised (Eisenman, 1992: 189).

8. Crow argues that the 'forced marginalisation of the artistic vocation' (1985: 244), implicit in the 1852 slogan 'l'art pour l'art', should not veil the fact that in the Second Empire leisure channelled energies turned from the banned public sphere and from the aridity of official art.

9. However, Marie Bashkirtseff's well-known image of well-dressed women painters in *L'Académie Julien* (*c.* 1880) dates from after the demise of the old Academy's monopoly.

10. Nochlin (1989) has argued with some force that the relative absence of work in Impressionism noted above is by no means total and especially does not extend to workers in the new service sector, many of whom were women – ballet dancers, barmaids, waitresses, singers, etc. (1989: 43). She shows that Berthe Morisot did explore the division of labour within women's work in her *Wet Nurse and Julie* (1875) (1989: chap. 2), a point which could also be exemplified through her *A Gathering of Laundresses* (1875). Within the latter the scale of the working women depicted is tiny, as though part of a romance of work, much like nostalgic visions of peasants.

6

THE POPULAR AND THE MIDDLEBROW

My aim in this chapter is to reassess the economy of symbolic goods. I shall be concerned especially with the division between the fields of restricted and expanded cultural production, or, in other words, between fine art and the culture industry. The fundamental opposition in the cultural field for Bourdieu stems from creators' social relations with their readers or patrons, that is, in Valéry's terms, between an art which is created by its public and art which creates its own public (1966b: 874). I shall develop further my view that in his work of unmasking ideologies of art Bourdieu has left unquestioned certain social classifications. These classifications or representations have as their stake the fundamental questions of the origin of art, and the nature of the charismatic individuals who produce it. While Bourdieu is perceptive in seeing bohemia as an inversion or reverse discourse of classical political economy, I want to problematise further the divisions of the cultural field between 'high' and 'low' culture. I shall suggest that Bourdieu is still under the spell of certain tacit assumptions maintained by the priests who monopolise cultural authority. In particular, Bourdieu's own line of inquiry needs to be deepened into a feminist materialism.

Bourdieu shockingly exposes the mysteries of the work of art by revealing the social consequences of the well-known economic barrier to creativity. In practice, this limits receptiveness towards what Max Raphael called 'the demands of art' to those who possess sufficient funds or a family to support them during the years when they are withheld recognition by the public. Only agents with these advantages can sustain themselves in the metropolitan centre, where they are better placed to experience and distil through the rules of art the great waves of collective effervescence. Granting this, it is essential to ask whether the divide between high and low culture is shaped simply by the material experience of class relations and the educational determinants shaping positions within the field. Bourdieu has certainly *begun* the very important task of periodising and mapping the location of cultural production. He notices, for example, that the French realist novel written outside the metropolis and by writers originating from the subordinate class became marginalised as a lesser, 'regional literature' after 1850.[1] Following the approach to Impressionism, I shall claim that in the novel gender divisions have also created specific trajectories within these wider laws of space and time. Given that Bourdieu has portrayed masculine domination as in many ways the paradigm of all power relations, it is odd that he has not yet integrated this analysis into his cultural theory.

How does Bourdieu think masculine domination works? His answer derives from taking Kabylia as a limiting case. Here masculine domination is the consequence of collective, public organisation, quite unlike its transitory expression within the psychoanalytic cure or poetic licence, through which it perpetuates its subterranean existence in the modern West. By thus highlighting the nature of masculine honour in a world where it is assigned the mark of a truly human existence, Bourdieu's account is distinguished from other feminist interpretations. It is especially through its powerful depiction of *society within the mind* that it achieves its impact. He makes us see the aura radiating from male power itself so that it creates a social unconscious, capable even of denying the fact of repression.

Such well-established power does not need ideologies (in the sense of legitimating theories). Nor does it depend simply on physical force. Instead, in Western soceties, masculine domination is accomplished by the workings of educational institutions and particularly through the cultural capital acquired by men. By contrast, in Kabylia, such domination is the 'natural attitude', the common-sense or doxic world-view that is anchored in everyday experience within structures in which gender is stringently and elaborately differentiated. For Kabylians it is taken for granted that to be male is to be a universal being, segregated by one's sense of honour from confrontation with the intimate, physical dimension of family existence. In turn, women are condemned to see themselves pejoratively, possessing the negative virtues engendered by their exclusion from the *agora* or public sphere and constrained to recognise their purely private and subordinate existence:

> [W]oman, who is bad by nature, has to be placed as soon as possible under the beneficial protection of man . . . [w]oman is like a young shoot which bends to the left; man is the guardian who sets it straight again. (1966a: 227)

Even the use of specific walls in the Kabylian house or the fountain in the Kabylian village are regulated by gender, however ironically approached. The gender divisions that in the West are residual but still active, as in the fear of putting a baby boy in pink clothes, are linked in Kabylia to a much more complex cosmology in which gender orders not only the entire agricultural calendar (sowing, harvesting, etc.), but all the domestic crafts, and especially the cooking practices of the household. Practice is governed by choices which will ensure matching: for example, a man who wants his penis to swell should choose foods that also swell in cooking or in the stomach (rice etc.). The substance of gender attributes is socially arbitrary. Hence Kabylians denigrate capacities such as quickness, cunning and calculative action, since for them these are linked to activities in the market-place undertaken by women, whereas in the West the same qualities are attributes of males and are prized.

Male domination possesses a further general trait that is revealed most sharply in Kabylia: that of the 'somatisation' of the relations between men and women. The social order literally makes its mark on the body. It thus transcends ideology. At the most simple, the bent bodies of all older women testify to years of decorously walking behind their men, their eyes downcast; the husbands, on the other hand, retain their straightness. Or male circumcision, apparently separating younger boys from older males, serves in reality to distinguish all males from females. Thus, attacking all natural essentialisms, Bourdieu notes that on the frail biological difference between the sexes is constructed a whole edifice of gender-differentiated experiences, which come to be felt as a second nature. The collective creation of the socio-somatic body he christens the 'institution effect'.

For Bourdieu, Kabylia demonstrates the familiar Janus faces of power, which he draws out with striking clarity. Its first face is revealed in the 'social unconscious' of male domination which associates it with all other noble, disinterested incitements to the exercise of power, in which power is considered as an element of a protective paternalism. The other face is harsher, deriving its character from violence and symbolic force. In this the male comes to stand for the legitimate power of the social itself, 'the pitiless and inexorable power of necessity' (1990b: 23), which requires the violence of the knife or the executioner and through which is exerted the force of the social over recalcitrant natural beings. Since women and children are part of the natural world of *laissez-faire* and *laissez-aller*, male power must be imposed by prising all the children – and especially the boys – from the shelter and sustenance of women.

Masculine domination for Bourdieu thus rests on an essentialism, just as race and class are forms of essentialism. The sexual habitus ensures the *misrecognition* of the consequences of the long process of socialising the body:

> In this case the work aimed at transforming into nature the arbitrary product of history finds its apparent foundation in the appearance of the body, at the same time as it creates very real effects on the body and inside the brain; that is to say, that both in reality and in the representations of reality, the thousand-year project of socialisation of the biological and of biologising the social, which reverses the relation between cause and effects, also makes apparent a naturalised social construction. . . . (1990b: 12)

Excluded from the public and sacred spheres where the universal character of the male sex manifests itself, Kabylian women are trained for inferiority by the inculcation of appropriate emotions of subordination: modesty, shame and timidity. Thus their *self-exclusion* completes the historical process of *structural exclusion*, and the genesis of the antagonistic image of women lies in these relations. Women are condemned through their submission to possess only negative virtues (such as sexual purity); to be endowed only with deferred power (such as 'the power behind the throne'); to be independent only through the ruses and other survival tactics which simultaneously incur scorn for their pettiness.

But, most importantly, it is male *libido dominandi* (love of domination) which ensures masculine investment in power, whether in the academic, artistic or political worlds. Bourdieu's is one of the richest accounts we have of the social psychology of patriarchy, not least in its use of Virginia Woolf's *To the Lighthouse* (1927) as a representation of the disenchanted female gaze. For Woolf's narrative devices not only create aesthetic distancing, through which all male societies can be perceived as the equivalents to the tribal worlds of savages, but they isolate both the passion with which men are involved in public life and the child-like egotism for which women castigate them. Yet the profound seriousness of the arenas within which men invest their energies enhances their dignity, while women's cultural energies are forcibly divided: a necessary consequence of their culturally induced preoccupation with children and matters of life and death.

Woolf, read from the position of professorial eminence, suggests the challenging view that men's possession of power is in itself attractive. It is the *libido dominandi* that creates an aura around male sexuality, while women, in turn, have the magical power to reflect back the male image as twice as big as it is 'naturally':[2]

> [Because of] the differential socialisation predisposing men to love games of power, women to love men who play them, the masculine charisma is partly the charm of power, the seduction that the possession of power exerts itself on the body, the sexuality of which is politically socialised. (1990b: 25)

In short, moving in the orbits of male power, women enhance men's quest for distinction:

> Everything leads one to suppose that the condition for women's liberation is a mastery of those mechanisms of domination which had, up to now, prevented us from seeing that culture – that is, the asceticism and sublimation through and by which humanity is inscribed – cannot be understood otherwise than by a set of social relations of distinction affirmed against a nature which is composed of dominated groups – women and poor people, colonised groups, stigmatised groups. . . . It is clear that without being in all cases and at all times totally associated with rebarbative nature, against which are organised the games of culture, women still enter into a dialectic of pretension and distinction more as objects than as subjects. (1990b: 31)

More as objects than as subjects . . . I shall return to the implications for women and culture shortly.

Bourdieu's 1990 account of Kabylia treats the control over women as so effective that their autonomy is virtually absent. His initial treatment of the gender division of labour in *The Algerians* (1961) characterises women's responses differently. Kabylian civilisation here possesses its *discontents*, such that women who can no longer tolerate their condition adapt the secret magical resources of their own gendered world to turn the evil eye or, in desperate cases, to provoke their husbands' death. In this earlier work, the prerogative of divorce from their wives is certainly a testament to male power, but it represents also a continued discrepancy between men's desires and women's compliance, with the use of gender solidarity on the part of women to protect little strategies of resistance. Bourdieu's acknowledgement of the ceaseless labour of Kabylian women and their total disappearance from all public life after marriage indicated a harsh realism about the massive stakes involved in Kabylian men's retention of their legally monopolised patriarchal power.

By 1990, perhaps to combat feminist utopianism, Bourdieu depicts most starkly only the collusion of women with their oppressors. Yet, despite this undoubted oversimplification, his conception of symbolic violence throws into relief the existence of inequalities of *power*. It is preferable to the mere *difference* theorised by Lacan's disciples and, for this reason, this complex approach offers a welcome contribution to feminist theory.

Bourdieu's treatment of masculine domination in contemporary Western societies is only fragmentary. Following his analysis, it could be argued that where education and the law have been wrested from overt patriarchal divisions, where capital can be accumulated as efficiently by Ms as by Mr Moneybags, and where the reserve army of unemployed labour can be of either sex, then the cultural obeisance to male power appears arbitrary. This creates a *generalised crisis*, even if not an explosive one. However, against the grain of most socialist feminism, which has presented the working class as the embarrassing site of traditional patriarchy, Bourdieu takes a different tack, highlighting how changes in the position of women have had divergent effects in different classes, not least in the increased enforced celibacy in the peasantry (see, for example, Bourdieu, 1990a). Particularly in the dominant class, female cultural capital, acquired through education, is converted into economic capital in highly paid jobs. Women's liberation thus has an accidental fall-out in the creation of a new strategic resource within bourgeois families for the social reproduction of their own power (1989: 376–411).

But while Bourdieu has usefully articulated the linkage of gender with class, he has still left unexplored many of the contradictions surfacing around gender within the 'sacred island' of culture. This terrain has become the seed-bed for proliferating crises, not unlike those conflicts of expectation and reality that created the instabilities he charted in the university world (1988a: 164).

Bourdieu's masculine domination and the cultural field

One of the resources men possess which Bourdieu has not theorised concretely is precisely their passionate involvement in the artistic *illusio* or game. Put another way, there exists also a *gendered* difference in what Bourdieu has called the 'production of belief', the collective processes through which a writer is attributed with an inner grace. Such a gendered belief was perhaps at stake in leading Mrs Gaskell in her preface to *Mary Barton* to disavow her mastery of political economy (1985 (1848): 38).

Huyssen has suggested that the whole epoch from 1850 to 1960 was premised on a form of masculine cultural domination in which the art of the masses was distanced *as though it were a woman* (1986). If modernism was precisely *valorised* by Adorno and others as the subversive 'Agent Orange' of the capitalist social order, the culture industry was dismissed in tropes which aligned it with feminine consumption and degraded femininity (see also Lovell, 1987). Mass culture was like the vamp, peddling style without substance, ministering to the sensual pleasures of entertainment but reneging on the austere and uncomfortable demands of art. Huyssen's interpretation of texts such as *Madame Bovary* (1856–7) falters uncomfortably over Flaubert's explicit identification with Emma, even with her love of romances, but he is right that modern literature certainly possesses many alternative examples of the dangerously seductive lure of popular culture. I need mention only Lewis Grassic Gibbon's contrast between Ake Ogilvie's poetry and romantic fiction in *Grey Granite* (1993 (1934)) or the earlier tragedy of development of George Douglas Brown's *The House with Green Shutters* (1901), in which a servile wife, enfeebled by a diet of fantasy from her romantic magazines, fatally weakens the promethean drive of a Scottish entrepreneur. Of course, the trope of a feminised mass culture is not the only means of valorising modernism: images of mass culture as a *plague* can also be found in the writing of American post-war intellectuals (Ross, 1987: 328–9). Nevertheless Bourdieu should have been alerted to the peculiar disadvantage under which women labour in struggles over consecration.

As Bourdieu points out, the art-worlds of modernity have been profoundly shaped by the priests or critics who possess the legitimate monopoly of judging or consecrating a writer. Such judges must produce rationales for their choices, but the terms in which they do so include folk versions of élite categories which retain an unavoidable imprecision and context-dependence. Thus the aesthetic concepts of 'beauty', '*soigné*' and 'finish', have specific meanings which shift according to the logic of the artistic epoch (1993a: 262). Consequently, the history of the whole artistic field is involved in any validating judgement. Moreover, despite artistic autonomy, the specialised language of aesthetics is itself shaped historically by struggles over the principles of vision and division, fundamental to which has been the drive to express a distance from the popular. Thus both within art and the wider intellectual or educational fields, the binary oppositions between brilliant and dull, distinguished and vulgar, personal and banal, original and common, fine and crude, etc., betray, through their linguistic origins, the way of life of a dominant – even noble – class (1984: 494; 1989: 31).

We can accept with Bourdieu that these terms set up their own constraining pressures, even if he forgets that they can also be *stretched* for new and democratic uses. He has, however, neglected the existence of a similar set of evaluative judgements in which masculinity is prized in the artistic field. These tended to marginalise women, not least within the early and high modernist movements.

The situation for women writers has been as difficult in France as in England, despite the early impact of de Staël's *Corinne* (1807) (Moers, 1978: 43, 183). Monique de Saint Martin's study (1990) shows that these obstacles persisted well after the appearance of George Sand, under the 'golden age' of Louis-Philippe's rule. By the end of the nineteenth century it was possible for a woman to be a writer publicly, but only at the cost of being associated with scandal; otherwise the shameful literary activity had to be kept secret (1990: 54). As a consequence, the emergence of an *autonomous* literary terrain was segregated from women's literary activities. Unless the woman writer had the protection of a distinguished male guardian, as in the case of the widow of Alphonse Daudet, her writing was classified as popular literature or journalism (1990: 55). Even then, women writers were still mainly from the comfortable sections of the bourgeoisie, especially from those which possessed cultural capital. Admitted in only tiny numbers to the Society of Letters, the chief explanation advanced was the view that women excluded themselves because they refused to write *for the sake of the work of art*, and stressed extra-literary ends. Saint Martin concludes:

> It is impossible to understand the differences separating the trajectories of literary men and literary women without taking into account the logic of the literary field which by its genesis and its functioning, its values and its representations tends to give more indulgence and more recognition to men than to women. (1990: 56)

Art and literature were taken more seriously and distinguished writers could acquire greater consecration in France than in Britain, as was obvious in the 'dialectical relationship' of Paris to London (Bradbury and McFarlane, 1976: 174). Paradoxically, the more effective exclusion of women in France serves as one measure of the greater social investment at stake.

In Britain, the relative prominence of Virginia Woolf and Katherine Mansfield should not obscure the marginalisation of the other modernist women writers: Dorothy Richardson, H.D. (Hilda Doolittle), Leonora Carrington, Edith Sitwell, Bryher (sic) and Dora Marsden. It is Woolf on whom Bourdieu draws for his female gaze at male power, for she is one of the '*lucides exclues*' (a term which he uses also of Flaubert). Woolf's negotiation of the public/private division aimed to introduce innovations in form–language which would suit the new subjects deriving from the repressed hopes and private worlds of consumption and desire. But her case is atypical: she can be regarded as one of Bourdieu's '*miraculées*', who escape their social fate. Clearly canonisation of Woolf was aided by her unusual range of literary assets, not least the number of her novels – neither too few nor too many – and by the importance of her early literary and social criticism in achieving her vindication through appeal to a female subculture (see Gilbert and Gubar, 1988: 166, 250; Lovell, 1987: 130–2). Moreover, Woolf's membership of the Co-operative Women's Guild gave her an angle of vision that included wider material and historical questions as well as feminist issues. Bloomsbury's links to the economic and social field of power itself is Woolf's asset, with its Whig roots among the great liberal professional and entrepreneurial families, and its paternalist concern with the underdog, conferring on her a position in a cultural division of labour that was remarkable (Williams, 1980: 159–69). More practically, Woolf's novels could be published by Leonard Woolf's Hogarth Press, while his support for her literary project gave her a social capital which should not be underestimated (Bowlby, 1988: 65; Moi, 1991: 1040).

Bourdieu fails to confront both the bumpier route to consecration for the other modernist *women* writers and the distinctive barriers for women presented by the linguistic innovation characteristic of modernism as a consequence of their relative exclusion from academic life. Further, although there were expressions of solidarity for women and although women figured as the financial patrons and even co-editors,

> the rise of the female imagination was a central problem for the male imagination. . . . Indeed it is possible to argue that a reaction-formation against the rise of literary women became not just a theme in modernist writing but a motive for modernism. (Gilbert and Gubar, 1988: 156)

D.H. Lawrence is of course a representative mysogynist. His mystical romanticism valorised women only insofar as they stayed as passive figures at home, while he loathed the modern 'half-women' who threatened to supersede them (1950: 31-4). Wyndham Lewis was a domestic tyrant: he refused to allow his wife to have children and gave away the illegitimate children of his mistresses, a stance entirely compatible with Vorticism's general response to feminism (Carey, 1992: 170). In this respect, the British movement shared the opinions of its Italian Futurist counterpart, for which Marinetti's Manifesto had issued a declaration of war against women (Apollonio, 1973). Ezra Pound shows the clearest strategic practice towards women in his tenure as literary editor of *The New Freewoman*.[3] Capitalising on Dora Marsden's dual commitments as editor both to feminism and to an imagism which would 'cleanse the poetic language of abstraction', he symbolically cleansed the paper of its feminism by persuading her to rename it *The Egoist* (Gilbert and Gubar, 1988: 162; Thacker, 1994: 76).

Pound's trophy in this victory was the triumph of a hard and rigorous aesthetic against the ' flaccidity' or 'soft mushy edges' of those of rival modernist groups (Thacker, 1994: 87). In the microcosm of the little magazine it can be judged with what astringency the feminine qualities Bourdieu has isolated in his essay on male domination are tested against the necessity and severity of the masculine world and found wanting (1990b: 23). Yet, equally, if art-worlds rely for their 'professional rationales' on the writing of sympathetic literary critics, as he has also proposed (1993a: 259–60), then he needs also to situate recent feminist critics – male and female – who have struggled to reject the old patriarchal 'sense of order' with its associated linguistic classifications.

Women and the social structures of modernism

There are other reasons why women's cultural activities have not fitted easily into the dissident culture of modernism. Modernism itself has two main sites: the mature money economy and the metropolis (see Bourdieu, 1992: 365–6; Simmel 1978: 477). Of course, the experience of city life has certain common elements for both sexes. Benjamin's brilliant comments on shock and on gambling and Simmel's observations about the speed of change from riches to poverty, the cool cynicism and the reduction of quality to quantity are gender-neutral. They are rooted in the nature of bourgeois commodity exchange and in the ebbs and flows of industrial production. But the bitterness of modernist critique stems particularly from the contrast between instrumental reason and Enlightenment reason, between linear clock time and the subjective sense of duration: contrasts stemming from masculine contexts of work and bureaucracy. For women, often still linked to a domestic culture permeated by use-values and by a sense of time linked to immediate human needs, these alienating elements were less heightened (Kristeva, 1986).

Raymond Williams (1989) stresses the importance of the contexts of modernism, with both banality and insight. It is blindingly obvious that modernist writing comes from a series of experiences of metropolitan capitalism that both heightens the distance between subjective meanings and the collective consciousness and provides the context in which social distance breeds despair and cynicism. Yet Williams shows in much more detail than Bourdieu that other forms of writing have persisted into twentieth-century Europe where these sites of modernity and their typical structures of feeling are absent, both in the rural periphery and in isolated industrial or mining communities (1980: 213–32). What is also more distinctive in Williams' conception of modernism is his focus on the nature of exile, and especially on expatriates' sense of a cosmopolitan mass in the poorer districts of London, Paris, Prague and Vienna. For even where modernism was the work of natives, it was often expatriates who provided the catalyst.[4] The modernist focus on the nature of the signifier, so important in the case of Dadaism and Futurism, had an elective affinity with the experience of non-native speakers, who were drawn to focus intellectually on the nature of language. Formalist games with the phonic qualities of words stem from this understanding of the arbitrary character of language – hence the experimental concern for 'rare rhythms' or for 'revolutions of the word' that unified much literary exploration (Williams, 1989: 46).

Bryher wrote, 'We were all exiles. . . . It is our destiny', and linked the loss of home to women's empowerment (quoted in Griffin, 1994: 6). Yet women were much less likely to be among bohemian exiles. There were rarely allowances available to young women as there were for young men to settle in strange towns and establish themselves without kin (Davidoff and Hall, 1987; Flint, 1993). Nor could they travel alone.[5] Moreover, modernist circles had their location in the cafés and taverns that provided conviviality within a male public sphere, as in the case of the Black Boar in Berlin for German Symbolism or the Café Guermont for Parisian Impressionism (Bradbury and McFarlane, 1976: 200; Wilson, 1992: 93). More strongly, the aesthetic of the initial movements, including Naturalism, was derived from moments of illumination within urban experience which possessed specific dangers for women writers. In this reverse process of crossing the tracks, women could less easily disguise themselves, as Jack London did to investigate the background to his *The People of the Abyss* (1903), nor could they become *flâneurs*, as did Morrison or Gissing in the East End. Even the subsequent turn to Symbolism required a level of philosophical competence which would have been beyond the reach of women, who had only recently been granted access to higher education (Gamboni, 1989: 32), while their physical seclusion was also matched by the policing of their reading. Indeed, despite the appearance of the 'new woman', the regulation of women and girls within the respectable bourgeoisie still extended to every item of their cultural diet (Flint, 1993: chap. 4). These modes of control extended into the 1920s and beyond.

In brief, Bourdieu has so far neglected the gender habitus of cultural power, to which movements of modernism became so frequently adapted. In this case, can the central classification of Bourdieu's cultural theory be sustained? Could it be that, in the case of women, cultural production has taken different forms, cutting across his polarisation between art (autonomous production) and entertainment (heteronomous production); sitting uneasily with his categories of commercial production: bourgeois art, middlebrow pastiche and the naive political moralism of industrial art (1993a: 45)? Is his denial of the existence of 'significant form' outside modernism merely a historical report on the efficacy of contemporary classifications, or does it represent a blindness in his own analysis? It is necessary to retrieve those cultural expressions which the modernist gaze passed over, but which continued to exist in both rural and industrial areas (Bourdieu, 1992: 365–6).

Feminist reappraisals of what Bourdieu calls the 'social novel' make this issue more pressing (1993a: 63). It is unnecessary to enter the debate between adherents of realism or modernism to recognise that a group of writers existed which counted amongst its members women endowed with considerable cultural capital, yet who have been in some way excluded from the bounds of high culture (Light, 1991: x, 6–8).[6] Indeed it is possible that the acquisition of university education by the first generation of women may even have *fuelled* the adoption of more esoteric literary forms by male writers who feared intensified competition, a development that would parallel the break with Realism that Bourdieu notes in the case of Impressionism (Gilbert and Gubar, 1988: 36).[7] Statistics from British studies can be assembled to suggest a different picture from Bourdieu of the so-called 'entertainment' section.

Cultural capital, women and popular genres: empirical studies

Historically, only 4 per cent of British canonised writers have been women.[8] Even in the most recent period, empirical analysis of British literature suggests that women are less likely to get Arts Council backing than are men. They thus miss out on the recognition which is frequently the first stage of the consecration process. There are proportionately fewer women (33 per cent) than men (67 per cent) who are awarded either Creative Writing Bursaries or Fellowships, and 73 per cent of the grants to publishers are for texts written by men as against only 27 per cent for texts by women (Arts Councils, 1981–91).[9] A further study of the 1970s Arts Council applications reveals that fewer women than men were successful in their bids for subsidies for current novels (24 as against 56) (McGuigan, 1981: 23–9). Sexual discrimination was also accompanied by other social and geographical imbalances, with successful applications massively biased towards the metropolis and the Home Counties and grants to writers being given to those already most materially well endowed.[10] One implication of this is that it is still more difficult for women than men to gain literary recognition – to 'make their mark', as Bourdieu says, or to reap the symbolic profits of their labour.[11]

Possibly as a consequence of this structure of the literary field, a greater number of women have turned to the despised middlebrow and popular literary genres. Public library loans in the popular genres do indeed reveal the disproportionate numbers of women authors successful in socially degraded literary forms. Thus in the year 1991-2, 40 (61 per cent) of the books most frequently borrowed were written by women and only 26 (39 per cent) were by men (Public Lending Right, 1993). Predictably, the books in most frequent demand were in the popular categories, and among these female authors figured more prominently than male.

Such patterns can all be explained without disrupting Bourdieu's formulation. What is unexpected in terms of his classification of the cultural arena is the fact that this category of popular and middlebrow writer also contains women who are the holders of considerable educational credentials and/or social capital. Biographies of twentieth-century romantic fiction writers provide an illuminating source of information on their intellectual formation (Vinson, 1983). As might be expected, the overwhelming number are women. If we take references within these biographies to educational qualifications as a measure of cultural capital, as indeed Bourdieu does himself in *Distinction*, then the relatively large number of women who have higher education becomes apparent. Thirty-three per cent of the British and 72 per cent of the American women writers have university degrees. They therefore possess the cultural capital which would normally be a key requirement for entry into the restricted literary field. This suggests that amongst those women 'living off' writing, there are a group with high qualifications who might otherwise have received the respect of those who 'live for writing', that is, engage in a legitimate cultural activity. As it is, they experience the cynical dismissal of the educated public that is the popular writers' fate. ('To be a best-selling writer', once remarked Ed McBain, 'is to be guilty of white-collar crime' (quoted in Worpole, 1984: 21).)

Taking the 1890s as the period when modernism emerges in Britain, an empirical study of the women writers born from 1870 can be undertaken using the biographical resource of the *Dictionary of Women Writers* (Todd, 1987). Omitting literary critics and historians, it is possible to survey the 155 remaining writers (novelists, playwrights, poets, children's writers) in order to discover the structure and volume of their economic, social and artistic capital.[12] First, there is extraordinary convergence with the positions of male authors as detailed by Bourdieu for France. Women writers, too, have been overwhelmingly located in London or the Home Counties. While a common pattern has been a retreat in later life to the country, which could well be linked to the British cultural pleasure in the pastoral, the crucial element is that writing from uninterrupted experience of the rural periphery is virtually absent in this period. What is even more striking is that writing from industrial cities and towns outside London is also extremely rare, even for women of bourgeois origin. This distribution of writers suggests that there are whole communities, occupations and patterns of material existence which have yet to be portrayed in literature.

Although 33 per cent are unstated,[13] the social origins of women writers are most often within the dominated fraction of the dominant class (38 per cent or 60/155). Of these, the families of liberal professionals count for 26 per cent or 41/155, clergy 6 per cent or 9/155 and the 'state nobility' (the military élite, civil servants and politicians) 6 per cent or 10/155. It is therefore evident that there is a close relationship with the older 'traditional intelligentsia' of Gramscian theory. Indeed, if we take the bourgeoisie proper in the sense of industrial or merchant capitalists and bankers – Bourdieu's dominant fraction of the dominant class – the site is surprisingly *rare* among the fathers of women writers in this period (only 6 per cent or 9/155). This contrasts with earlier cultural groups, such as the Pre-Raphaelite painters and poets, whose social origins were within the class of industrial manufacturers (Williams, 1980). Perhaps also surprising is the fact that slightly more of the women writers come from the aristocracy or large landowning class (8 per cent or 12/155) than from the working class (6 per cent or 10/155) or the petty bourgeoisie (6 per cent or 9/155). In brief, British women writers in the period of modernity come from the privileged strata, however fraught and dissentient their relationship with them. They have acquired the sense of distinction which goes with this habitus, despite their other resentments, competitive failures or unhappiness. In this respect, too, they duplicate the pattern of male writers (Bourdieu, 1993a; Charle, 1981; Gamboni, 1989).

In their choice of husband or partner, these patterns emerge even more strongly, especially the predominance of the dominated fraction of the dominant class. Some of these writers did not marry; 13 (or 8 per cent) are stated to be single, with a further 22 whose status in this respect is less clearly defined. Of those who did marry, or who cohabited, 34 per cent (53) of their partners – by far the largest number – are from the liberal professions, and 10 per cent (16) from the civil service, army or politicians. A tiny number – 4 per cent (6) – come from industry or banking. *Only one writer was married to a man doing manual labour* (Jessie Kesson). A similarly small minority of partners as of fathers comes from the petty bourgeoisie (5 per cent or 7). The number from the aristocracy (or owners of large estates) had declined amongst the husbands in relation to the fathers from 12 to 3 (2 per cent), while none were clergymen. Finally, only one of the partners was a farmer, a fact which also documents the predominantly urban character of this group. To use a rather different language of class, the brief details described in these writers' biographies allow us to glean that, whatever the personal tragedies or economic difficulties, their existence has passed within the broad borders of the upper middle class.[14]

Bourdieu has pointed to the high cultural capital of modernist artists and writers in France from the 1850s onwards. The similarities in this sample of women writers, despite its inclusion of a minority from the popular genres, is quite remarkable. Seventy-nine of the women (51 per cent) had acquired cultural capital through university, art school and drama college, of whom a further 7 also possessed postgraduate degrees. Thus these are not uneducated writers nor are they autodidacts, unaffected by the scheduled learning of the school. The key role of Oxbridge in particular in the production of writers is also immediately apparent, with as many as 30 writers (19 per cent) having attended Oxford or Cambridge colleges, 7 of the writers graduating from Somerville alone. The most typical trajectory was a period of study at Oxford (22), Cambridge (8) or London University (15) preceded by attendance at private schools, either independents or Girls' Public Day School Trust (23 or 15 per cent). Of course, generational membership is crucial in this respect, since access to universities has become progressively easier and families more prepared to pay for or support their girls' higher education. In the earlier period, of women born between 1870 and 1895, there were relatively few women with higher education. Consequently as many as 35 (23 per cent) of the writers listed had secondary education only, followed in the case of those with social capital, by finishing schools (7 or 5 per cent) or travel abroad (18 or 19 per cent). Even as recently as the upbringing of the detective novelist Baroness (P.D.) James (born 1920), however, families might be unprepared to finance their daughters at university, as in her case, while many of the earlier writers such as Radclyffe Hall (1880–1943) had been educated only by governesses (13 or 8 per cent of the total sample). Despite these, and the many important exceptions who did not go to university (including Woolf, Lessing, Spark and Prawer), the most frequent trajectory is the passage from boarding or high school, through one of the élite universities, before beginning a writing career. The rigorous formal education appropriate to a ruling class is thus combined with the esprit de corps of the reputable schools and colleges, producing the sense of distinction which facilitates achievement in the arts.

Even in the small number of writers with a lower-class background, cultural capital has in most cases been achieved by meritocratic ascent. The case of Margaret Forster might be mentioned here, whose father was a fitter and who proceeded to grammar school, Somerville and teaching before starting her literary career. Consequently, the numbers of women writers who – like Shelagh Delaney – failed the 11+ or who were never considered worth educating – like Flora Thompson – are a tiny fraction: a minority of a minority. Whatever the barriers to women's consecration as writers or their marginality in terms of modernism, in the post-war period they have not been negligibly endowed with (certified) cultural capital.

A recurrent feature of women writers' lives is the fact that they have – what might be called flippantly – trouble with patriarchy. Unlike Mrs Gaskell or Sarah Stickney Ellis, the personal lives of later women writers are strewn with affairs, unhappy marriages or, in a minority of cases, the experience of lesbian attachments. The diversity of subjective meanings in these areas makes it extremely unwise to pretend to calibrate such experiences exactly, but if to the single, divorced, those with affairs or unhappily married we added the small number of illegitimate writers instanced in the biographies, half the writers fail to occupy normatively approved positions (78). It is difficult to estimate whether writing is a cause or consequence in these patterns, nor do we have comparative studies of male writers that might help to evaluate their meaning. Nevertheless, these dossiers of loss and frequent isolation do suggest that the woman writer has an understanding of the family which is at odds with the contemporary nostalgia for the patriarchal past. It is from these personal dislocations as well as the experience of different modes of production that the most significant works have emerged.

What has emerged with crystal clarity from the above survey of modern women writers is that there are vast tracts of British culture that have not yet been recorded in literary writing: ways of life and structures of feeling which have not yet been submitted to scrutiny. It is not just a question of the multiplicity of working-class perspectives that are missing, nor even the absence of black women writers, but that the nature of the industrial bourgeoisie and its impact on the country is itself still largely unrepresented. And when such areas *have* thrown up writers (for example, Phyllis Bentley, Jessie Kesson), it is they who are more exposed to the gaps in the collective literary memory.

Bourdieu's category of 'middlebrow'

It is particularly interesting that, in the case of women's writing, canonisation can often occur late, and may be the work of a pioneering critic working outside the politics of the mainstream (as in the case of Emily Brontë, consecrated much later than Charlotte Brontë (Leavis, 1979: 60) or Mrs Gaskell, whose reputation owed much to Williams (1961). I want to discuss a category of accessible women authors, more or less contemporary with high modernism, whose concerns are not uniquely those of the private sphere and who, for this reason, are engaged in a 'woman to people discourse' as much as a 'woman to woman discourse' (see Lovell, 1987: 87–8). Whilst thus widening the subject of the novel they also demonstrate considerable narrative skills. Nor is their storytelling totally devoid of modernist technique, for devices such as the presentation of multiple realities, or even a Joycean stream of consciousness, are accommodated within a realist form. But the important point is that, in contrast with the most experimental products of modernism, which are dependent on decoding strategies accessible only to the few contemporary artistic producers, these writings bear some continuities with the realist works of the last century. Unlike the formulaic romance, this literature is free of the banality, the absence of risk and the collusion with a dominant ideology which ensues when a writer is solely concerned with instrumental values or, to paraphrase Weber's sharply polarised dichotomy, 'living off' rather than 'living for' writing (Gerth and Mills, 1947).

It is necessary now to reassess Bourdieu's cultural theory in the light of this writing. He notes that middlebrow art, like legitimate art, is the product of professionals, but that it derives from 'competition for conquest of the market' and that it is linked with the 'self-censorship' of the writer so as to appeal to the average reader (1993a: 125–6).[15] The middlebrow and the work of 'pure art' are twins: both reveal a similar focus on professional technique and the logic of pure art leads the artist as much as the writer of popular fiction to by-pass serious economic and political issues (1993a: 128).[16] My suggestion is that this is too restrictive a view of the middlebrow and that it risks contributing to the very reification of cultural divisions Bourdieu desires to expose.

The inter-war novels of writers such as Winifred Holtby, Margaret Kennedy and Catherine Carswell, even some of Daphne du Maurier's writing (for example, *Rebecca* (1938)), cannot be described in these terms. Many of these novels are organised around a critical view of social and sexual inequality. Some are structured by a (middle-class) radicalism, and by the pacifism and internationalism generated by the First World War (Holtby, Jameson, West, etc.), others, like the works of Du Maurier and Compton Burnett, are informed by a paternalist conservatism. These ways of seeing are encoded within pliable realist forms which sketch out the lines of an extensive totality, even while they may lack the coruscating dialogues or layered complexity of design of, say, Joyce's *Ulysses*. But as Alison Light has cogently argued, the 'historical squint' at canonical cultural élites has left aside other groups and obscured the ways in which such women writers were seeking to re-inscribe their own experiences of modernity within forms which were very familiar (1991: 8). High and low may thus share more than is at first suspected. Indeed, as in the writers above, the division between realism and modernism is itself one of the first classificatory victims of the critical encounter.

What if these so-called middlebrow novels represented also a repressed tradition of the new? Indeed, it is possible that they were suspect in literary terms precisely because, despite the freshness of their subjects, they sold well. What appears in the twentieth century as 'middlebrow' exists as the 'social novel', whose death Bourdieu describes in the face of the late nineteenth-century rise of modernism. These female authors do not inhabit a *literary* space. For the most part living outside the arenas of the traditional ruling class, lacking the metropolitan and country houses of the ruling élite, the education at major public schools, they also lacked the power to cross the magic boundary into art.

Many of these uncanonised novels have their origins in the great impulse towards radicalism of the inter-war period with its manifestations in the democratisation of education, the seizure of power at local level to extend popular housing and the feminisation of the public sphere through which would be extended to women the rational culture and choices of the bourgeois citizen. Thus, for example, Holtby's *South Riding* (1954 (1936))[17] is focused on 'the drama of English local government' and concerns the transition from the administration of the county by the feudal landed gentry ('whose God is order') to a new, bureaucratised progress. This is not the 'classless commonwealth of equals' which is the dream of both the heroine, a head-teacher, and her friend, a socialist printer. One narrative strand concerns the sense of loss at the destruction of hopes for 'a new order of government, planning dignity, planning beauty, planning Enlightenment' (1954: 126). But tradition no longer works either, its harsh loss signified by the rejection of the romance form, for the unfulfilled love between the gentleman farmer and the young head-teacher is cut short by his death: passion and social position are doomed to be at war. Nevertheless, *South Riding* is the story of a new drama being played out: 'daily revolutionising the lives of . . . men and women' yet 'part of the unseen pattern of the English landscape' (1954: 5). From the Byzantine complexity of local interests, some meaning is saved. A new village is constructed out of wasteland to rehouse slum-dwellers. The trained energy of educated women can be put to realistic projects. Declaring that 'I'm a spinster and, by God, I'm going to spin' (1954: 67), the head-teacher channels her formidable work ethic into creating a democratic secondary school. The ending celebrates her rejection of suicide as she turns once more to healing the severed high and low cultures of Yorkshire life. If she will not cheat the working-class scholarship girl with her love of Shakespeare, she will also encourage her pupils to enjoy 'the dogs, the speed-track, the films'.

In this context, the uncanonised voice of Rebecca West can also be remembered. In *The Judge* (1980 (1922)) she produced a narrative of infractions of patriarchy which has a tragic realism. Much as the warnings of a wise woman might, it serves as a double admonition, both to transcend 'the old sexual story' but – more strikingly – of the dangers of flouting the patriarchal law and community common sense. Told partly through flashbacks, its principal dichotomy is between the compliant woman (Ellen's mother) and the transgressive woman (her fiancé's mother, Marion), both profoundly damaged in different ways by their men and the gender order. The 17-year-old Ellen defines her mother as a good child who has never snatched – ' a specialist in disappointment' (1980: 193) – who has reaped only a harvest of respectable self-annihilation. She dies anonymously as number 93 in a public hospital gulag:

> [A]nd they looked for one moment into the long cavern of a ward, lit with the dreadful light that dwells in hospitals, while the healthy lie in darkness, that

> dreadful light which throbs like a headache and frets like a fever, the very colour of pain. This light is diffused all over the world in these inhuman parallelogrammatic cities of the sick. . . . (1980: 183)

But this novel principally concerns those women who fly in the face of the patriarchal sense of order. Ellen's lover, Richard, is an illegitimate child. His mother's sin was the infraction of his father's feudal arranged marriage for the sake of a more passionate alliance; defined socially, therefore, in terms of excess, her punishment exerts a horrific cost. Seven months pregnant, she is stoned by the villagers and barely survives without miscarriage: she is thus driven to seek refuge from further sanctions by a marriage of convenience with her lover's butler. After her son is born, this servant's duplicitous rape – a 'black sacrament' – produces another, unloved child who grows up indebted, unemployed, friendless. Marion herself exists through the concentration of every social impulse and sexual need into the love for her illegitimate son. The transgression of the normal patriarchal law creates an answering disharmony between the illegitimate and the legitimate sons. Richard, enjoying a surfeit of maternal love, possesses the flaw of contemptuousness beneath apparent heroism. As the recipient of devotion, he has the strength for the chemist's lonely, intensive work, and is rewarded with the highest scientific honours and a contract with 'illimitable power . . . over men and machines' (1980: 339). But even through his engagement he possesses a passion for his mother which approaches sexual intimacy. After her suicide, this erupts in fratricide and a pact of death with Ellen. Thus despite her feminist disavowal of both older women's trajectories – 'neither the dirty bed of gratification nor the harsh pallet of renunciation' (1980: 80) – Ellen is still destroyed by her love.

In these two examples, we can recognise powerful storytelling that can communicate to any intelligent reader. In explaining them it is possible to employ Bourdieu's own idea of symbolic domination, but to extend it towards a view of centre–periphery relations in which the periphery offers a different canon rather than being simply belated. The implications of Bourdieu's study of the modernist cultural fields can then be drawn out in ways that he has not yet pursued. Specifically, it is necessary to forgo the assumption that difference is always *detrimental to the periphery*, and to break with the kind of thinking in which everything new radiates from the centre. Castelnuovo and Ginzburg describe the older assumptions:

> In the case in which one comes to recognise different canons, these will hardly be examined in their turn except on the basis of the dominant paradigm, by a procedure which gives birth to judgements of decadence, corruption, qualitative decline, vulgarity. (1981: 58)

These writers have taken issue with this point in their study of medieval European art history, using as example the case of the 'active resistance' of the twelfth-century autonomous artists in the periphery at Chartres cathedral (1981: 60–1). They suggest instead that innovation has many sources and that it often springs from 'encounters of two cultures' (1981: 62), from changes of public or changes in the artists' region.

In both cases of peripheral writer mentioned above, the women lacked sufficient means to support themselves without writing for a living: they were not inheritors. Both West and Holtby had cultural capital: West had been educated at a good Edinburgh school, despite the genteel poverty of a family abandoned by an ex-army officer turned journalist. She herself took up journalism (for the *Freewoman* and *Time and Tide*), while also being the mother of an illegitimate son.[18] Holtby had an Oxford education at a time when this was still rare for women, just missing a First.

Holtby also possessed considerable social and symbolic capital: both her mother's and her father's family were long-established gentlemen farmers; she lived as a child on a farm of 900 acres in the East Riding of Yorkshire, which was (and still is) feudal, self-enclosed and clannish. The claims on her time demanded by a conscience trained by rural paternalism were later to conflict with the time for more aesthetic interests (Brittain, 1940), and the choice of a more accessible form for her writing perhaps springs from this same distance from egoistic individualism. Yet her family's life was also fundamentally changed by modernity in the form of an agricultural workers' strike which ruined her father financially and from which he never recovered.

This family trajectory of decline is overlaid by her own academic and professional success, as she became a headmistress, like her main protagonist. Holtby's writing was also mediated by an artistic group of educated Northern women, among them Vera Brittain, Phyllis Bentley and Storm Jameson, who acted as 'cultural accumulators', much as Bourdieu argues for the artistic habitus common to the Flaubert group in the second bohemia. Against the poets' colonies of Oxford, then, the distinctiveness of their origins and their feminism provided a sustaining wider identity for each writer.

Popular art and cultural distinction

The model of the cultural field that Bourdieu has adopted must be understood as a historical socio-analysis of the repressions of a culture and a society. It is a cultural theory delivered in an ironic mode and stripped of any prescriptive or valorising dimension. Bourdieu's aim, then, is to follow the Durkheimian *Rules*, that is, to make an objective analysis of judgements of aesthetic value, in other words, 'to classify the classifiers' (Durkheim, 1974: 87; Wolff, 1983: 48–9). In doing so, he proposes a theory of the nature of popular culture, characterising it solely by its ethical/political concerns, chief of which is the aim of integrating art and life. However, his studies of the historical genesis of art and literature have not yet elaborated on the *clashes over cultural value* in which some popular genres of writing are systematically excluded from the literary field, or their producers neglected. In contrast, within the parallel field of the critical analysis of religion, sociological studies of disputes have adopted a less restrictive approach. Troeltsch, for example, described sectarians' disputes with the Churches about theological and pastoral principles such as the nature of a poor church.

In Bourdieu's analysis of the art-worlds of capitalist societies, *there is no popular art* (1992: 83; 1993c). This view has been opposed most vigorously by Shusterman, who has accused Bourdieu of accepting too readily the dominant class's hostility to popular art, evident in the diatribes against kitsch in the works of leading American writers such as Gans and Greenberg:

> Bourdieu . . . rigorously exposes the hidden economy and veiled interests of the so-called disinterested aesthetic of high culture but nonetheless remains too enchanted by the myth he demystifies to acknowledge the existence of any legitimate popular aesthetic. (1992: 172)

Against Bourdieu, Shusterman has argued brilliantly for the claims of rap as a complex, politically responsive, popular art-form in the hands of its most talented performers. At best, he argues, Bourdieu's arguments about the absence of popular art apply only to French society and French cultural institutions, which may indeed have obscured the artistic expression of working-class experience. In fact it is clear that Bourdieu accepts the maturity of the popular arts in pre-capitalist societies, but that he denies the possibility of their existence within capitalist modernity. This position is at odds with other historians, notably American, who are increasingly unwilling to demarcate a stable, elevated tradition separate from degraded popular genres, arguing that such classifications are in a state of constant evolution (Levine, 1988: 241; Ross, 1989). The case of jazz in the United States offers further evidence for Shusterman's case. Jazz grew up precisely in working-class urban areas like St Louis, rather than in the pre-capitalist cotton fields of Alabama. It is a musical expression which depends equally both on tradition and on the prnciple of innovation and it is jazz that is at the root of much so-called commercial music (Ross, 1989: chap. 3). Yet when Bourdieu discusses jazz in the French context of *Distinction*, he refers to it solely as an area to which heresiarch bourgeois children take flight, seeking refuge from overcrowded areas of consecrated art. He argues further:

> We could say of certain populist exaltations of 'popular culture' that they are the 'pastorals' of our epoch. . . . As an inverted celebration of the principles that undergird social hierarchies, the pastoral confers upon the dominated a nobility based on their adjustment to their condition and on their submission to the established order (think of the cult of *argot* or slang and, more generally, of 'popular language', of the *passéiste* extolling of the peasants of old or, in another genre, of the glorifying descriptions of the criminal underworld or, today, of the veneration of rap music in certain circles. (Bourdieu and Wacquant, 1992: 83)

The rationale for Bourdieu's position derives from both Marxist and Weberian cultural theory (see, for example, Goldmann, 1964b: 56, who makes a similar dismissal of all popular literature). His approach differs from that of straightforward materialism in that he does not see financial barriers as the main obstacle to consecrated production. His argument can be summarised briefly.

First, the cultural producers of the dominant class have themselves produced a counterfeit popular art, for by attaching the label 'popular' onto their works, they can be credited with a distinguished disinterestedness (1984: 567). Thus in one dialogue with Bourdieu, it is argued that what is passed off as popular is in fact a *populist strategy*:

> [Interviewer, Didier Eribon] If every cultural practice is a means of creating distance (you even say that Brechtian distanciation is a distancing from the people), then the idea of . . . access to art for all, has no meaning. That illusion of cultural communism has to be denounced.
>
> [Pierre Bourdieu] I have myself shared in the illusion of 'cultural communism'. . . . My whole book [1984] argues that access to a work of art requires instruments that are not universally distributed. And consequently that the possessors of these instruments secure profits of distinction for themselves, and the rarer these instruments are (such as those needed to appropriate avant-garde works) the greater the profits. (1993c: 1)

There are echoes here of Marx's attack on Suë in *The German Ideology* (Colletti, 1977) for disguising his *Les Mystères de Paris* (1844) as a genuinely popular novel when it was the work of a middle-class professional writer. Bourdieu rightly notes Brecht's simultaneous identification with drama, repudiation of current consecrated culture and legitimating turn to the working class, but such little duplicities, of course, neither invalidate the plays nor prove the absence of a popular reception.

Secondly, there is a claim that the existing popular culture in bourgeois societies takes other forms than those of art, a view of which Williams in *Culture and Society* (1961) was the most notable exponent, although he was later to abandon it (1980: 213–32). For this reason Bourdieu argues that working-class culture can be brought to view only through practices that occur under the aegis of social science, and not through the industrial novel or, today, rap.

Thirdly, there is a pre-eminence of the professional in all forms of modern art, with the exception of naïfs, who lack any viable independent existence. Bourdieu's concept of artistic habitus and practice also depends on a model of the professional artist gauging his actions in the light of knowledge of the prior history of art. This model of practice relies, I suspect, on Bourdieu's tacit theoretical debt to Weber. Weber claimed that musical developments in the West had been structured through a radically anti-traditional organisation and technique, which were pioneered by professionals within the churches (1958). For example, in the Western religious and secular musical structures a revolutionary new harmonic system based on thirds and fifths had ushered in a contrapuntal polyphony, with its characteristic forms such as the fugue, sonata and symphony. But Weber's assessment of a rational progression of musical form was also blind to the new and traditional popular music which emerged autonomously alongside the main professional centres in the West and which, like jazz later, was to be increasingly recuperated within Western music. Bourdieu does instance cases of such recuperation, but his account lacks any adequate assessment of *what* is to be recuperated. This is a theory of parasitism in which the host organism has only a shadowy presence.

Bourdieu's position has certain justifications. There are enormous obstacles for painters and writers produced from within the working class. The simplicity of realist form adopted by writers with manual occupations can be explained precisely because this is most easily mastered in the absence of the time necessary to develop a literary habitus. Even within these terms, women's occupations and experience have only rarely been considered sufficiently dignified to merit the attention of readers (Corrigan, 1991). The 'proletarian' writing of Greenwood (*Love on the Dole* (1986 (1933)), Smedley (*Daughter of Earth* (1977 (1929)), Commons (*Kiddar's Luck* (1951)) and others conforms to a realism which is modelled on the autobiography, for precisely this reason. Indeed, in a view very similar to Bourdieu's, Roy Johnson has argued that there is only one British working-class novel which could be said to have any value in literary terms: Lewis Grassic Gibbon's *A Scots Quair* (1975: 94). In effect, Johnson is using an appeal to cultural capital to explain the absence of literary skills. Despite these apparent 'materialist' credentials in the stress on education and craft skills, Johnson's arguments (unlike Bourdieu's) seem to rest on élitist premises: both are ultimately too restrictive.

It is not that Bourdieu denies the existence of a popular *culture*, as will be readily grasped if his work on photography and on other forms of consumption is understood. It is rather that he regards socialisation into language as a socialisation into the recognition of symbolic power. The only circumstances in which such power is effectively subverted are in the tightly circumscribed areas in which the working class has an autonomous domain – in cafés, prisons and the underworld, where slang expresses 'a vision, developed essentially to combat feminine (or effeminate) "weakness" and "submissiveness" through which the men most deprived of economic and cultural capital grasp their virile identity and perceive a social world conceived purely in terms of toughness' (1991: 96).

Bourdieu's argument rests too much on a zero-sum formulation.[19] For despite these constraints of language, British historical studies have shown how independent cultures emerged in factories and mines, particularly where these have been located within a homogeneous community, or linked with workers' libraries. Even the existence of a *dominated* language cannot inhibit all popular artistic developments within it. Again, it is no accident that in Britain the richest of these developments have leant on the culturally rich vernaculars of the Scottish and Welsh (Ortega, 1982: 141). The training necessary to express such popular literary and artistic needs depends on the availability of some leisure, but not essentially on professional skills (see, for example, Becker, 1982; Levine, 1988; Moorhouse, 1991: 174, 180).

In brief, Bourdieu's arguments are powerful but finally unconvincing. It is mistaken to exclude from consideration the novels of miners (such as Lewis Jones, who wrote *Cwmardy* (1979 (1937)) in trade union meetings) or the autobiographical novels of Afro-American women such as Maya Angelou, who wrote her extraordinary *I Know Why The Caged Bird Sings* (1972) after full-time work as a bus-conductress. If the education of a Proust is the only possible twentieth-century equipment for writing, then not only the writing of working-class authors, but the writings of many young people, ethnic minorities – even the post-colonial novelists – would have to be dismissed: indeed the *absence of any discussion of youth culture*[20] is significant given Bourdieu's enormous span of subjects. Thus, in this respect, we should seek to explore the cultural field quite differently from Bourdieu, by challenging his category of 'entertainment' and leaving open the possibility that works of artistic value might appear outside the field of bohemia and modernism. In other words, we should develop the theory of plebeian intellectuals, so far only used by Bourdieu in the analysis of philosophy and fascism (see the discussion on Heidegger in chap. 1 above).

In Britain, we can trace one such line of descent, creating an alternative canon which is by no means a secure component of the Great Tradition, yet from which the popular romance, the detective novel and even the American dime novel have constantly drawn. The tradition of working-class novels began with the great unfinished *Sunshine and Shadows* (1849–50), by the wool-comber and architect of the Chartist Land Plan, Thomas Wheeler. Although its lack of an ending suggests an uneasy rupture with more orthodox devices of narrative closure, its harsh images of the confining nature of early industrial capitalism, its redundant and harried artisan hero, its extraordinary dystopia of cottonopolis and metropolis show the working class becoming for the first time the subject of its own literary experiments. Wheeler's novel is at the furthest pole from the enclosed, almost parochial class realities of later industrial fiction. It creates an epic perspective on the colonial world arena, as in the vivid narrative of transportation to the West Indies where the hero sees the substitution of one form of unfree labour (indentured) for another (slavery), and reflects on the similarities between the Caribbean worker and the British factory-worker.

The best-known of this tradition is Robert Tressell's *The Ragged Trousered Philanthropists* (1965 (1914)), in which a vigorous, Bunyanesque prose is deployed to undo the misrecognition of social reality sown in the minds of the 'philanthropic' housepainters by their tabloid *Daily Obscurer*. In the difficult path of wresting thought from common-sense the novel is used – with flat characters and immense objective detail – as sermons had been used to popularise Puritanism. Part of this relies on the caricatural assembly of minor characters so as to undermine the doxic respectability of the ruling class. Hence such figures as Sir Graball d'Encloseland (the squire), Slyme (the slavish model worker), Misery (the foreman who delivers work known to be shoddy), Rushton, Didlum and Grinder (the decorating firm) and the Church of the Shining Light (an organisation for hypocrisy and mystification), all of whom derive from the long plebeian habit of cocking a snook at authority. *The Ragged Trousered Philanthropists*' greatest strengths are in its depiction of its central figures' degradation of labour – the worm in the bud of craft skills. Owen, its housepainter hero, is the living embodiment of an ideal of workmanship but condemned to forgo the exercise of his knowledge. In particular, the novel reveals the paradox of a global system of communication which makes available to workers Persian and Indian designs, but at the same time denies their capacity to develop or reproduce them. Hence the poignant pleasures of decorating the Moorish room for an exceptional customer where the creative side of his skill can be shown. The division of labour and decline of craftsmanship had been described many times, but it has been rarely expressed with such inner passion before.

Lewis Grassic Gibbon's *A Scots Quair* (1993 (1932–4)) is justifiably the most securely consecrated of these fictions, not least for its depiction of the 'elimination of the Scottish peasantry' in *Sunset Song*. But it is also technically ambitious, for Gibbon's use of classic realism is intertwined with modernist techniques, such as *Cloud Howe*'s polyphonic voices. Its power derives from the complexity of its vision, and especially from the conflict between the naive belief in progress of its youthful factory labourer and the cyclical peasant stoicism of his country mother, creating an unresolved and dialectical tension within the novel.

The limited canonisation of Gibbon should not distract from the wealth of other working-class novels – using modernist and realist devices, both pessimistic and visionary. In terms of the current interest in cultural hybridity, an earlier generation of powerful migrant authors should be remembered: James Hanley, for his Liverpool/Irish novels (*Boy* (1931) or *An End and a Beginning* (1990 (1958) for example); or Patrick MacGill for his novel cycle *Children of the Dead End* (1980 (1914)), *Moleskin Joe* (1980 (1915)), *The Rat-pit* (1983 ((1915)) and *Glenmornan* (1983, (1919)), a composite picture of the 'fistic' culture, the hopes, and above all the stoic resilience of the Irish navvies whose historic contribution was to build the reservoirs, railways and hydroelectric works of Scotland. It also tells the story – to illuminate, to advise, to warn – of the Irish women hired in gangs for Lowland potato picking and more selectively for sexual services. Written at a time when 17,000 women were reckoned to be prostitutes in Glasgow alone, *The Rat-pit*, especially, reveals the traps specific to female migrant workers, the links binding manufacturing and sexual wage-labour.

The novels of diaspora, proletarianisation and work have been largely the products of men. For this reason, Ethel Carnie (Holdsworth)'s *This Slavery* (1925) is unusual. It centres on women workers in a Lancashire textile mill. Their experience is conveyed through the story of two sisters: Hester, who enters a loveless marriage to a mill master, and Rachel, who becomes a strike leader. At the climax, as the workers starve in a bitter strike, Hester unexpectedly retails news gained confidentially from another employer; thus, despite her own death, she helps the strike succeed. In this novel, it is a woman, Rachel, who criticises the economistic narrowness of many trade unionists, and Rachel who reads *Capital* and dreams. Less lyrical but more compelling than her dreams are the novel's small realist details, of women's tiredness, for example, or of hunger: 'We seem to do nothing but talk and think about grub. . . . Our bodies get in the way. We're a set of pigs kept grovelling in the ground.' Or again, in ironical reflections on workers' endurance: 'To starve quietly, unobtrusively and without demonstration, is perhaps the greatest art civilisation has forced on the masses' (1925: 190).

It appears that Shusterman is right when he argues that in Bourdieu's sociology of art there is no possibility of canonising existing popular culture. But this is not because Bourdieu rules out a priori such a possibility. It is more likely to be due to the better-entrenched 'nobility of culture' in France than in Britain or America. To this extent it could be argued that in his cultural theory Bourdieu has been partially 'captured' by dominant ideology himself . Bourdieu's classification of the cultural field – like Goldmann's before him – leans too much on the values of the priestly or mandarin strata. It must problematise these further. In doing so it should further reveal the objective force that such values acquire in the distinction between high and low culture, operating so as to censor out classifications of popular genres and authors in terms of literary value. It might thus reveal further the relationship between plebeian intellectuals, folk history and folk dreams, already broached by Bourdieu in his theory of working-class culture and carnival. For, as Ricoeur (1994) has suggested, from these texts, too, there is generated an important source of the social 'imaginary' or utopian hopes.

Conclusion

Bourdieu fails to ask whether the lower survival-value of women's texts might not be symptomatic of their lesser capacity to represent themselves rather than be represented, as Said has concluded is the case with Orientalism. A major achievement of feminist literary theory is to have shown how women's texts have been excluded from the arena of consecrating activities. Due to somewhat different mechanisms, the similar exclusion of the literature of labour has necessitated its periodic recovery (Klaus, 1982).

I have challenged Bourdieu's view that in capitalism it is impossible to find popular art alongside the literature of the dominant class and gender. Rather than argue that it is only after a revolutionary transformation of schoolteaching that working-class children will have the tools for deciphering art, I want to claim that the production of such artistic texts exists already, but in a hidden and unconsecrated manner. For this reason, popular and women's writing is doomed to be seen as 'ethical' or 'political' rather than literary.

Notes

1. In this respect, Bourdieu deepens the historical study of Lukács, who had shown that realism represents in literature the experience of a transition from peasant or feudal societies to capitalist ones and that realism in Russia (Tolstoy) or Norway (Ibsen) occurred later because of the uneven development of capitalism.

2. Bourdieu does not comment on the impulses to parricide which male domestic tyranny also provokes (1992: 175).

3. The Vorticist journal, *Blast* (1914–15) was also the site of anti-semitism, containing Pound's lines 'Let us be done with Jews and jobbery,/Let us SPIT upon those who fawn on the JEWS for their money' (quoted in Dasenbrock, 1985: 88).

4. The metropolis was the centre of migration. Indeed, London had more Scots than Aberdeen, more Irish than Dublin and more Catholics than Rome in 1890 (Bradbury and McFarlane, 1976: 180). Paris, with its art-loving expatriates, lodgers and unstable households, was already showing the cracks in both extended and nuclear families as early as the 1880s (Herbert, 1988).

5. One of the attractions of Cook's first package holidays in the 1850s in Britain was that they offered single women the possibility of travelling abroad (Urry, 1990: 24).

6. For these purposes I am adopting the definitions of modernism proposed by Brecht and Lunn, which emphasise the importance of defamiliarisation by means of form (Lunn, 1982: 2 and chap. 2).

7. I cannot assess the situation in France, but the writing of Monique de Saint Martin has suggested that the first generation of French women intellectuals (Weil, de Beauvoir, etc.) possessed considerable cultural capital themselves, and had families who were both well educated and moved in artistic circles. The downward economic mobility of their families appears to have been an experience they shared, permitting the pioneering daughters to continue their studies (Saint Martin, 1990). This may also have been the case in Britain.

8. This statistic derives from the data-base of the *Dictionary of National Biography* in the University of Glasgow.

9. Information on the gender distribution of *applications* is excluded from these reports.

10. Unsurprisingly, the beneficiaries had occupations within the liberal professions and especially within lecturing or teaching, rather than employment in manual or petty-bourgeois jobs (McGuigan, 1981: 63–4). Similar *backgrounds* for writers have been shown in France (Charle, 1981: 12).

11. For analysis of the growing feminisation of the cultural field, see Collins (1989) and Zukin (1988).

12. It should be noted that the criteria for selection are not made entirely clear. Writers in the popular genres are quite properly not excluded for this reason alone, but they are sometimes included simply because of their personal following or historical interest rather than on literary grounds (for example, Ngaio Marsh, Enid Blyton). However, this only affects at most 29 or 19 per cent of the 155 writers in this period.

13. In these cases, the occupations of the writers' fathers are not specified with precision in Todd's biographies.

14. Information is not yet available for a comparative assessment of male writers.

15. Q.D. Leavis herself identifies middlebrow novels with their possession of a 'herd instinct', characterised by their belief in social hierarchy and a distrust of art. However, she also proposes a category including Wilder, Cather and Priestley: respected middling novelists of blameless intentions and indubitable skill, 'thoughtful', 'cultured', 'impressive' but lacking interest for the highbrow reader (1979: 43). But Leavis also defended the 'proletarian' writing of Grace Lumpkin (Mulhern, 1979: 147). It is in the light of this heterodox judgement that we might challenge the apparent transparency of this distinction between middlebrow and art.

16. However, the middlebrow contrasts with aestheticist assumptions. More paradoxes exist: the 'logic of the dialectic of distinction is continually liable to degenerate into an anomic quest for difference at any price' (1993a: 117), while middlebrow publics may also read the great works of the past, although these are always much too old-fashioned and much too easily-accessible to 'prove' their cultivation (1984).

17. This was a Book Society choice for 1936 (Brittain, 1940: 409).

18. Of West, Shaw remarked: 'She could handle a pen as brilliantly as ever I could, and much more savagely' (quoted in Marcus, J. (1982) *The Young Rebecca*, Bloomington: Indiana University Press, p. ix).

19. There is a brief discussion of the nineteenth-century regional or industrial novel in *The Field of Cultural Production* (1993a), but it is subsumed under the category of 'entertainment', even if only ironically.

20. Paradoxically, Bourdieu's early reception in Britain was via Stuart Hall at the Centre for Contemporary Cultural Studies, where youth culture was carefully mapped.

7

BOURDIEU, THE POPULAR AND THE PERIPHERY

In this chapter, I want to situate further Bourdieu's view of the aesthetic of popular art. I shall argue that he has depended on a contrast between the popular and the cultivated which is rooted in his anthropological studies of Algeria and especially in his fine-meshed investigations of the peasant ethos, a perspective he also explored in the French rural context in *Photography* (1990c). But what is missing from all his work is a detailed feel for the nature of popular culture within urban modernity. I shall proffer some preliminary studies of writing which remedy this deficiency. These will differ in time and space, but they are attempts to explore the 'mysteries of the city' within the novel or autobiographical form.

If Bourdieu is unjustified in calling Kant a formalist, he is more plausible when, describing his aesthetic condemnation of the 'facile' or the 'charming', he reads this as a systematic opposition to popular taste. The 'distance' from the real removes the possibility of any simple, commonly shared emotions or ideas. Equally, the remoteness from emotion that characterises second-order interest in form or style is celebrated for its *rarity*. Taking Kant's denigration of the 'sensual' and 'agreeable' as a denial of the claims of ethnic or community arts, the Kantian conception of the beautiful is criticised in *Distinction* as based on a presumptuous claim to identify the truly human or universal art.

The popular aesthetic – in Bourdieu's view – 'can only invert the relationship which is the basis of the aesthetic sociodicy by a strategy of reduction or degradation, as in slang' (1984: 491). Bourdieu reconstructs the anti-aesthetic of popular taste in an ideal-typical fashion, that is, in opposition to the aesthetic. The dominated class *rejects* in art anything that is too concerned with *form or stylisation*. If the aesthetic incorporates a Cartesian impulse towards radical doubt, popular taste avoids anything that transgresses community beliefs and hallowed moral attitudes. Recalling the Academy's old hierarchies of importance which had ranked subjects of public importance over domestic interiors or still life, popular judgements profoundly question the portrayal of trivial subjects for the sake of experimental form-languages. For naive taste is perceived as engaged seamlessly with 'life' itself: the inventive arrangement of colour and shape (or narrative and dialogue) is always subordinated within it to the objective of questioning and crystallising dilemmas of practical action. This aesthetic honours the collective impulse to celebrate the feasts and festivities which spice ordinary lives. It seeks to encapsulate social hopes. But popular distrust of the powerful also surfaces in the myriad ways in which the contemporary great figures are debunked and reminded of their material bodies or specific interests. Popular works embody a conditional and utilitarian aesthetic; that is to say, their choice of images is powerfully determined by their interests or conception of social needs (see 1990c: 87).

The field of symbolic goods

Cheap fiction – romances, science fiction and thrillers – are all part of production of luxury goods and therefore exist on the wider field of cultural production. Since they lack marks of distinction, they are doomed to be pulped quickly by the publisher. In exploring this field, Bourdieu throws out a few fascinating comments on popular fiction. First, he notes that, unlike the couturier's aspirations to create art, the writer of popular fiction is free of the legitimate hierarchy. Chandler's explicit disavowal, as a mystery story writer, of any interest in the 'cult of the classics' exemplifies this. Such a writer, Chandler states, need not dwell in the shadow of the past (Bourdieu, 1975b: 17). However, the popular can be reincorporated into legitimate discourses by a 'thesaurisation' process:

> [T]o the degree that the Western enters into history, the history of the Western enters into the Western itself, producing some that are no more than literary games with historical references. The scholarly system itself is entwined with popular forms at this stage, either by supplying writers with scholastic capital en route to the genre's canonisation, or by supplying consumers with certain cultural competencies [who] . . . amuse themselves with risky investments. (1975b: 19)

So the process of social alchemy that in the field of couture can turn an object into art by the magic of the couturier's label has its equivalent in popular fiction. An authorised reader, radiating distinction, can recuperate the works of popular writers. Similarly, the young of the dominated fraction of the bourgeoisie can transform even flea-market goods into art by embracing them with a bohemian nonchalance that transforms poverty into creditable originality (1975b: 8).

In brief, within the huge field of symbolic goods, value is related to the time a product lasts or its felt durability, criteria which are intricately linked to the distinction of either producers or consumers. Initially – but only initially – the survival value of such goods is dependent on the choices of those with symbolic rather than economic capital. The exceptional instances of the canonisation of works with a popular base are described by Bourdieu as part of this same logic.[1]

However as already noted – this theory is like a net that catches a certain size and type of fish. In being fashioned to focus on the importance of the aesthetic attitude, Bourdieu provides very little detail about the works that were popular amongst both educated and uneducated audiences at an earlier historical moment, prior to modernism – Mozart's opera, for example, or Dickens' novels. Further, despite his schematic comments above, there is very little exploration of popular genres themselves in contemporary societies. Yet the recurrent history of the novel is of authors driven to defamiliarisation so as to reveal personal or community experience or make a political point, rather than for the sake of the artistic device alone (Tolstoy being perhaps an extreme case) (Armstrong, 1987; Medvedev and Bakhtin, 1978: 61). Bourdieu has hardly started the work of mapping the contemporary field of popular culture in these terms, but rather assumes a priori that all popular culture will be devoid of formal interest and written with withered ideological matrices. I am thinking of the complex range of ideological references which give the comics of Robert Crumb their depth, or the powerful depictions of class and sexuality in a handful of Catherine Cookson's novels.

Finally, as Bourdieu outlines its underlying relations, the field is skewed politically across a Left–Right axis, so that the dominated pole of legitimate works is associated with the Left, and bourgeois art with the Right. In fact, the different political magnetic fields that operate in the popular arts have hardly been charted. The traditional political divisions do not capture the nature of the concerns of popular art. In the period since modernism, cultural forms have been artificially fragmented into 'torn halves': 'high culture' has been concerned with representations of alienation and estrangement, while popular culture has been the site of representations of community and love. Yet within the genres of the latter – and for all their retention of specific denigrated forms – there sometimes persists an interest both in critique and in resources for hope, not least through the reaffirmation of ideal laws of social behaviour (Bloch, 1986; Jameson, 1981: 287-99).

I shall now assess less abstractly some of the facets of such popular culture. Where Bourdieu evokes only pub songs, stand-up comics, circuses and holiday photographs as popular embodiments of alternative communal genres, I shall look at both the fossilised and more inventive or complex types of popular writing. In particular, I want to address this writing in relation to its *representations of urban life*. To a degree that intellectuals might find surprising, popular writing has as an important theme the nature of communities and their history. Particularly given the crises of working-class reproduction or the decline of the 'red neighbourhood' – to which Bourdieu also alludes – it is helpful to view these stories as offering phenomenological experience of the changing texture of civic life. For this is envisaged as a framework for individual 'belonging' or dependence as well as for free development through the urban public sphere. The metropolis is therefore the object of both pride and criticism. Such writing often foregrounds the nature of women's experience and it is evident that for many writers in the texts that follow there is a concern to record a folk memory of the treatment of women which is too often ignored in standard histories. Moreover, it is perhaps symptomatic of the crisis of modernism that dilemmas of narrative technique are often circumvented by the adoption of a different cultural mode, that of working-class autobiography or the narrative forms closest to it, organised around the learning processes of a central character. Yet I shall contest the view that within these writings historical events can simply be read in terms of nostalgia, despite the fact that this is a common explanation of other 'theatres of memory', such as industrial museums (see, for example, Urry, 1990: 130). I shall argue instead that such popular documents often become most powerful when they seek to uncover the 'mysteries of the city', and that they can therefore be allied with the critical realism of the canonised novel form.

The aesthetic representation of place in popular writing has been explored through works which derive from different periods and different social positions within modernity. The following is a mapping exercise which starts with Bourdieu's positioning of popular writers in terms of a functional aesthetic – a concern with political/ethical questions rather than art. But I want to encourage a more sensitive and nuanced analysis concerning the nature of such cultural documents, much as Ginzburg does when he investigates the precise nature of the contact with written and oral influences in the case of a sixteenth-century religious sceptic: the miller, Menoccio, later the victim of the Inquisition (1980: 33).

The older family sagas and romances of women's magazines still survive. These serve the purposes of a technology of forgetfulness as much as a technology of remembrance (Benjamin, 1973b). In other words, along with the pleasures of melodrama, the aesthetics of necessity depend upon retaining unquestioned certain stock ideological motifs. In England, this has depended upon a symbolic elastoplast in which the injuries of class are healed through an imaginary invocation of a rural arcadia. In Scottish writing, there had emerged through the nineteenth century a provincial or 'kailyard' literary tradition typically relying on images of harmonious social relations. Such portrayals highlighted the personal bonds within an idealised small town, where the forms of collective deprivation and loss envisaged in the industrial city are prevented. As heir to this, the invocation in Emma Blair's *The Sweetest Thing* (1993) of a 1920s and 1930s small-town intimacy depends upon a well-worn contrast between the ultimately benign fate of an impoverished working-class family, who are the beneficiaries of the gentry paternalism of the country town, and the perpetual job insecurity, family disorder and chaos experienced by workers in Glasgow. It starts, like a fairy-tale, with loss and lack, delineating the destruction of a united family through the early death of a miner and the unhappy consequences for both his children and his widow of her precipitate and unsuitable remarriage to a horse-dealer. A Scottish *Hamlet*, however, is forestalled in favour of narrative devices that are both familiar and reassuring. In particular, a crucial magic helper is introduced as a *deus ex machina* in the figure of a Liberal laird whose need for servants ensures the end of the family's economic troubles. The ending also follows the 'Damascus'-like conversion of the philandering horse-dealer. It is his renewed and gentler affections which save his wife.

But even through such atrophied conventions, some lines of new interrogation still surface. In *The Sweetest Thing* (meaning 'love'), the central realist passages reconstruct with indignation the paradoxes inherent in the hidden relations of gender and especially the savagery of supposedly civilised society towards unmarried mothers. Having slept once with a boyfriend who goes off to sea, the pregnant 15-year-old twin daughter is denounced from the pulpit for her infraction of official community morality. The lapse is translated into the act of a 'moral defective' and, despite her family's active support, the culprit becomes subject to incarceration and discipline within a State asylum (Blair, 1993: 177). In effect, this narrative focuses on the legal switch from government *through* families to government *of* families (Donzelot, 1980). Using overt representations of the provisions of the 1913 Scottish Mental Deficiency and Lunacy Act, the story relates the submission of the pregnant girl to hard labour and to the forcible administration of ECT after the birth, events which are followed by her suicide. Within the stock formulaic narrative, an unexpected vigour and passion is produced about the treatment of a vulnerable minority of women. The narrative action is organised in part through a critique of Calvinism, and especially of the asceticism that leads one protagonist, the town's Presbyterian minister, to crush the object of his own disavowed sexual yearning by denouncing her to the authorities. Moreover, the unusual subject for a popular novel provokes certain connotations. Not least, it serves to raise questions about the State's interests in the 1990s concerning its policies for single mothers.

For Emma Blair, Glasgow is 'The City of Dreadful Night'. Yet popular narratives have also been premised on much more complex and ambiguous views of the metropolis. Partly as a limiting case, I want to take the much earlier representation of the immigrant Jewish community in the early 1900s: Israel Zangwill's almost forgotten *The Children of the Ghetto* (1909). This poses a particularly interesting contestation of dominant individualist perspectives in two main respects. First, it presents employment and wealth as fundamentally discrete from wisdom, scholarship or intellectual ability. Secondly, the celebration of family and community integration in this narrative severs the narrative convention in which love is linked to marriage.

The novel reveals the nature of Jewish life in the East End of London where Jews were taking refuge from Polish ethnic cleansing. It represents the process of capital accumulation in the ghetto itself, with one fraction becoming a class of employers and building bridges to the wealthier English Jewry outside the ghetto, while the other becomes a proletarianised (or subproletarian class). It reveals also the collective consciousness of the community, shaped by a patriarchal Law and by a division of labour still deeply imbued with pre-capitalist assumptions. In essence, it is a narrative revolving around the intense conflicts within the community as to the degree to which they should now cling to a Law and culture that has set them apart as 'a peculiar people' (1909: 1). For the novel is basically organised around the realist project of explaining the community to the implied reader, who is not him- or herself Jewish but who is rather clearly envisaged as a Christian or non-religious outsider. At the same time the novel has a hegemonic agenda of its own, in that its closure implicitly underlines orthodoxy. Zangwill's text takes on the role of pastoral advice which a wise woman might proffer for internal consumption.

Its known community encompasses the whole of the ghetto, focusing especially on two families, those of a Rabbi (Reb Samuel) and those of an unemployed worker (Moses Ansell). It is their vicissitudes that are most closely followed. These are partially material struggles for survival as Moses' ineffectual attempts at hawking reduce his motherless daughter Ethel, and his other infants, to perpetual anxiety about bread and fuel. But they also revolve around political and moral struggles over the degree to which Jews should continue to uphold the old order of the Law. This theme underlies the dilemma of the Rabbi's beautiful and able daughter, Hannah, who is married with an engagement ring in a mock betrothal by a playful friend, Sam Levine, intending to taunt his fiancée. An old guest proficient in the law discloses the contractual reality of the marriage jokingly performed. Although Sam and Hannah discover they can be divorced, when Hannah falls in love with David Brandon, a Cohen (priest), the divorce returns to haunt her, for a Cohen is forbidden to marry a divorced woman. Reb Samuel, who reveals this horrific prohibition, is, on the one hand, called to keep both the letter and the spirit of the law, but, on the other hand, knows that he dooms his daughter to terrible unhappiness by forbidding her marriage. David Brandon persuades Hannah to elope with him for America where his identity as a Cohen will not be known. Hannah agrees and the narrative seems to be one in which the individuals' rights – enshrined in the ethic of romantic love – will prevail over older orthodoxy. Brandon, a lax Jew who is nevertheless not amoral, puts forward powerful arguments about the need for the law to change to fit new conditions of social existence. But with the approaching Feast of the Passover, Hannah is wracked by her conscience, deciding silently to reject the invitations of her lover to leave. When he calls for her outside the house, she shuts him out, shouting to her parents that the noise is only 'a rough Christian' outside the door.

Perhaps deliberately disrupting the received traditions of European Romanticism, for Zangwill, it is the lover who is seen as the tempter and the father and patriarchal social order which is necessary and just. Thus the Jewish community is represented as inside the order of necessity, the Name of the Father, the good, while the lover is represented as outside, lax (a 'link Jew') – his situational ethics rejected as the slippery slope to relativism. He is portrayed as the voice of a baleful *ressentiment* – the ungracious rebel, pretender for the father's power. Ultimately, then, Hannah sides with orthodoxy and the detailed requirements of community existence. This alone, she discovers, has allowed the Jews to retain their pleasures – of food, visual richness, synagogue chants and purim balls – together with their traditional moral laws, providing a sustaining culture which enfolds within its bonds of acceptance even those in the most extreme material misery. Thus the Jewish nomos is defended against the various heterodoxies thrown up by capitalism (accepting Sabbath work etc.) and modernity. The second strand around the vicissitudes of the hapless Ansell family amplifies this point, showing the beauties of communal life that are available to lighten the poorest with both fasts and feasts, while linking these to Messianic hopes. The novel begins with a motif of loss as little Esther spills her soup-kitchen broth; it ends with Esther being given charity to buy her family Passover fried fish. In its stress on doctrinal rigour the novel reflexively links its own perspective to the intense religiosity of the poor: turning centrally to their activities in the ghetto and away from the 'lax', more assimilated English Jewry. Its principle is unswervingly ethical, as Bourdieu suggests is the case with popular culture. Hence its distanced portrayal of the Zionist poet whose bohemian ego is disclosed ironically through its fissiparous consequences, and hence, also, its sympathetic portrayal of the factory-workers' leader, whose socialism is viewed as the intellectual inheritance of traditional Jewish concepts of solidarity. Given this logic, it is no accident that only those who attempt to change their social position by breaking with the ghetto meet tragic fates.

Zangwill's novel presents a conservative critique of aspects of modernity, despite its insistence that the 'wise man may go in rags' and its careful portrayal of scholarly and talented men who cannot feed their families. Yet it complies with an inherently Enlightenment project in its aspiration to record all the debates that rocked the ghetto. And it is this fidelity to the precise character of the contemporary arguments that enables the reader to refuse the authorial viewpoint and which therefore links the novel form to the sceptical rationality attributed to it by Bakhtin.

The autobiography lends itself to the same concerns about the nature of cities. A characteristic of recent popular literature is its dual focus – a desire to explain what it feels like to live in poverty but also to explain the particular lived experience of working-class girls. If some of these autobiographies provide the same sort of 'objectivation' of the effects of unemployment and poor housing as do good interviews (compare Bourdieu, 1993b: 903–25), it is because this is a world absent from contemporary literary fiction, for reasons described in Bourdieu's account of the high–low divide.

Helen Forrester's memoirs (1995) of Liverpool in the 1930s focus on the city from the perspective of the third of its inhabitants who were unemployed. It is the childhood she lost as the oldest girl that still rankles. This is nevertheless a sharp description of the material basis of experience which insists on a minute inventory of all the apparatus of poverty. We note the abrupt list of meagre provisions which she would have issued to the poor: the comb, because this could never be afforded, the newspapers that would serve triple functions – as bedding, warm underclothes and as handkerchiefs – and so on. Or the pithy comment that the poor possess nothing and so have enormous amounts of free time. Throughout the narrative there is an oscillation of perspectives that is in itself both an index of realism and a sign of symbolic violence – the author insistently emphasises her difference from the local working class through her Oxford accent, which struck the discordant note with her dishevelled and ugly appearance and provides the same measured and gracious tones for the representation of family dialogue. For this is a tale of the catastrophe that strikes a middle-class family and – perhaps in part because of this – reveals the world of the poor more sharply as a world of continuous exclusions. Unwanted by the Church because of her appearance, denied access to free museums because of the pram, banned from night school by the younger children's needs – in effect the public sphere has become inaccessible:

> The Oxford accent coming from the bundle of rags and bones like me must have really puzzled him. It had not, however, impressed the commissionaire and given me entry to the museum. So much for the public cultural emporia. (1995: 135)

Her father's old school tie fared rather better. It is this that finally evokes an esprit de corps between ex-pupils and which thus opens the door for recruitment to a clerical job.

Finally, the autobiography can take the form of the 'mysteries of the city', the modern equivalent of the 1840s American dime novels. Within its structure, the full nature of the ghetto is revealed only gradually, as the story takes on a detective form. The narrator of Meg Henderson's *Finding Peggy* (1994) becomes a female Sam Spade, whose archaeology of the city becomes also a struggle to reveal the buried experiences of stigmatisation. Concerned with recording the subjective meaning of living in degraded enclosures, Henderson deploys for her dialogues forms of working-class speech. In this respect she radically delegitimises the genteel element that continues to cling to Helen Forrester's autobiography. Although it has nothing in common with the heroic industrial novel of the 1911–40 period, which points to the culmination of community struggles over production, it shares with it the same urgency to create representations of figures who have so far existed only outside literature. In this respect it could be considered under the heading that Bourdieu (1993b) uses to describe his project of interviewing: it is a tool of collective auto-analysis. Hence the fondness of local readers for their regional authors. The shelves of Glasgow literature in libraries and bookshops are not just a provision for tourists but also derive from a desire to discover oneself through a historical sense of space (see Public Lending Right statistics).

Finding Peggy is structured in part around the story of the heroine's alcoholic father and her strong 'earth-mother', constantly waging war with bureaucrats for the sake of her neighbours. A minority of a minority as a Catholic and a skilled worker, the father is an artisan in the dying trade of shoe-making. He is out of touch with the new, an embodied memory of past ways of doing things, who is perceived by the author as a failure. Although he is a force pulling the mother down – and the image of his falling drunkenly into an unmade hole in the road typifies this most graphically – there is only an absent hero to take his place. Perhaps as a rupture with the outdated romance, the reader is provided with a photograph of the author's husband, but his personality and work are left unspecified. Her heroic quest for self and family discovery is therefore accomplished painfully alone, taking the place of the odyssey of the young man in folk-tales.

The whole focus of the novel is to provide what might be called the socio-genesis of a wrecked clan. To further objectify the autobiographical author, it might be added that she escaped into the expanded middle class at a period when there was some upward mobility available through work even for those, like her, whose education was blocked by enforced domesticity. Yet her own survival is only etched out more clearly in the context of the city and the ruins of the whole family network. The story proceeds from the reconstruction of the lost past and especially of the entry into the city of the wayward farmer's son together with the Ulster bacon-curer and Dundee weaver's daughters who made up her family: a clan divided by the Protestantism of her mother's side from the Catholicism of her father's. She inherits this contempt for the 'wild Irish pigs' (as her grandmother calls her father's relatives) but preserves secret respect for their ingenuity, their capacity for entertainment and enjoyment. Within the mother's family, a further division between the 'fair yins and the dark yins' created a binary opposition within the heart of the child's world, transcended only by the unity of the competitive games played mentally by the whole family against outsiders, proving their superiority. Within this rooted inner-city family, too, the rituals and close solidaristic ties are shattered by the economic vicissitudes of the clan. Using a common motif of disintegration, *Finding Peggy* starts abruptly with the literal collapse of the immediate residential community of family and neighbours in the inner-city tenement and its resettlement on a more fragmented basis in the post-war city housing schemes. But in this case the enclosure is Blackhill, 'a ghetto replacing a ghetto', contaminated by its proximity to the prison and polluting gasworks. The search for a way out of the ghetto turns out to cost the inner solidarity of the clan. For her mother's quest to both right the wrongs of others and to improve her family's lives through moves to better housing schemes had inadvertently left her sister vulnerable to an untrustworthy husband and hostile environment.

The heroine looks back from her escape to the wasted lives connected with hers – her aunt, dying tragically aged 37 in childbirth, and her mother, as a consequence, becoming depressed, mad and dying early herself. The narrative quest of the mature 'I' is to discover the repressed events that the family had hidden and, not least, the cause of her aunt's death. The truth that emerges is one that shows the interconnections of the whole city, low and high. The novel expresses the nature of class experiences not through the point of production but through the forms of consumption and status.

Popular literature often uses as a device the debunking of pretentiousness and cynical awareness of professional interests. Unravelling Peggy's early death means unmasking those who keep distasteful episodes hidden. Thus the heroine, now a medical technician, must take on the medical profession, the apex of the local power. She does so at first in comic mode, inducing a pleasure allied to carnival release as she describes the severity with which she tells off an orderly who is interfering with her ECGs, only to discover that he is the new professor of orthopaedics. The second assault is tragic, as she confronts the whole armoury of a cohesive occupation as it seeks to first cover up, then exonerate those involved in her aunt's unnecessary death. Confronting the GP responsible for the birth, she discovers that a medical student had taken his place at the time of delivery: later, that the student had 'butchered' the woman and that family members had been bribed to keep silent. Most shocking of all, she learns from the ranting doctor in his salubrious drawing-room what she had already gleaned at work, namely that a profound form of ethnocentrism exists in which the people of Blackhill are written off as vermin, equivalent to Jews for Nazis. For his was a rhetoric which systematically reduces the social to the natural and caricatures a whole community in Darwinian terms as composed only of those with low intelligence, high fertility, murderers and thieves (Henderson, 1994: 280). What shines through after the various rationalisations of the botched-up event have been discredited is this overwhelming 'racism of class', to use Bourdieu's phrase. Thus the end of the novel possesses the same kind of conclusion that Hammett's *Red Harvest* does: this event has been hauled to the surface, but the causes that set it in motion are still present. 'Then you'll have your city back, all nice and clean and ready to go to the dogs again', says the detective in Hammett's *Poisonville* (1982: 181): *Finding Peggy* reveals the same putrid opposition at the heart of the city.

It is common to refer to the museumisation of the past and the other signs of the heritage industry as providing a false set of banal signifiers which obscure and mask the nature of historical reality (Urry, 1990; Wright, 1985). In the sense that this popular literature of community might be understood as the inferior, banal and commodified form of high culture, equivalent to costume history or Georgette Heyer romances, it might be taken as the literary equivalent of the latest tourist 'sight'. However, as Urry has recently argued, the preservation of fragments of the past may have a different function and be put to different practices (1995: 7). The same might be said of the popular novel. It operates as a site for ideological perspectives but also for preservation of certain important folk memories. The sociologist might then see these texts as revealing important perceptions of the subjective experience of class, not least its hidden injuries. We can learn from the novel not just the nature of the 'imaginary community' of nation (Anderson, 1983), but also about the imagined local community, against which the actual community reveals its deficits. In general, we might take issue with Bourdieu when he dismisses all popular literature of this sort as populist, and seeks the sociological interview alone as the locus of the democratised hermeneutic (1993b: 923). The popular novel may be entirely formulaic or it may, despite its conventions, provide a phenomenologically enriched understanding of the world. It needs only the sociologist to complete its significance, by providing an objectivation of the author. This task has yet to be fully undertaken in the instances above.

Modernism within the periphery

Bourdieu has drawn attention to the formalist aesthetic of the metropolitan centres of advanced capitalism and disclosed its origins within the deracinated, educated bourgeoisie. He has not studied closely, however, those contexts *within the periphery* where the older communal concerns of art lingered on. The Scottish Renaissance was one such movement. This broad grouping of writers active in the inter-war years – Sorley MacLean, Hugh MacDiarmid, Neil Gunn, Lewis Grassic Gibbon and Naomi Mitchison – operated as a group sharing similar interests in the political fate of Scotland and in the need for a nationally autonomous, democratic and non-capitalist social order that would supersede the insecurities of employment and sharp inequalities of the time. To varying degrees, they were modernist in their interest in new technique: MacDiarmid's conversion to Scots in 'The Watergaw', along with significant works by James Joyce and T.S. Eliot, leading some to christen 1922 the *annus mirabilis* of modernism (Crawford, 1992: 261). The Scottish group themselves were often intensely critical of each other and were devoid of the game-like aesthetic playfulness that Bourdieu has noted in the institutionalised avant-gardes of the restricted field.

The reason lies, I suggest, because of the uneven development of the periphery, the memory of pre-capitalist forms within the experience of these writers and the availability of an older model of 'bard' or 'seer' (Nicolson, 1992: 4). In other words, the restricted or educated field lacked the *distance* from the popular field that was found in Paris. As a consequence the position in the field of power of these writers was different. Where Andy Warhol was partying in the 1970s with the 'rich' (amongst them princesses, the New York and Dublin bourgeoisie and the 'tin king of Bolivia' (Warhol, 1989: xv, 18)), Hugh MacDiarmid was still living a meagre existence in a country cottage (he died only in 1978). Equally, Lewis Grassic Gibbon and Neil Gunn died young and uncelebrated, while Naomi Mitchison, despite her position as a member of the Scottish progressive intelligentsia and her activity as a laird, had to wait for her 96th year for any acclaim. Thus although these writers are now in the process of canonisation, most or all of their lives were lived as unconsecrated figures.

In certain respects their Scottish radicalism aligned them with the deracinated dominant class of the Parisian avant-garde. Like them, they were anti-academic, anti-Christian and anti-bourgeois; they attacked the preceding literary generation (especially the late nineteenth-century Scottish writers of the kailyard school) and stood aloof from contemporary mass culture. Amongst these writers were those who possessed the self-image of a suffering Old Testament prophet. MacDiarmid, for example, lashes the whole Scottish nation with warnings as to the wrong paths it has taken ('A Drunk Man Looks at the Thistle' (1926). This could certainly be interpreted as a narcissistic strategy of distinction. Yet his egoistic misanthropy is also a self-protection for a poet who is only just surviving, forced to live off orange-box furniture. Hence MacDiarmid's alliance with the dominated ('Highbrowism plus Communism'), on which he comments: 'The interests of the real highbrow and the working-class are identical' because both have an interest in resistance to intellectual short-circuits. It was particularly at the outset of the Second World War that he developed most clearly his equivalent to a theory of active practice (1943: 336; Cribb, 1983: 93).

This was a transitional generation of poets and novelists, living in rural areas,[2] who wanted to redeem the lost or dying low cultural vernacular of the Scottish regions, against the monopolisation of the high culture terrain by English. In the subsequent generation the city location of Scottish writers, especially in Glasgow, Paisley and Renfrew (Tom Leonard, James Kelman, Alasdair Gray, etc.), was to allow them to turn to living vernacular forms. They thus avoided the opacity of vocabulary which characterised Hugh MacDiarmid's initial turn to a synthetic Scots, a poetic language which was stripped of the English of the élite, but stripped, too, of any substantial links with the urban population of the twentieth century. This was an experimental stage which he was to abandon for a more widely comprehensible 'Englished Scots' (MacDiarmid, 1943: 31).

It was a fate that Gunn, Mitchison and Gibbon bypassed by dint of mixing Scots and English or that was solved by MacLean with dual versions of his poems. MacLean, for example, wrote in Gaelic for the then-declining native Gaelic-speaking constituency in the Islands but also wrote for a wider readership with his English translations. It was thus a specifically avant-gardist cul-de-sac that trapped MacDiarmid when he went down the route of using an etymological dictionary to revive words, which he then 'swallowed whole', on occasion letting the logic of the dictionary dictate the logic of the poems (Buthlay, 1989: 193). It was through such linguistic changes that MacDiarmid freed his writing of stock romantic imagery. He also initially differentiated himself by these means from an older generation of Scottish poets, such as the more influential John Davidson, who had developed an English that would register the rigours of existence for Greenock ship-builders and 'thirty-bob-a-week' clerks. It was Davidson, the ex-chemist, who had drawn MacDiarmid towards a 'poetry of fact' that would encompass the developments of the natural sciences (Lindsay, 1961: 22, 49).

This is not the place to develop an extended analysis of MacLean or of MacDiarmid's Caledonian Anty-Syzergy (a synthesis of 'extremes'), his alternative to the diluted Burns who was served up to an arrogant and self-vaunting bourgeoisie on Burns Nights. MacDiarmid represented an extraordinary combination of Lowlands Scottish folk culture and Calvinism, but also Russian, French, German and other European poets read in the original, not least the avant-garde. Moreover, he was intolerant of any notion of two cultures, developing a range and power that is missing in his earlier, lyrical Scots modernist poems. Further, he developed a fraught and critical relationship with political organisations. A founder member of the Scottish National Party (MacDiarmid, 1943: 43), he had the distinction of having been expelled from both the Communist Party for nationalist deviations and from the SNP for his communism. Even more against the grain of other Left intellectuals, he rejoined the Communist Party precisely at the time that the Moscow leadership was ordering tanks into Budapest. But through all his twists and turns, naivety and misanthropic egocentrism, MacDiarmid retained a set of broad public concerns that differentiates his poetry sharply from the tone and especially the paternalism that permeates his 1930s English contemporaries, whom he reviled as public school Marxists, mystics and lightweights (1943: 167–70; see, for example, the poems on pp. 300–1 and 319).

Sorley MacLean similarly directs his poems at the tragic repercussions of the Scottish Clearances, and the depopulation and decline of a culture, as well as at the Spanish Civil War, the deaths of soldiers in Egypt in the Second World War, and the Easter Rising. MacLean is able to reproduce the historical consciousness of the Highlanders – and especially the voice of the male crofters who have been left behind after the waves of emigration. His poems possess a grandeur and epic depth which resemble those of the poets of rural Algeria (Bourdieu, 1961).[3]

Finally, I think it is important to note further, also with Bourdieu in mind, the uncharacteristic social origins for these poets. Robert Crawford has recently aligned MacDiarmid with the marginal figures who have moved from one continent or nation to another to make their mark within modernism: Joyce, with his similar use of demotic languages, 'nigger English', etc.; Pound as the 'wild boy of Wyoming'; Eliot from the urbane East Coast of America to London (Crawford, 1992: 263). This misses the distinctive *structural location* of the most significant of the Scottish Renaissance writers. MacLean is a schoolmaster's son (the grandson of a protesting crofter) from the small island of Raasay, who lived among his family in Skye for many years. Grassic Gibbon was the child of tenant farmers. MacDiarmid's relatives were weavers and farm labourers, his father was a postman; his and Grassic Gibbon's origins are thus not too distant from the artisan realists of the second bohemia (Bourdieu, 1992: 111). Moreover, MacDiarmid grew up in the Borders town of Langholm, which itself represented an active front of resistance to English culture (MacDiarmid, 1943: 3). From Langholm, he possessed the general democratic culture, rooted in a radical anti-gentry strand of Calvinist thought, but which was inherited in his own family from parents who were set apart by their seriousness. The library of Thomas Telford, the engineer, was immediately at hand for MacDiarmid as a boy; poetry became simply what he was good at, just as a carpenter might be skilful with his hands. We should note also the aberrant *reception* of the poet, for unlike the strategies of distinction that placed poets of bourgeois origins under some compulsion to look for distinguished readers, as an ex-teacher, MacDiarmid's reputation was made perhaps as much by his supporters in the EIS (teachers' union) through their *The Scottish Educational Journal* as by his literary godfathers – A.R. Orage and John Lehmann (Kerrigan, 1989: 182). Lastly, it was only his extraordinary *material circumstances* in Shetland (living in a virtually rent-free cottage) that allowed him to remain a poet on a poet's income.

In brief, MacDiarmid was both a proletarianised intellectual and a miraculous survivor. Like the others within the Scottish Renaissance group, his poetry has to be understood not just simply in terms of its bearers within the industrial city but also through its links to an underdeveloped or declining commercial section of the economy. The colonial linguistic context was simultaneously alienating and empowering: forcing creative mixtures (Crawford, 1992: 105). The history of both the 1920s and the 1980s West of Scotland writers' movement suggests that Bourdieu's accounts of the symbolic violence exerted in dominant linguistic markets are unduly restrictive about the potential for the survival of alternatives.

Notes

1. For a challenging alternative view, see Lovell (1987: 100–2), who argues that the literary survival value of women writers must be explained in terms of their authorship of more than one work, their skill in appearing to avoid or mask didacticism, and, lastly, their capacity to address their works to a readership wider than that of women; a woman-to-man discourse rather than a woman-to-woman discourse.
2. Gibbon was an exception, despite his country childhood.
3. See especially 'The Island' (1991: 59), 'The Cuillin' (1991: 79–81), 'The Ship' (1991: 29–35), 'Dogs and Wolves' (1991: 135).

CONCLUSION

Bourdieu's project has been shaped over the years to show – as Marx had done earlier – that the bourgeois theory of the market equality of individuals veils the existence of social distinctions. The field research on which *Distinction* is based reveals that supposedly natural or individual tastes are in fact founded on social constructions which have been elaborated over generations, through the habitus. Where Marx had analysed only the inequality of the capital/labour contract, Bourdieu has shown the re-emergence of inherited distinction in the different relation to both pedagogic knowledge (cultural capital) and the area of artistic production and consumption. He has challenged meritocratic beliefs with a theory of cultural legitimation based on the fact that, in becoming the spiritual core of bourgeois individuality, art and literature have become sacralised. The adornment of such consecrated knowledge enhances the dignity of the person, leaving those deprived of it with an internalised consciousness of ignorance. Baudelaire remarked that the bourgeoisie would be enormously strengthened if they possessed not only money but knowledge (1972: 47). Bourdieu shows that this has in fact come about.

Bourdieu has developed a theory of practice and a concept of the habitus which is adequate to the complexity of social reality. Whilst grounded on the dull material compulsion of everyday economic needs, this approach addresses a realm that goes beyond the ideological battle into the arena of doxic assumptions that are 'written on the body' itself. In my view, this theory of practice does provide us with a genuine advance over preceding social and cultural theory in that it is rigorously determinist, yet it also conceives of agents as active, transformative figures. It is thus entitled to the use of the term 'practice', which has an honourable descent from Marx's *Theses on Feuerbach*. Bourdieu's synthesis rejects either objectivist or subjectivist alternatives, much as an important line of cultural theory has refused the choice of either of the two paradigms, structuralism and culturalism, in the period after Althusser. Like Williams' cultural materialism, Bourdieu's theory is irreconcilably opposed to the total colonisation of the subject by ideology, as in Lévi-Strauss's structuralism, and it is the critique of this 'new idealism' that he makes in his 'work of the break' (1968), which sought to reintroduce the agent's practice (see Boyne, 1993). Like Giddens, he became deeply critical of 'the lost harvest' of structuralist promise (Giddens, 1987: 195). Both sociologists take from historical materialism the significance of space and time in social life (Giddens, 1981) and have criticised structuralism for its over-reliance on Saussurean linguistic positivism as a model of linguistic transformation and social action. But Bourdieu provides a more fertile soil for sociology than structuration theory. It saves the best aspects of Lukács' Hegelian Marxism but fuses it with a much more elaborated notion of socialisation. In particular, Bourdieu maps anthropology onto historical materialism to give a fuller account of culture. It is thus no accident that some of the most brilliant of his insights into the restricted field of art recall the Bakhtin/Voloshinov school and its work of criticising formalism (Medvedev and Bakhtin, 1978).

Bourdieu is concerned to carry what he calls this 'troublemaking' practice of sociology into the most intimate and seemingly private areas of collective life, such as the family photograph taken by the father of the peasant family. In order to do so he will need to assess the distinctive characterisations of art that emerged initially with Romanticism. These are the charismatic theory of authorship, the autonomous character of the artistic/literary field and the notion of the fresh eye. I have argued on this that Bourdieu's questioning of the cultural field and its typical ideologies is important, although he has not yet provided a sufficiently rich and detailed account of the nature of popular art-forms. However, his view that the 'illusory' beliefs in authorship are simply this society's 'magic' is more contentious.

It is now possible to weigh up the gains and losses in Bourdieu's attempt to dissect, through phrases like 'the invention of the artist's life', the nature of bourgeois art-worlds. Bourdieu's skill is in revealing the hidden prerequisites for active participation in legitimate art in the period after 1850, not just the possession of a high degree of educational capital – ensuring a 'code of codes' – but also a specific location in space and time. He shows convincingly that the objective consequence of the commoditisation of literature and the increasing number of the 'literary proletariat' was the segregation of the culturally well-endowed authors from the rest, within a restricted field.

Bourdieu has commented in his account of pre-capitalist Kabylia that peasant practice has to be grasped in terms of cosmological classifications of time and space. In his work on the development of modernism he has also focused on time: he writes of the social ageing of modernist movements as they move from heterodoxy and rupture to consecration, of the permanence of artistic revolution, of the transience of judgements of value, such that those, like Cladel and Champfleury, who lack the artistic perspective to seize the moment in the competitive struggle have to flee, beaten, to the country. In other words there is here a phenomenology of avant-gardes which is based on lived time, with its strange oscillations between the speed and contingency of shifting judgements and the eternal consecration for the 'creators' (see, for example, 1993a: 52–3).

This same phenomenology of time is used in the work on contemporary class realities where Bourdieu (1974) develops Bachelard's theme of the 'causality of the probable'. Elegantly avoiding both finalism (voluntarism) and mechanistic determinism, he develops the notion that the habitus of each individual is regulated by the probable fate of the group. Their habitus ensures that the dominant class alone experience time as endowing them with a secure future. Against them, he contrasts both the subproletariat (especially of migrants), who have no future and who respond by giving themselves up to dreams and to the fatalism of natural fertility, and the petty bourgeoisie, who, still experiencing the moral rigour of early ascetic Puritanism, contrive literally *to make themselves small* in terms of size of families and appetites in order to undergo their project of an upward trajectory. Condemned to a present of the constant striving for the future, they experience also the loss of their past, since it is this striving that will alone dominate their memories. In contrast, and with relevance to modernism as well as finance and science, the haute bourgeoisie can afford to speculate, to risk 'everything' – since precisely in being secure they will *never* risk *everything* (1974).

In describing the post-1850s division of the field, Bourdieu delineates also an ideology about art that defined it rhetorically as the opposite form of production from that based on instrumental rationalisation. In other words, he has outlined a discourse about high and low in which 'art' or 'serious writing' *de facto* excluded both producers and consumers from the dominated class as part of the logic of a minority culture.

By reconstructing the historical genesis of art for art's sake, Bourdieu reveals that this became a classification of immense power. He understands it to have the same level of pervasive acceptance as other social classifications that became entrenched in the same period, such as 'scientific' racism (Orientalism, anti-semitism, etc.), which were only contested by exceptional minorities. Because it was a generally shared social representation of culture it was irrelevant if one or two critics refused to define art in terms of style and an educated culture, or if a handful of artists had non-élite origins, as in the case of James Joyce or D.H. Lawrence. A realist portrayal of a mill town such as Ethel Carnie's *This Slavery* (see chapter 6) was ineligible to fit the category 'art'. Because the discourses of art and literature were based on rarity, they were, in his view, closed to participation by the subordinate classes. Consequently popular culture could only exist within this moral economy as a 'reverse ethnocentrism', by which he means that popular 'art' signalled a magical liquidation of the nature of the relations between the classes underlying dominant classes' concern for style (1971: 1373).[1] I have challenged this view of high and low by revealing what it left out, although Bourdieu may reject such critical investigations as failing to take account of the symbolic power of such social classifications.

Bourdieu's alternative to the charismatic magic of creation requires substituting a theory of *refraction* for the the liberal individualism implicit in sacralised art. His socio-analysis demands that the author should be seen as subject to social determinants, deriving from his or her position within the cultural field, the amount of social, economic and cultural capital he/she possesses and the trajectory experienced within a specific family. Rather than portraying art as the outcome of a mystical experience, the artist is engaged in a series of struggles to make a mark. 'Natural' distinction is now revealed to be the appearance of an artistic agent who is most endowed with a knowledge of the history of the field, and for whom a good fit exists between the structure of the works and the perspective of a category of consumers (1993c: 143–4).

Such an approach permits an explanation of art which is remote from the idealising conception of the ideology of art. One of its merits is that it insists on attributing material and professional interests to artists, thus undermining the trope whereby the working class only have material and sectional interests while the middle class have ethical objectives. A further merit: Bourdieu sees the artist in his/her active practice as no longer merely the site for the play of discursive forces, in contrast with the Foucauldian version of authorship. He is therefore persuasive when he envisages this science of literature and art having emancipatory consequences:

> [P]aradoxically, sociology frees us by freeing us from the illusion of freedom, or, more exactly, from the misplaced belief in illusory freedoms. (1994a: 15)

However, Bourdieu goes beyond refraction to an *extreme disenchantment* derived from a tragically neo-machiavellian view of the working of social mechanisms. It is this which has provoked resistance. Such resistance, he acknowledges, has its origins in the fact that the author gives voice to *universal interests*, even though, historically, artistic alliances with the dominated classes have been so fragile. This is an important concession. For Bourdieu's disenchantment is too radical, in danger of always effacing moments when artists may bear witness to the truth so as to highlight only how they use artistic works for status purposes or accommodate to power. I have argued that we need also to see some artistic movements as being the modern equivalent to a poor church. Rather than throw out the baby with the bathwater in an unremittingly tragic view of the logic of consecration, we need to ask for how long and under what circumstances do groups of mature artists serve the role of disclosing the real (Habermas, 1987) or acting as a critical subculture (Crow, 1985)?

I am also less convinced by Bourdieu's wholesale 'vulgar' critique of Kant. It does seem to me that we can keep a modified sense of genius even if this conception has to be rethought so as to bypass Kant's own retention of élitist and masculinist assumptions from the court tradition. Here we might transfer into art the account Bourdieu (1987b) himself gives of religious prophetic movements, which, he argues, become possible once *social needs* have created the suspension of everyday life. Of course, the art-worlds of such charismatic prophets or geniuses also have other social pre-conditions – material necessities, a minimal use of conventions or artistic rules, collective structures of support (Becker, 1982).

Much of the shock of *The Rules of Art* comes from the radicalism with which it approaches modernist artists' interests in distinction. Artists' groups are treated rather like skilled industrial workers striving to retain their conditions of life by demarcation rules and restrictive practices. In their case, these are transmitted through the institution of art in the form of increasing the cultural capital for entry (esoteric language, the cult of spontaneity), the tactic of denying the social world (as in the adoption of the psychological novel (Huysmans) or the Symbolist painting (Redon)) and the dangerous anti-bourgeois strategy of 'flaunting . . . convergences' between the political vanguard and the artistic avant-garde (while actually maintaining a prudent sense of distance (1993a)):

> Members of the dominant class appear distinguished because, being born in a distinguished position – their habituses – their constituted social nature – is immediately adjusted to the immanent demands of the game and they are thus able to affirm their distance from others without having to do so, that is to say, with the naturalness that is the mark of the distinction called 'natural'. (1987a: 21–2)

By such means is the reader cruelly shaken out of the 'love of art' in which art had become the spiritual 'soul' of the bourgeoisie. It was with precisely the same revulsion that artists in Berlin, before the destruction of the Wall, came at night to paint a long yellow horizontal line through the graffiti which was increasingly becoming celebrated for its own sake. 'The Wall is not about Art', they scrawled.

However, in the face of an undiscriminating aesthetic populism, which conflates commercial and aesthetic considerations, it is perhaps time to re-evaluate this stance.[2] I suggest, then, without wanting to return to Romantic ideology, that it is now necessary to emphasise once more that artists are still potentially the prophets of late bourgeois society. We can thus restore to them (in a less idealising manner) the significance of 'bringing newness into the world', of daring to criticise when others keep quiet and of giving shape to those anticipations of the future that are based on a feasible utopia (Bloch, 1986; Ricoeur, 1994). This means taking further some of Bourdieu's brief comments on cultural production within the periphery and from less well-represented groups within the terrain of 'art'.

In other words, my anxiety with Bourdieu is that he remains too close to the Althusserian sense of institutional ideology, with its passive view of authorship. We need to propose a more active sense of the author as possessing in his or her artistic practice the capacity to (partially) see through and develop the great cultural discourses of his/her period. It would be a paradox if the work of sifting through popular genres for distinctive products ('frail fetishes') were to be abandoned out of a dislike for the bourgeois humanist individualism of auteurism. In searching for a solution to this I want to stress the *potential* of Bourdieu's logic of practice. For within Bourdieu's own theory of social agents there is a conception of the skilled nature of all human agents which applies also to artists (1990a: 55). We can emphasise the historical genesis of the artist but also his/her strategic choices – just as Williams stressed the need to look at an active composition as well as the conditions of composition, at the structure of feeling and the lived experience which shaped that activity as well as the hegemonic ideas.

I have argued that the literary terrain was one that the working-class writers themselves saw as a site for the crucial struggle over representations: first, in Wheeler's eyes, to cancel out hostile images of 'the democrat in warpaint' and then to create new and fertile forms to foster Chartist ideas. It is this dissident internal transformation of culture for quite different popular ends that Bourdieu does not theorise. A similar case can be made about middlebrow fiction by women writers (chapter 6), a more surprising gap given his earlier illuminating study of photography as a middlebrow art (1990c (1965)). In other words, he weakens his description of both the restricted and the expanded field by systematically neglecting those junctures at which literature and art acquired an emancipatory consequence. If we are to regard literature and art as a cult which neglects or even neutralises the extraction of vast amounts of surplus-value from the dominated class and peoples, we need also to look at the way its 'magic' can be stolen for other purposes. In particular, we need to study those networks camped outside the gates of the consecrating institutions. Furthermore, Bourdieu appears to make the institution or field too pervasive if he does not admit that there can be 'literature' and literary critics who have broken with formalism. In this sense, Bourdieu, Baldick and others influenced by structuralism have overemphasised the degree of ideological insulation and integration within the autonomous art-world and underemphasised the different practices elsewhere. Lamont's astringent criticisms about the limits to the sacralisation of art and its effects are worth recalling in this context, as is the fact that, en route to consecration, art has not always been the product of small enclaves but has frequently debated popular ideas and has often created a popular following.[3]

Bourdieu's work, I suggest, is neither élitist, nor relativist, as has sometimes been claimed (see Lash, 1993). However, it does have some weaknesses, which are the obverse of its strengths, and these have been the focus of the case-studies. A more specific criticism of the kind outlined already has been raised by Bürger, who has quite rightly attacked Bourdieu's *Distinction* for its view that the work of art is merely a form of fetishism (see 1984: 250: 'culture might be devoid of intrinsic interest'). Bürger contends that the modernist canon has been the creation of dissidents. It is noteworthy that in fact Bourdieu has amended his formulation in later works to defend the 'frail fetishism' of these works, while insisting on a genetic analysis. Bourdieu is approaching a Durkheimian explanation of canonised art, in which he conceives of it in terms similar to the analysis of religion in *Elementary Forms*. I am reminded in his recent response (1992) of Durkheim's view that

> religious thought is very far from a system of fictions, the realities to which it corresponds can still only be expressed in religious form when transfigured by the imagination. (1995: 367–8)

In his latest arguments, then, Bourdieu may be tacitly conceding that *Distinction* overemphasised the formalist character attributed to the consecrated canon and may instead seek to see art and literature as the main area of struggle over social representations.

As Bourdieu's work has progressed, he has held out less and less hope that the cultural sphere might contribute to further democratisation. Although his initial works emphasised radical pedagogy, his later work views authentic popular culture as the product of social research itself or as restricted to small enclosures. However, despite his understandable refusal to engage in prediction, his theory of practice already suggests junctures at which love of one's fate – working-class *amor fati* – no longer holds. In particular, the new model of domination premised on market consumerism is only feasible so long as expectations do not depart too savagely from real experience, and there is reason to think that this situation has already been reached in many inner-city areas. It is at this point that artistic and literary texts could be put to quite a different use. As Bourdieu has emphasised, material struggles are not just the product of material conditions but are also the outcome of beliefs (1983: 2). Artists still play an important role in effecting those beliefs and legitimating those struggles, even in an era of a shadowy transnational capitalist class.

It is this concern with the suspension and production of belief that is the organising principle of Bourdieu's sociology of culture. For if his subjects can understand reflexively the mechanisms that create the reproduction of the haute bourgeoisie, which he has himself exposed, these determining forces will lose their effectiveness.

Notes

1. For the same reason, rejection of the formalism inherent in production within the restricted field often served merely as another form of reverse discourse. In this respect, the aesthetic populism of some recent critics shows the symbolic violence exerted by the former by simply turning it on its head.

2. Bourdieu himself may be re-evaluating it, too: see his dialogue with the artist Hans Haake, in which they discuss the changes in the field of power in America and the removal of subsidies for certain types of art (1995).

3. As representatives of popular literature, Bunyan, Defoe, Richardson, Balzac, Dickens and Tolstoy can all be mentioned, but the total list is much greater.

BIBLIOGRAPHY

(All publishers are in London, with the exception of Polity (Cambridge) and those specified beneath)

Works by Pierre Bourdieu (single-authored)

Bourdieu, P. (1961) *The Algerians*, New York: Beacon.

Bourdieu, P., with Darbel, A., Rivet, J.P. and Seibel, C. (1963) *Travail et travailleurs en Algérie*, Paris: Mouton; partially translated as (1978) *Algeria, 1960*, Cambridge, Cambridge University Press.

Bourdieu, P. (1966a) 'The Sentiment of Honour in Kabyle Society', pp. 191–242 in J.G. Peristiany (ed.), *Honour and Shame*, Chicago: University of Chicago Press.

Bourdieu, P. (1966b) 'Champ intellectuel et projet créateur', *Les Temps Modernes*, 22, fév.: 865–906.

Bourdieu, P. (1968) 'Structuralism and the Theory of Sociological Knowledge', *Social Research*, 35 (4), Winter: 681–706.

Bourdieu, P. (1971) 'Disposition esthétique et compétence artistique', *Les Temps Modernes*, 295, fév.: 1345–78.

Bourdieu, P. (1974) 'Avenir de classe et causalité du probable', *Revue Française de Sociologie*, XV: 3–42.

Bourdieu, P. (1975a) 'L'Invention de la vie de l'artiste', *Actes de la Recherche en Sciences Sociales*, 2, 67– 94.

Bourdieu, P., with Delsaut, Y. (1975b) 'Le Couturier et sa Griffe', *Actes de la Recherche en Sciences Sociales*, 1, 7–36.

Bourdieu, P. (1977) *Outline of a Theory of Practice*, Cambridge: Cambridge University Press.

Bourdieu, P. (1980a) 'The Production of Belief', *Media, Culture and Society*, 2: 261–93.

Bourdieu, P. (1980b) *Le Sens pratique*, Paris: Minuit (translated and revised as (1990) *The Logic of Practice*, Polity).

Bourdieu, P. (1980c) 'Le Mort saisit le vif', *Actes de la Recherche en Sciences Sociales*, 32–3: 3–14.

Bourdieu, P. (1983) 'The Philosophical Institution', pp. 1–9 in A. Montefiore (ed.), *Philosophy in France Today*, Cambridge: Cambridge University Press.

Bourdieu, P. (1984) *Distinction*, Routledge.

Bourdieu, P. (1987a) *Choses dites*, Paris: Minuit (translated as (1994) *In Other Words*, Polity).

Bourdieu P. (1987b) 'Legitimation and Structured Interests in Weber's Sociology of Religion', pp. 119–36 in S. Lash and S. Whimster (eds), *Max Weber, Rationality and Modernity*, Allen and Unwin.

Bourdieu, P. (1987c) 'The Force of Law: Towards a Sociology of the Juridical Field', *Hastings Journal of Law*, 38: 209–48.

Bourdieu, P. (1988a) *Homo Academicus*, Polity.

Bourdieu, P. (1988b) *The Political Ontology of Martin Heidegger*, Polity.

Bourdieu, P. (1988c), '*Vive la Crise*! For Heterodoxy in Social Science', *Theory and Society*, 17: 773–87.

Bourdieu, P. (1989) *La Noblesse d'état*, (*The State Nobility*), Paris: Minuit.
Bourdieu, P. (1990a) *The Logic of Practice*, Polity.
Bourdieu, P. (1990b) 'La Domination masculine', *Actes de la Recherche en Sciences Sociales*, 84: 2–31.
Bourdieu, P., with Boltanski, L., Castel, R., Chamboredon, J.-C. and Schnapper, D. (1990c) *Photography: A Middlebrow Art*, Polity.
Bourdieu, P. (1990d) 'Les Conditions sociales de la circulation internationale des idées', *Romanistische Zeitschrift für Literaturgeschichte*, 14 (1/2): 1–10.
Bourdieu, P. (1991) *Language and Symbolic Power*, Polity.
Bourdieu, P. (1992) *Les Règles de l'art* (*The Rules of Art*), Paris: Seuil.
Bourdieu, P. (1993a) *The Field of Cultural Production*, Polity.
Bourdieu, P. (1993b) *La Misère du monde* (*This World of Suffering*), Paris: Seuil.
Bourdieu, P. (1993c) *Sociology in Question*, Sage.
Bourdieu, P. (1994a) *In Other Words*, Polity.
Bourdieu, P. (1994b) *Raisons pratiques* (*Practical Reason*), Paris: Seuil.
Bourdieu, P. (1996) *The Rules of Art*, Polity.

Co-authored Works by Pierre Bourdieu

Bourdieu, P. and Darbel, A., with Schnapper, D. (1991) *The Love of Art: European Art Museums and their Public*, Polity.
Bourdieu, P. and Haake, H. (1995) *Free Exchange*, Polity.
Bourdieu, P. and Mammeri, M. (1978) 'Dialogue sur la poésie orale en Kabylie, *Actes de la Recherche en Sciences Sociales*, 23; 51–66.
Bourdieu, P. and Passeron, J.C. (1964) *Les Héritiers*, Paris: Minuit; translated as *The Inheritors* (1995) Chicago: University of Chicago Press.
Bourdieu, P. and Passeron, J.-C. (1990) *Reproduction in Education, Society and Culture*, Sage.
Bourdieu P. and Saint Martin, M. de (1978), 'Le patronat', *Actes de la Recherche en Sciences Sociales*, 20–1: 3–83.
Bourdieu, P. and Sayad, A. (1964), *Le Deracinement: La Crise de l'agriculture traditionelle en Algérie* (*The Uprooting: The Crisis of Traditional Agriculture in Algeria*), Paris: Minuit.
Bourdieu, P. and Wacquant, L.J.D. (1992) *An Invitation to Reflexive Sociology*, Polity.
Bourdieu, P., Chartier, R., and Darnton, R. (1985) 'Dialogue à propos de l'histoire culturelle', *Actes de la Recherche en Sciences Sociales*, 59: 86–93.

Other works

Abercrombie, N. and Urry, J. (1983) *Capital, Labour and the Middle Classes*, Allen and Unwin.
Abercrombie, N., Hill, S. and Turner, B. (1980) *The Dominant Ideology Thesis*, Allen and Unwin.
Adorno, T. (1973) *The Jargon of Authenticity*, Routledge.
Adorno, T. (1996) *Aesthetic Theory*, Athlone Press.
Alverman, D. (1960) 'Algeria over France', *New Left Review*, 6, Nov.–Dec.: 36–46.
Anderson, B. (1983) *Imagined Communities*, Verso.
Anderson, P. (1984) 'Modernity: An Unfinished Project', *New Left Review*, 144, Mar–Apr: 96–113.
Anon., (1960) [No title] *Les Temps Modernes*, Aug.–Sept.: 193–7.
Apollonio, U. (1973) *Futurist Manifestos*, Thames and Hudson.
Armstrong, N. (1987) *Desire and Domestic Fiction*, Oxford: Oxford University Press.
Arts Council for England and Wales (1981–91) *Annual Reports*, London.

Arts Council for Scotland (1983–4) *Annual Reports*, Edinburgh.

Baas, J. (1985) 'Edouard Manet and *Civil War*', *Art Journal*, 45, Spring: 36–42.

Bakhtin, M. (1968) *Rabelais and His World*, Cambridge, Mass.: MIT Press.

Baldick, C. (1983) *The Social Mission of English Criticism*, Oxford: Clarendon Press.

Balibar, E. and Macherey, P. (1981), 'On Literature as an Ideological Form', pp. 79–99 in R. Young (ed.), *Untying the Text*, Routledge and Kegan Paul.

Balibar, R. (1986) 'National Language, Education and Literature', pp. 126–47 in F. Barker (ed.), *Literature, Politics and Theory*, Methuen.

Battersby, C. (1989) *Gender and Genius*, The Women's Press.

Baudelaire, C.-P. (1972) *Selected Writings on Art and Artists*, Harmondsworth: Penguin.

Baudrillard, J. (1975) *The Mirror of Production*, St Louis: Telos.

Becker, H. (1982) *Art-Worlds*, Berkeley: University of California Press.

Benjamin, W. (1973a) *Charles Baudelaire: A Lyric Poet in the Era of High Capitalism*, New Left Books.

Benjamin, W. (1973b) *Illuminations*, Fontana.

Benjamin, W. (1979) *One-Way Street*, Verso.

Bennett, T. (1981) 'Marxism and Popular Fiction', *Literature and History*, 7 (2), Autumn: 138–65.

Berman, M. (1983) *All That Is Solid Melts into Air*, Verso.

Berman, M. (1984) 'The Signs in the Street', *New Left Review*, 144, Mar.–Apr.: 114–23.

Bernstein, B. (1975) *Class, Codes and Control, Vol. 3*, Routledge and Kegan Paul.

Bhabha, H. (1993) *The Location of Culture*, Routledge.

Blair, E. (1993) *The Sweetest Thing*, Bantam.

Bloch, E., Adorno, T., Lukács, G., Benjamin, W. and Brecht, B. (1977) *Aesthetics and Politics*, Verso.

Bloch, E. (1986) *The Principle of Hope, Vols. 1–3*, Oxford: Blackwell.

Blunt, A. (1970) *Art and Architecture in France, 1500–1700*, Harmondsworth: Penguin.

Bowlby, R. (1985) *Just Looking: Consumer Culture in Dreiser, Gissing and Zola*, Methuen.

Bowlby, R. (1988) *Virginia Woolf: Feminist Destinations*, Oxford: Blackwell.

Bowness, A., Gowing, L. and James, P. (1964) *54–64: Painting and Sculpture of a Decade*, Tate Gallery, *Catalogue raisonné*.

Boyne, R. (1993) 'Pierre Bourdieu and the Question of the Subject', *French Cultural Studies*, 4, 3 (October): 241–51.

Bradbury, M. and McFarlane, J. (1976) *Modernism*, Harmondsworth: Penguin.

Bredo, E. and Fineberg, W. (1979) 'Meaning, Power and Pedagogy', *Journal of Curriculum Studies*, 11 (4): 315–32.

Brittain, V. (1940) *Testament of Friendship*, Macmillan.

Brown, M.R. (1978) *The Image of the 'Bohemian' from Diaz to Manet and Van Gogh*, New Haven, Conn.: Yale University Press.

Brubaker, R. (1985) 'Rethinking Classical Theory: The Sociological Vision of Pierre Bourdieu', *Theory and Society*, 14: 745–75.

Brubaker, R. (1993) 'Social Theory as Habitus', pp. 212–34 in C. Calhoun, E. Lipuma and M. Postone (eds), *Bourdieu: Critical Perspectives*, Polity.

Buck-Morss, S. (1989) *The Dialectic of Seeing*, Cambridge, Mass.: Harvard University Press.

Bürger, P. (1984) *The Theory of the Avant-Garde*, Manchester: Manchester University Press.

Bürger, P. (1990) 'The Problem of Aesthetic Value', pp. 23–34 in P. Collier and H. Geyer-Ryan (eds), *Literary Theory Today*, Ithaca, New York: Cornell University Press.

Buthlay, K. (1989) 'MacDiarmid's Conversion to Scots', pp. 189–200 in H.W. Drescher and H. Volkel (eds), *Nationalism in Literature: Scottish Studies*, Verlag Peter Lang.

Calhoun, C. (1993) 'Habitus, Field and Capital: The Question of Historical Specificity', pp. 61–89 in C. Calhoun, E. Lipuma and M. Postone (eds), *Bourdieu: Critical Perspectives*, Polity.

Calhoun, C., Lipuma, E. and Postone, M. (eds) (1993) *Bourdieu: Critical Perspectives*, Polity.

Callinicos, A. (1989) *Against Postmodernism*, Polity.
Carey, J. (1992) *The Intellectuals and the Masses*, Faber.
Castelnuovo, E. and Ginzburg, C. (1981) 'Domination symbolique et géographie artistique', *Actes de la Recherche en Sciences Sociales*, 40: 51–72.
Caughie, J. (ed.) (1981) *Theories of Authorship*, Routledge.
Charle, C. (1981) 'Situation du champ littéraire', *Littérature*, 44: 8–20.
Clark, T.J. (1980) 'Preliminaries to a Possible Treatment of *Olympia* in 1854', *Screen*, 21 (1): 18–42.
Clark, T.J. (1982a) *Image of the People: Gustave Courbet and the 1848 Revolution*, Thames and Hudson.
Clark, T.J. (1982b) *The Absolute Bourgeois: Artists and Politics in France, 1848–51*, Thames and Hudson.
Clark, T.J. (1985) *The Painting of Modern Life: Paris in the Art of Manet and His Followers*, Thames and Hudson.
Clay, J. (1985) 'Ointments, Makeup, Pollen', *October*, 3–43.
Cockcroft, E. (1992) 'Abstract Expressionism as a Weapon in the Cold War', pp. 82–90 in F. Frascina and J. Harris (eds), *Art in Modern Culture*, Phaidon.
Codd, J. (1990) 'Making Distinctions', pp. 132–59 in R. Harker (ed.), *Introduction to the Works of Pierre Bourdieu*, Macmillan.
Colletti, L. (ed.) (1977) *Karl Marx: Early Writings*, Harmondsworth: Penguin.
Collins, R. (1989) 'Femmes, stratification sociale et production de la culture', *Sociologie et Sociétés*, XXI (2): 27–45.
Cork, R. (1994) *Bitter Truth: The Avant Garde and the Great War*, New Haven, Conn. and London: Yale University Press.
Corrigan, P. and Sayer, D. (1985) *The Great Arch*, Oxford: Blackwell.
Corrigan, M. (1991) 'Tales of Toil', *Voice Literary Supplement*, April: 19–20.
Cribb, T.J. (1983) '*The Cheka's Horrors* and *On a Raised Beach*', *Studies in Scottish Literature*, XX: 88–100.
Crane, D. (1987) *The Transformation of the Avant-Garde*, Chicago: University of Chicago Press.
Crawford, R. (1992) *Devolving English Literature*, Oxford: Clarendon Press.
Crow, T. (1985) 'Modernism and Mass Culture in the Visual Arts', pp. 233–66 in F. Frascina (ed.), *Pollock and After*, Harper and Row.
Crowther, P. (1993) *Critical Theory and Postmodernism*, Oxford: Oxford University Press.
Crowther, P. (1994) 'Sociological Imperialism and the Field of Cultural Production: The Case of Pierre Bourdieu', *Theory, Culture and Society*, 11 (1), Feb.: 155–70.
Dasenbrock, R.W. (1985) *The Literary Vorticism of Ezra Pound and Wyndham Lewis*, Baltimore: Johns Hopkins University Press.
Davidoff, L. and Hall, C. (1987) *Family Fortunes*, Hutchinson.
Debord, G. (1977) *The Society of the Spectacle*, Practical Paradise Publications.
Denning, M. (1987) *Mechanic Accents: Novels and Working-Class Accents in America*, Verso.
Dews, P. (1987) *Logics of Disintegration*, Verso.
DiMaggio, P. (1986) 'Cultural Entrepreneurship in 19th Century Boston: The Creation of an Organisational Base for High Culture in America', pp. 194–211 in R. Collins et al. (eds), *Media, Culture and Society: A Critical Reader*, Sage.
Donzelot, J. (1980) *The Policing of Families*, Hutchinson.
Durand, J.C. (1989) 'The Market in Painting and the Artistic Field in São Paulo', *Sociologie et Sociétés*, XXXI (2): 103–13.
Durkheim, É. (1974) *Sociology and Philosophy*, Glencoe, Ill.: Free Press.
Durkheim, É. (1981) *The Division of Labour*, Macmillan.
Durkheim, É. (1989) *Suicide*, Glencoe, Ill.: Free Press.
Durkheim, É. (1995) *The Elementary Forms of the Religious Life*, Glencoe, Ill.: The Free Press.
Durkheim, É. and Mauss, M. (1963) *Primitive Classification*, Cohen and West.

Eadie, W. (1990) *Movements of Modernity: The Case of Glasgow and Art Nouveau*, Routledge.

Eagleton, T. (1976) *Marxism and Literature*, Methuen.

Eagleton, T. (1984) *The Function of Criticism*, Verso.

Eagleton, T. (1990) *The Ideology of the Aesthetic*, Oxford: Blackwell.

Eisenman, S.R. (1992) 'The Intransigent Artist, or How the Impressionist Artists Got their Name', pp. 189–98 in F. Frascina and J. Harris (eds), *Art in Modern Culture*, Phaidon.

Elias, N. (1978) *The Civilizing Process*, Oxford: Blackwell.

Featherstone, M. (1990) 'Perspectives on Consumer Culture', *Sociology*, 24 (1), Feb.: 5–22.

Featherstone, M. (1993), 'Cultural Production, Consumption and the Development of the Cultural Sphere', pp. 265–89 in R. Munch and N. Smelser (eds), *Theory of Culture*, Berkeley: University of California Press.

Felski, R. (1989) *Feminist Aesthetics*, Cambridge, Mass.: Harvard University Press.

Ferguson, H. (1990) *The Science of Pleasure*, Routledge.

Ferry, L. (1993) *Homo Aestheticus*, Chicago: University of Chicago Press.

Flint, K. (1993) *The Woman Reader: 1837–1914*, Oxford: Clarendon Press.

Forrester, H. (1995) *Twopence to Cross the Mersey*, HarperCollins.

Foucault, M. (1967) *Madness and Civilisation*, Tavistock.

Foucault, M. (1970) *The Order of Things*, Tavistock.

Foucault, M. (1981a) 'The Order of Discourse', pp. 48–78 in R. Young (ed.), *Untying the Text*, Routledge and Kegan Paul.

Foucault, M. (1981b) 'What is an Author?', pp. 282–91 in J. Caughie (ed.), *Theories of Authorship*, Routledge.

Foucault, M. (1989) *The Archaeology of Knowledge*, Routledge.

Fowler, B. (1991) *The Alienated Reader*, Brighton: Harvester.

Frascina, F., Blake, N., Fer, B., Garb, T. and Harrison, C. (1993) *Modernity and Modernism: French Painting and the Nineteenth Century*, New Haven, Conn.: Yale University Press in association with The Open University.

Frisby, D. (1985) *Fragments of Modernity*, Polity.

Frow, J. (1987) 'Accounting for Tastes: Some Problems in Pierre Bourdieu's Sociology of Culture', *Cultural Studies*, 1 (1): 59–77.

Gamboni, D. (1989) *La Plume et le pinceau: Odilon Redon et la littérature*, Paris: Minuit.

Garnham, N. (1993) 'Bourdieu, the Cultural Arbitrary and Television', pp. 178–92 in C. Calhoun, E. Lipuma and M. Postone (eds), *Bourdieu: Critical Perspectives*, Polity.

Garnham, N. and Williams, R. (1986) 'Pierre Bourdieu and the Sociology of Culture', pp. 116–30 in R.E. Collins (ed.), *Media, Culture and Society: A Critical Reader*, Sage.

Gaskell, E. (1985) *Mary Barton*, Harmondsworth: Penguin.

Gellner, E. (1988) *Plough, Sword and Book*, Collins Harvill.

Gerth, L. and Mills, C.W. (1947) *From Max Weber: Essays in Sociology*, New York: Oxford University Press.

Gibbon, L.G. (1993) *A Scots Quair* (*Sunset Song*, *Cloud Howe*, *Grey Granite*), Edinburgh: Canongate.

Giddens, A. (1981) *A Contemporary Critique of Historical Materialism, Vol. I*, Methuen.

Giddens, A. (1986) 'The Politics of Taste: *Distinction*, *The Social Critique of the Judgement of Taste*', *Partisan Review*, 53: 300–5.

Giddens, A. (1987) 'Structuralism', pp. 195–223 in A. Giddens and B. Turner (eds), *Social Theory Today*, Polity.

Gilbert S. and Gubar, S. (1988) *No Man's Land: The Place of the Woman Writer in the Twentieth Century, Vols 1 and 2*, New Haven, Conn.: Yale University Press.

Ginzburg, C. (1980) *The Cheese and the Worms*, Routledge.

Goldmann, L. (1964a) *The Hidden God*, Routledge.

Goldmann, L. (1964b) *Pour une sociologie du roman*, Paris: Gallimard.

Grana, C. (1964) *Modernity and Its Discontents* (originally *Bohemians versus Bourgeois*), New York: Harper Torchbooks.

Green, N. (1990) *The Spectacle of Nature: Landscape and Bourgeois Culture in Nineteenth Century France*, Manchester: Manchester University Press.
Greenberg, C. (1961) *Art and Culture: Critical Essays*, New York: Beacon.
Griffin, G. (1994) 'Introduction', pp. 1–14 in G. Griffin (ed.), *Difference in View: Women and Modernism*, Taylor and Francis.
Grignon, C. and Passeron, J.-C. (1989) *Le Savant et le populaire*, Paris: Seuil.
Habermas, J. (1987) *The Philosophical Discourse of Modernity*, Polity.
Habermas, J. (1988) *On the Logic of Social Sciences*, Cambridge, Mass.: M.I.T. Press.
Hall, S, (1986) 'Cultural Studies: Two Paradigms', pp. 520–38 in N.B. Dirks, G. Eley and S.B. Ortner (eds), *Culture/Power/History: A Reader in Contemporary Social Theory*, Princeton: Princeton University Press.
Hall, S. (1981) 'Notes on Deconstructing the Popular', pp. 227–40 in R. Samuel (ed.), *People's History and Socialist Theory*, Routledge.
Halsey, A.H.., Heath, A.F. and Ridge, J.M. (1980) *Origins and Destinations*, Oxford: Clarendon.
Hamilton, G.H. (1954) *Manet and His Critics*, New Haven, Conn.: Yale University Press.
Hammett, D., (1982) *The Four Great Novels*, Pan.
Hanson, A.C. (1977) *Manet and the Modern Tradition*, New Haven, Conn.: Yale University Press.
Harker, R., Mahar, C. and Wilkes, C. (eds) (1990) *Introduction to the Works of Pierre Bourdieu*, Macmillan.
Harrison, C., Baldwin, M. and Ramsden, M. (1981) 'Manet's *Olympia* and Contradiction', *Block*, 5: 34–43.
Harvey, D. (1989) *The Condition of Postmodernity*, Oxford: Blackwell.
Heidegger, M. (1962) *Being and Time*, SCM Press.
Heinich, N. (1987) 'Arts et sciences a l'âge classique: Professions et institutions culturelles', *Actes de la Recherche en Sciences Sociales*, 66–7: 47–78.
Henderson, M. (1994) *Finding Peggy*, Corgi.
Herbert, R.L. (1988) *Impressionism*, New Haven, Conn.: Yale University Press.
Holdsworth, E. (pseud. E. Carnie) (1925) *This Slavery*, London Publishing Company.
Holtby, W. (1954) *South Riding*, Glasgow: Fontana (Collins) (1936).
Huss, R. (1993) 'Ajax Agonistes: Review of *Les Règles de l'art* and *The Field of Cultural Production*', *Times Literary Supplement*, 24 Sept.: 11.
Huyssen, A. (1986) *After the Great Divide*, Macmillan.
Jameson, F. (1981) *The Political Unconscious*, Methuen.
Jameson, F. (1983) 'Postmodernism and Consumer Society', pp. 111–25 in H. Foster (ed.), *Postmodern Culture*, Pluto.
Jameson, F. (1984) 'Postmodernism: Or The Cultural Logic of Late Capitalism', *New Left Review*, 146: 53–93.
Jameson, F. (1991) *Postmodernism or the Cultural Logic of Late Capitalism*, Verso.
Jencks, C. (1986) *What is Post-Modernism?* Academy Editions.
Jenkins, R. (1992) *Pierre Bourdieu*, Routledge.
Johnson, R. (1975) 'The Proletarian Novel', *Literature and History*, 2, Oct.: 84–94.
Kant, I. (1952) *The Critique of Judgement*, Oxford: Oxford University Press.
Kasl, R. (1985) 'Edouard Manet's *Rue Mosnier, Le Pauvre*, a-t-il une patrie?', *Art Journal* (Chicago), Spring: 49–58
Kemp, T. (1969) *Industrialisation in Nineteenth Century Europe*, Longman.
Kemp, T. (1971) *Economic Forces in French History*, Dennis Dobson.
Kerrigan, C. (1989) 'The Ugsome Thistle', pp. 181–9 in H.W. Drescher and H. Volkel (eds), *Nationalism in Literature: Scottish Studies*, Verlag Peter Lang.
Klaus, H.G. (1982) *The Socialist Novel in Britain*, Brighton: Harvester.
Kracauer, S. (1975) 'The Mass Ornament', *New German Critique*, 2: 67–76.
Kristeva, J. (1986) 'Women's Time', pp. 187–213 in T. Moi (ed.), *The Kristeva Reader*, Oxford: Basil Blackwell.
Kroeber, A. (1963) *Style and Civilisations*, Berkeley: University of California Press.

Lajer-Burcharth, E. (1985) 'Modernity and the Condition of Disguise: Manet's *Absinthe Drinker*', *Art Journal* (Chicago), Spring: 18–26.

Lamont, M. (1992) *Money, Morals and Manners: The Culture of the French and American Upper Middle Class*, Chicago: University of Chicago Press.

Landes, J. (1988) *Women and the Public Sphere*, Ithaca, New York: Cornell University Press.

Lash, S. (1990) *The Sociology of Postmodernism*, Routledge.

Lash, S. (1993) 'Pierre Bourdieu: Cultural Economy and Social Change', pp. 193–211 in C. Calhoun, E. Lipuma and M. Postone (eds), *Bourdieu: Critical Perspectives*, Polity.

Lash, S. and Urry, J. (1987) *The End of Organised Capitalism*, Polity.

Lawrence, D.H. (1950) *Selected Essays*, Harmondsworth, Penguin.

Leavis, Q.D. (1979) *Fiction and the Reading Public*, Harmondsworth: Penguin.

Lefebvre, L. and Martin, H.-J. (1976) *The Coming of the Book*, New Left Books.

Levine, L. (1988) *Highbrow/Lowbrow*, Cambridge, Mass.: Harvard University Press.

Lewis, H. (1988) *Dada Turns Red*, Edinburgh: Edinburgh University Press.

Lidsky, P. (1970) *Les Écrivains contre la commune*, Paris: François Maspero.

Light, A. (1991) *Forever England*, Routledge.

Lindsay, M. (ed.) (1961) *John Davidson: Poems*, Hutchinson.

Lipuma, E. (1993) 'Culture and the Concept of Culture in the Theory of Practice', pp. 14–34 in C. Calhoun, E. Lipuma and M. Postone (eds), *Bourdieu: Critical Perspectives*, Polity.

Loesberg, J. (1993) 'Bourdieu and the Sociology of Aesthetics', *English Literature and History*, 60: 1033–56.

Lovell, T. (1980) *Pictures of Reality*, British Film Institute.

Lovell, T. (1987) *Consuming Fiction*, Verso.

Lukács, G. (1968) *History and Class Consciousness*, Merlin.

Lukács, G. (1969) *The Meaning of Contemporary Realism*, Merlin.

Lukács, G. (1978) *Studies in European Realism*, Merlin.

Lukes, S. (1973) *Émile Durkheim*, Harmondsworth: Peregrine.

Lunn, E. (1982) *Marxism and Modernism*, Verso.

Lyotard, J.-F. (1987) *The Postmodern Condition*, Manchester: Manchester University Press.

MacDiarmid, H. (1943) *Lucky Poet*, Methuen (Edinburgh: Carcanet, 1994).

MacDiarmid, H. (1967) *Collected Poems*, rev. edn, Macmillan.

MacDonald, M. (1979/80) 'Cultural Reproduction: The Pedagogy of Sexuality', *Screen Education*, 32/33, Autumn/Winter: 141–53

McGuigan, J. (1981) *Writers and the Arts Council*, Arts Council of Great Britain.

Macherey, P. (1978) *A Theory of Literary Production*, Routledge.

MacLean, S. (1991) *From Wood to Ridge: Collected Poems in Gaelic and English*, London: Vintage.

Marcus, L. (1992) 'Feminist Aesthetics and the New Realism', pp. 11–25 in I. Armstrong (ed.), *New Feminist Discourses*, Routledge.

Martin, J.L., Nicholson, B. and Gabo, N. (1971) *Circle: International Survey of Constructive Art*, Faber and Faber.

Marx, K. (n.d.) *The Communist Manifesto*, Moscow: Foreign Languages Publishing House.

Marx, K. (1973) *Grundrisse*, Harmondsworth: Penguin.

Marx, K. and Engels, F. (1976) *On Literature and Art*, Moscow: Progress.

Medvedev, P.N. and Bakhtin, M.M. (1978) *The Formal Method in Literary Scholarship: A Critical Introduction to Sociological Poetics*, Baltimore: Johns Hopkins University Press.

Miller, M.B. (1981) *The Bon Marché: Bourgeois Culture and the Department Store*, Princeton: Princeton University Press.

Moers, E. (1978) *Literary Women*, The Women's Press.

Moi, T. (1985) *Sexual/Textual Politics*, Methuen.

Moi, T. (ed.) (1986) *The Kristeva Reader*, Oxford: Blackwell.

Moi, T. (1991) 'Appropriating Bourdieu: Feminist Theory and Pierre Bourdieu's Sociology of Culture', *New Literary History*, 22: 1017–49.

Moretti, F. (1983) *Signs Taken for Wonders*, Verso.

Moore, B. (1978) *Injustice*, Macmillan.
Moorhouse, H.F. (1991) *Driving Ambitions: An Analysis of the American Hot Rod Enthusiasm*, Manchester: Manchester University Press.
Mulhern, F. (1979) *The Moment of 'Scrutiny'*, New Left Books.
Nice, R. (1978) ' A Vulgar Materialist in the Sociology of Culture', *Screen Education*, 28, Autumn: 23–33.
Nicolson, C. (1992) *Poem, Purpose and Place: Shaping Identities in Contemporary Scottish Verse*, Edinburgh: Polygon.
Niebuhr, R. (1957) *The Social Sources of Denominationalism*, New York: Meridian.
Nietzsche, F. (1961) *The Genealogy of Morals*, New York: Mercury.
Nochlin, L. (1989) *Women, Art, and Power and Other Essays*, Thames and Hudson.
Nora, F. (1967) 'The Neo-Impressionist Avant-Garde', pp. 51–64 in T.B. Hess and J. Ashbery (eds), *Avant-Garde Art*, Collier-Macmillan.
Orr, J. (1986) 'Modernity and Modernisms', British Sociological Association Conference Paper, March, Edinburgh.
Ortega, R.L. (1982), 'The Language of the Working-Class Novel in the 1930s', pp. 122–44 in H.G. Klaus (ed.), *The Socialist Novel in Britain*, Brighton: Harvester.
Palmer, B. (1975) 'Class Conception and Conflict', *Review of Radical Political Economy*, 7 (2): 31–4.
Palmer, J. (1978) *Thrillers*, Edward Arnold.
Parker, R. and Pollock, G. (1981) *Old Mistresses*, Pandora.
Piaget, J. (1971) *Structuralism*, Routledge and Kegan Paul.
Poggioli, A. (1968) *The Theory of the Avant-Garde*, Cambridge, Mass.: Harvard University Press.
Pollock, G. (1988a) 'Agency and the Avant-Garde', *Block*, 15, Spring: 4–15.
Pollock, G. (1988b) *Vision and Difference, Femininity, Feminism and the History of Art*, Routledge.
Prawer, S. (1976) *Karl Marx and World Literature*, Oxford: Oxford University Press.
Public Lending Right (1993) Public Library Statistics for 1991–2, Stockton-on-Tees, Cleveland.
Reff, T. and Valdès-Forain, F. (1995) *Jean-Louis Forain*, Memphis, Tennessee: The Dixon Gallery.
Ricoeur, P. (1994) 'Imagination in Discourse and Action', pp. 118–35 in G. Robertson and J. Rundell (eds), *Rethinking Imagination*, Routledge.
Rigby, B. (1993) 'Heteronomy and Autonomy in Bourdieu's *Les Règles de l'art*', *French Cultural Studies*, 4 (3), October: 271–81.
Ringer, F. (1992) *Fields of Knowledge*, Cambridge: Cambridge University Press.
Robbins, D. (1991) *The Work of Pierre Bourdieu*, Milton Keynes: Open University Press.
Rodinson, M. (1974) *Islam and Capitalism*, Allen Lane.
Rose, M. (1991a) 'Post-Modern Pastiche', *British Journal of Aesthetics*, 31 (1), Jan.: 26–38.
Rose, M. (1991b) *The Post-Modern and the Post-Industrial*, Cambridge: Cambridge University Press.
Ross, A. (1987) 'Containing Culture in the Cold War', *Cultural Studies*, 1 (1): 328–48.
Ross, A., (1989) *No Respect: Intellectuals and Popular Culture*, Routledge.
Rushdie, S. (1988) *Satanic Verses*, Viking.
Said, E. (1993) *Culture and Imperialism*, Chatto and Windus.
Saint Martin, M. de (1990) 'Les "Femmes Écrivains" et le champ littéraire', *Actes de la Recherche en Sciences Sociales*, 83: 52–6.
Sanguineti, E. (1973) 'The Sociology of the Avant-Garde', pp. 389–97 in E. Burns and T. Burns (eds), *The Sociology of Literature and Drama*, Harmondsworth: Penguin.
Sartre, J.-P. (1981) *The Family Idiot*, Chicago: University of Chicago Press.
Schapiro, M. (1978) *Modern Art*, Chatto and Windus.
Schellenberg, J.A. (1978) *Masters of Social Psychology*, Oxford: Oxford University Press.
Schiller, F. (1954) *On the Aesthetic Education of Man*, Routledge and Kegan Paul.
Schorske, C.L. (1961) *Fin-de-Siècle Vienna: Politics and Culture*, Weidenfeld and Nicolson.

Shiach, M. (1993) ' "Cultural Studies" and the Work of Pierre Bourdieu', *French Cultural Studies*, 4 (3), October: 213–23.

Shiff, R. (1992) 'Defining "Impressionism" and the "Impression" ', pp. 181–8 in F. Frascina and J. Harris (eds), *Art in Modern Culture*, Phaidon.

Shusterman, R.M. (1992) *Pragmatist Aesthetics*, Oxford, Blackwell.

Shusterman, R.M. (1993) 'Légitimer la légitimation de l'art populaire', *Politix*,4: 153–67.

Simmel, G. (1978) *The Philosophy of Money*, Routledge.

Sklair, L. (1991) *Sociology of the Global System*, Brighton: Harvester.

Smoluchowski, L. (1987) *Lev and Sonya: The Story of the Tolstoy Marriage*, Sidgwick and Jackson.

Snee, C. (1979) 'Working-Class Literature or Proletarian Writing', pp. 165–92 in J. Clark, M. Heinemann, D. Margolies and C. Snee (eds), *Culture and Crisis in Britain in the 1930s*, Lawrence and Wishart.

Sohn-Rethel, A. (1978) *Intellectual and Manual Labour*, Macmillan.

Soper, K. (1991) 'Postmodernism, Subjectivity and Questions of Value', *New Left Review*, 186, Mar.-Apr.: 120–8.

Sorokin, P. (1964) *Social and Cultural Mobility*, Glencoe, Ill.: Free Press.

Spivak, G.C. (1988) *In Other Worlds*, Routledge.

Thacker, A. (1994) 'Our War is With Words', pp. 75–91 in G. Griffin (ed.), *Difference in View: Women in Modernism*, Taylor and Francis.

Thompson, E.P. (1961) 'Review of Raymond Williams' *Long Revolution*', *New Left Review*, 8, Mar.: 34–9; 9, May–June: 34–9

Thompson, E.P. (1968) *The Making of the English Working Class*, Harmondsworth: Penguin.

Thompson, E.P. (1979) *The Poverty of Theory*, Merlin.

Todd, J. (1987) *A Dictionary of Women Writers*, Routledge.

Tomaselli, K. (1989) *The Cinema of Apartheid*, Routledge.

Tressell, R. (1965) *The Ragged Trousered Philanthropists*, Panther.

Troeltsch, E. (1931) *The Social Teachings of the Christian Churches*, Allen and Unwin.

Trotsky, L. (1960) *Literature and Revolution*, Ann Arbor: University of Michigan Press.

Urry, J. (1990) *The Tourist Gaze*, Sage.

Urry J. (1995) 'Touring Cultures', unpublished paper, *Theory, Culture & Society* Conference, 10–14 August, Berlin.

Varnedoe, K. and Gopnik, A. (1990) *High/Low*, New York: Museum of Modern Art.

Viala, A. (1985) *Naissance de l'écrivain*, Paris: Minuit.

Vinson, J. (1983) *Biographies of Twentieth-Century Romance and Gothic Writing*, 2nd edn, St James Press.

Wacquant, L. (1993a) 'Bourdieu in America: Notes on the Transatlantic Importation of Social Theory', pp. 235–64 in C. Calhoun, E. Lipuma and M. Postone (eds), *Bourdieu: Critical Perspectives*, Polity.

Wacquant, L. (1993b) 'On the Tracks of Symbolic Power: Prefatory Notes to Bourdieu's *State Nobility*', *Theory, Culture & Society*, 10 (3), Aug.: 1–17.

Warhol, A. (1989) *The Andy Warhol Diaries*, Pan.

Weber, M. (1952) *Ancient Judaism*, Glencoe, Ill: Free Press.

Weber, M. (1958) *Rational and Social Foundations of Music*, Carbondale, Ill.: Southern Illinois University Press.

Weisberg, G. (1980) *The Realist Tradition*, Bloomington: Indiana University Press.

West, R. (1980) *The Judge*, Virago.

Wheeler, T. (1849–50), *Sunshine and Shadows*, Northern Star (microfiche).

White, H. and White, C. (1965) *Canvases and Careers: Institutional Change in the French Painting World*, New York: John Wiley and Sons.

Whitman, W. (1969) *Penguin Critical Anthologies*, Harmondsworth: Penguin.

Willett, J. (1979) *The New Sobriety*, Thames and Hudson.

Williams, Raymond (1961) *Culture and Society*, Harmondsworth: Penguin.

Williams, Raymond (1965) *The Long Revolution*, Harmondsworth: Penguin.

Williams, Raymond (1979) *Politics and Letters*, Verso.
Williams, Raymond (1980) *Problems in Materialism and Culture*, Verso.
Williams, Raymond (1981) *Writing in Society*, Verso.
Williams, Raymond (1989) *The Politics of Modernism*, Verso.
Williams, Rosalind (1982) *Dream Worlds: Mass Consumption in Late Nineteenth Century France*, Berkeley: University of California Press.
Willis. P. (1977) *Learning to Labour*, Westmead, Farnborough: Saxon House.
Wilson, E., (1988) 'Picasso and Pâté de Foie Gras: Pierre Bourdieu's Sociology of Culture', *Diacritics*, 118 (2), Summer: 47–60.
Wilson, E. (1992) 'The Invisble Flâneur', *New Left Review*, 191, Jan.–Feb.: 90–110.
Wolff, J. (1983) *Aesthetics and the Sociology of Art*, Allen and Unwin.
Wollen, P. (1980) 'Manet: Modernism and Avant-Garde', *Screen*, 21 (2) Summer: 15–26 (see also T. Clark (1980) 'Reply to Wollen', *Screen*, 21 (3) Winter: 97–100).
Worpole, K. (1984) *Reading by Numbers*, Comedia.
Wright, P. (1985) *On Living in an Old Country*, Verso.
Zangwill, I. (1909) *The Children of the Ghetto*, Dent.
Zeldin, T. (1977) *France, 1848–1945: Vol. II: Intellect, Taste and Anxiety*, Oxford: Oxford University Press.
Zola, E. (1993) *The Masterpiece*, Oxford: Oxford University Press.
Zukin, S. (1982) 'Art in the Arms of Power: Market Relations and Collective Patronage in the United States', *Theory and Society*, 11: 423–51.
Zukin, S. (1988) *Loft Living: Culture and Capital in Urban Change*, Radius.

INDEX